This book, 'A Gentle Man Passed By', has been compiled, edited and published by Colm McCarroll.

Colm spent more than forty years in the publishing business and was Managing Director of the 'Derry Journal Group of Newspapers' when it was sold in 1998. He established the 'Derry News' which was launched in 2001 and thrives to this day.

He played on the Ulster Interprovincial team in 1983, reached the final of the South of Ireland Championship in 1982, won the City of Derry Scratch Cup, Ballybofey and Stranorlar Scratch Cup (twice), North-West Scratch Cup (twice), Guinness Scratch Cup at Rosses Point (twice) and the Donegal Scratch Cup (twice). He was also an Ulster selector in the 1980's.

Every penny collected from donations and sales of this book will go to THE MICHAEL DOHERTY FUND. The beneficiaries are the Patients Comfort Fund, Nazareth House, Fahan, Co. Donegal, Arthritis Ireland and Parkinson's Ireland.

To support it would be a testament to the generosity of the community in general and the golfing fraternity in particular. Details as to where you can make a donation are given on the back inside cover.

First published in April 2017

Copyright © Colm McCarroll, 48 Talbot Park, Derry, BT48 7TA
Compiled, edited and published by Colm McCarroll
Proofread by Sara Plower
Designed and produced by Colm McCarroll junior
Illustrations created by Niall McCarroll
Cover by Mary Doherty, Managing Director, Red Dog Design Consultants,
23, Blackpitts, Dublin.
Tel: 0035314163288. E-mail: shona.byrne@reddog.ie

Distributed by Newspread, Altnagelvin Industrial Estate, Trench Road, Derry BT47 2ED
Tel: 02871320700

Amazon sales through Jenni Doherty of Little Acorns Bookstore,
The Yellow Yard, Palace Street, Derry, BT48 6PS; Tel: 07776117054;
Email: littleacornsbookstore@yahoo.co.uk

A CIP record for this book is available from the British Library.

The right of Colm McCarroll to be identified as the person who compiled and edited
this book has been asserted by him in accordance with the Copyright, Designs and
Patents Act 1988.

With support from Guildhall Press, Derry, and printed by W&G Baird Ltd, Greystone
Press, Caulside Drive, Antrim BT41 2RS

ISBN: 978 1 911053 255

ACKNOWLEDGMENTS

When you undertake a book of this size, you have to call on the very best. I am indebted to my life-long friend, Don O'Doherty, for his huge contribution. Nothing was too much for him and when you had to go at the pace we had set for ourselves, it is people of Don's quality, enthusiasm and generosity who were needed. Happy Days, Don!

To those who recalled their memories of Michael and to those who supplied photographs, your generosity of spirit was much appreciated. And from the content received it clearly demonstrated the affection they had for Michael.

The youngsters who served their 'time' under Michael left me in no doubt how much they admired, respected and indeed loved their 'boss'. Their tributes speak volumes.

The Doherty family couldn't do enough for me. Every request, every phone call, every e-mail had an immediate response. Thanks, in particular, to Veronica, Mary and Jim for their invaluable help and to Patricia for her willingness to lend a hand.

Having spent a lifetime in the publishing business, I knew who to contact if I needed advice. Paul Hippsley and Joe McAllister of Guildhall Press could not have been more helpful. And talking to my old friend Bill Breslin from Newspread, who will look after the distribution of 'A Gentle Man Passed By', took me back to the days when business was not quite so cut-throat. Thanks also to Artie Duffy of the Derry Journal for his help.

I have left my son Colm to the last. When Sheila and myself went out to visit him in Tenerife in early January, I told him of my plan to publish a book in Michael's memory. At that stage we had no idea what size or shape it would take. His words were, "No problem Dad, I will give you a hand". This tribute to Michael could not have happened without him. In my forty and more years in the publishing business, I have not come across anybody to match him. I am so grateful, I really can't find words to express my gratitude to him.

Some of the photos that appear in this book date right back to 1976 in a very different age of photographic development. You will understand that the quality of these images reflect the technology of the time.

She was always there to protect him. This beautiful photo speaks for itself. All through his married life, Michael had Veronica's loving support and as his illnesses wore him down, she was his 'rock', caring for his every need. She will miss him terribly.

A stalwart of the game

A tribute by Peter Allis

How sorry I was to hear of the death of Michael Doherty.

He was the sort of professional that made our association so splendid and worthwhile. He cared about everybody, he tried his best, he was honest and true, knowledgeable, wasn't jealous keeping his information and ideas to himself – he passed them on to others. He was, indeed, a man for all seasons and an absolute stalwart of the game. A man from another time who will be sadly missed.

Peter Allis

Tribute from the legendary Norman Drew

ALONG WITH MICHAEL and Arthur Gilliland, I was an Assistant Professional at North-West in the early 1950's. We played a lot together and I remember him as a capable and effective player who could compete with anyone at a high standard. I also remember him beating me at the 19th in a Northern Branch event in the mid-fifties.

On another occasion after a tournament at Prehen in Derry, some of the lads stayed on late playing snooker at which Michael was also very useful. Myself and my partner played Michael and his partner with ourselves winning the match. The stake was for a pound note, which I got Michael to sign. And would you believe it, I still have that pound to this day.

Norman Drew, former Ryder Cup (1959) and Walker Cup (1953) representative for Great Britain and Ireland, winner in 1959 of the Yorkshire Evening News Tournament, the Irish Dunlop tournament and the Irish PGA Championship; winner of the Irish Amateur Open (1952,1953), North of Ireland (1950,1952) and East of Ireland (1952).

You make a difference

Arthritis Ireland

Speaking about the launch of 'A Gentle Man Passed By' John Church, Arthritis Ireland CEO, said: "We are honoured to be nominated as one of the charities to benefit from this special book commemorating Michael's life and his many achievements. At Arthritis Ireland, we are working single-mindedly to transform the experience of people living with arthritis and those who care for them. Every day, we work in communities across the country providing community-based education programmes to help people effectively manage and control this devastating disease. Without the support and generous donations of people like Michael's family we could not do what we do and make a difference to the people living with arthritis all over Ireland."

For more information visit the Arthritis Ireland website www.arthritisireland.ie or call their Helpline on 1890 252 846.

The Parkinson's Association

The Parkinson's Association of Ireland are delighted to be the benefactors of this book, 'A Gentle Man Passed By'. Not only will this book raise much needed money, as we do not receive any government funding and are reliant on donations, it will also raise awareness about Parkinson's Disease and the battle a diagnosis brings.

This year marks the 200th anniversary of the discovery of Parkinson's Disease. The Parkinson's Association of Ireland and its seventeen branches around the country will work tirelessly to ensure resources are given to this under resourced sector.

Paula Gilmore CEO.

Image of my dad

I first met Michael Doherty when I was nine years old. It was in an age when you wouldn't dream of calling your elders by their Christian names. Children were seen and not heard. But first impressions are indelible, so I knew from a young age he was someone special. I think I was about ten when he took me aside and told me that he wasn't all that fussed about the 'Mister' title and maybe I should call him Michael. It took me a month or so to pluck up the courage but he was the first adult I called by his Christian name in my life.

And that just summed him up. As I was to find out over the next sixty years, he was the living image of my dad and I just can't pay him a bigger compliment than that. He was caring, intelligent, professional, witty and knowledgeable. I am so lucky to have met two people who had such a profound influence in my life. Through Michael's ingenuity, I have had the privilege to travel to new and fascinating places. I have been gifted with the opportunity to meet so many treasured friends.

Sowed the seed

It was Andy Meenagh, the Michael Doherty Tour organiser since 2009 who put the notion in my head about gathering a record of a unique trip which had been going non-stop since 1976. It would require some leg work, but it could be done with a bit of effort. But it all changed when Michael died last year.

The book that I had planned to celebrate his special annual tour was no longer going to be enough. I felt compelled to expand it into a celebration of his life, his influence on the development of golf in the North-West since he became the youngest professional in Europe at the age of 17 and to pass that information on for posterity. So few knew of his huge influence in every aspect of the game of golf.

11 under par

I knew how good a player he was. Remembered for a superb short game, his best round came on a sunny evening at Lisfannon where he pencilled in a wonderful round of 63. And that was when the par of North-West was 74. For those who know the course, the present 1st, 7th, 12th and 17th holes were par fives at the time – that meant that Michael went round in 11 under par! When it came to golf instruction he was in a class of his own, particularly in regard to the short game. Many, many times I availed of his expertise. I remember during the 1995 trip to California, we were playing a delightful course in Carlsbad, 'Aviara'. I had plugged my tee shot in a greenside bunker and had to get it out.

Ask CA

Michael, who was spectating that day, said to me "CA, you played that shot with an open face. When a ball is plugged you hood the face instead". Hard as it is to believe, I wasn't aware of that. So I put down another ball, plugged it in the sand, closed the face and tried again – I holed it! All we could do was laugh, but when the laughter was over I asked him why he had not imparted that pearl of wisdom many years before. The reply was so typical of Michael – "Ask CA, and you shall receive".

Another treat he had in store for us when we were in Carlsbad was a visit to the headquarters of Callaway. Typical of the 'old pro', he had set it up but kept it a surprise. My memories of the visit are as clear today as they were more than 20 years ago. Parked in the CEO's spot was a black Porsche, with the registration, ELY 1 – obviously Ely Callaway was in the building but too busy to meet us.

Fort Knox

It was like visiting Fort Knox, the security was unbelievable. We were instructed that no cameras could be used as we entered the busy production area where hundreds of Callaway staff were assembling both woods and irons. It was all very interesting and all new to us. We were particularly impressed with the secret laboratory which was sited in a discreet section of the huge building. It was there that the Callaways you would use 10 years later were being developed.

Ryder Cup referee

To be honest I was not aware of how influential Michael was in the PGA. There was a simple reason for that – he just didn't mention it. I was aware that he was highly thought of and a highly respected administrator. He was chairman of the Ulster branch of the Professional Golfers Association for many years and during that time he represented the Irish PGA on the Executive Committee of the PGA for eight years. He was elected captain of the Irish PGA in 1976.

A great moment for Michael came in 1977 in the Ryder Cup at Lytham and St. Anne's. Along with the five times British Amateur champion Michael Bonallack, he officiated at the match between the legendary Jack Nicklaus and Bernard Gallacher. Thankfully no adjudications were needed in a match that was won by Gallacher by one hole.

Rapport

For Michael a most gratifying aspect of the encounter between Nicklaus and Gallacher was the rapport between the two players. Recalling the occasion he said that there was none of the cut-throat 'dog eat dog' attitude that you get nowadays. He was privileged to hear most of the banter between the two players who were preoccupied with their tax affairs. Apparently Nicklaus offered some timely advice to the young Scot.

And then when Peter Allis and Frank Hannigan, president of the USPGA came to visit him at City of Derry in 1977, we began to realise we had something of a celebrity on our hands. Hannigan had run the United States Golf Association for many years and had been employed that week by the BBC as a rules expert during the British Seniors. Their visit spoke volumes.

And when asked to write a Foreword for this special book, 'A Gentle Man Passed By', Peter Allis said that he was privileged to do so.

Club pro of the century

Michael participated in PGA Pro buying groups and became a director, along with several local business men, of Criterion Sports, a firm manufacturing golf clubs in the 1980's and early 1990's. He was a gifted club-maker.

During the PGA's centenary year in 2001 Michael was voted 'Club Professional of the Century' by his peers in Ireland at a dinner in the Burlington Hotel and in 2007 the Londonderry Rotary Club awarded him with the Paul Harris Fellowship in recognition of his outstanding contribution to the community in Derry and the North-West.

Prolific writer

Writing and photography were two of his favourite pastimes. He was a prolific writer with a gentle style unique to himself. Some of the best laughs I had with Michael were during his editorship of 'Fore' magazine, a quarterly publication which kept City of Derry members right up to date. It was printed on the 'Journal' press in the late 1980's and early 90's.

My father, Tom Cassidy (the editor of the 'Derry Journal') and myself were the assistants, following the boss's orders without question. Apart from his many other talents, he had the skill to bring his great little concept to the finishing line.

City of Derry Pro-am

Among his many other achievements was the setting up of the City of Derry Pro-Am in 1992. It was to prove yet another resounding success with the likes of Ryder Cup star Philip Walton among its entrants.

When Michael organised a golfing trip to Scotland in 1976 he was not to know that it was the birth of an annual golfing tour which is thriving to this day. The itinerary was superb – Carnoustie, Downfield, Western Gailes and the home of golf, St. Andrew's. Who else could have organised such a feast of golf? A great new adventure had begun.

I really look forward to all of the forthcoming tours. I will try my heart out to win and who knows, miracles can happen. But what I really look forward to is meeting old friends, sharing a few memories, creating a few more and celebrating yet another fabulous Michael Tour.

The PGA celebrated its centenary in 2001. The renowned professional, Bobby Browne, presents Michael with the award for "Club Professional of the Century".

A great family legacy

Kevin lives in Dublin with Johanna, James and Ruby. He is a writer and professional musician who insists that, even though he didn't learn music from his father per se, Michael did teach him how to swing.

Mary runs creative agency Red Dog in Dublin, which she founded in 1993, after she graduated from art college. Her Dad was always incredibly encouraging and interested in Red Dog. She spent many of her weekends as a young teenager behind the counter of the pro shop selling tees, chocolate and green fees. From time to time she was brave enough to try to sort out the Pringle jumpers and the mis-matched waterproofs! She remembers very, very long summer days waiting for her father to finish up as she was anxious to get home and get ready for the White Strand disco. She lives in Dublin with husband Sean and their two young sons Sam and Oisín.

May he rest in peace

Patrick McConalogue

I HAD THE privilege of knowing Michael for over 50 years. I am proud to say that he was my brother-in-law and a gentleman till the very end.
The words of John Taylor are fitting when it comes to Michael's passing. "While we are mourning the loss of our friend, others are rejoicing to meet him behind the veil."
May he rest in peace…..
Patrick

Frank Friel

I KNOW HOW much Frank Friel did for the Doherty family during the last years of Michael's life. I spoke to Veronica about him one day and she told me about him helping out in every way possible. No task was too much for him. Frank, you should feel very proud. As Feargal Sharkey once sang – "a good heart is hard to find".

Patricia and her husband Paul live in Derry and spend their summers in Kerry. Like her father Patricia is an avid traveller. She also enjoys spending time on the beaches of Donegal, in all weathers, with her golden retriever. Like her older siblings, Patricia spent many Saturdays and Sundays in the Pro shop and accompanied Michael to many trade shows (even causing him to miss the ferry home on one occasion!). She is currently Head of Department of Business Studies in LYIT having held similar roles in Sligo and Dublin.

Jim works as a manager in the Health Services and has a business and management coaching service. In early years he often worked with Michael at City of Derry and was Technical Manager in Criterion Sports Golf Equipment Manufacturers, which was set up by Michael and business friends in the late 1980's in Buncrana. He lives in Donegal and is married to Maeve with two children - Ellen is studying engineering at university and Michael is at secondary school. He occasionally dusts off the old Criterion Classics and Scorcher golf clubs and tries to recapture what he learned in those lessons taught to him on late summer evenings by Michael at Prehen.

Commentating on their early days, Rosamund, sister of Michael and Ginger, said that they had a fabulous childhood. Buncrana was a brilliant place to grow up - you had the shorefront, the cinema and the 'Plaza' dance hall within walking distance of each other. Regarding Michael - he was the perfect brother for all of her life as was 'Ginger' and she misses them so much.

A gifted all round sportsman

A proud Buncrana man Michael began his golfing career at the local North West Golf Club where he was apprentice to the legendary Norman Drew, Walker Cup, Ryder Cup and World Cup golfer. As it happens, Norman had the unique distinction of beating the great Jack Nicklaus to the impregnable trio of achievements. A gifted all round sportsman, excelling at tennis, billiards and snooker, after dinner speaking and columnist could be added to the list. It also, of course, goes without saying that he was a fine playing professional until an arthritic condition virtually ended his successful playing career.

In the workshop Michael was advanced in all the modern techniques of treating clubs, his colouring, polishing and sculpturing of wooden clubs being one of his specialities.

National recognition

In July 1975, Michael achieved National recognition when he was elected Vice Captain of the PGA (Irish Section), to be followed by the ultimate accolade of Captain in 1976. His crowning glory was to be chosen as the 'Club Professional of the Century' especially as he was the choice of his fellow professionals.

While Michael's achievements are legion we can mention a 'short list' beginning with the launching of a club periodical 'Fore', a splendid comprehensive account of club activities, topical current features and rich historical reminiscences which made consuming reading for all members.

The coup of bringing Peter McEvoy to adorn the Desmond Trophy was another feather in Michael's cap, McEvoy being the outstanding amateur in England and with the immortal Joe Carr being one of the two amateur golfers from these shores to complete the four rounds of the Augusta Masters. It would be remiss not to mention that our own Colm McCarroll robbed Peter of a hat trick of victories in the Desmond Trophy beating him at the first tie hole with a a superb birdie 3.

Don O'Doherty, a life-time friend

Pictured at a PGA function held in London at which Bobby Charlton was guest of honour. From left, David Jones, Bobby Browne, Brian Campbell, Michael, Stephen Watson, Bobby Charlton, Jim Adgey and Christy O'Connor junior.

Denis 'Ginger' Doherty meets Gordon 'Ginger' Strachan. The former Scottish international and manager of the Scotland national team didn't realise he was in the company of one of the great Irish musicians of all time.

Michael's nephew James McHugh is a well-known caddie on the European Tour. His introduction to golf came when he caddied for Michael on Wednesday afternoons, the pro's half-day off. He worked for Michael making Criterion clubs for a year when he was 18. Under Michael's help and guidance, he was introduced to the world of caddying where he worked at St. Andrew's for several years before graduating to the 'Tour'.

Deep sense of fun

We first met Michael when we joined City of Derry in the very early 80's, the beginning of a long and lasting friendship. Michael went out of his way to make us most welcome but we quickly discovered that he was more than this iconic and respected golf professional. He had this deep rooted sense of fun and mischief which was just what we needed.

The three boos

Golf was important to us but not as important as the years of fun we have had with Michael at Prehen and further afield. He introduced us to the 3 boos - you were allowed to shout boo on your opponent's back swing at any given moment during the round. (editor's note – try that on me McCourt and I'll wring your neck) On Saturdays and Sundays he would always be standing by the side of the 16th green - if you hit the green, you got presented with a 'Milky Way', birdie the hole, the prize was a 'Bounty'.

Four dumb Derrymen

On one particular Saturday he announced that rather than chocolate, we were playing for a sponsored holiday in Florida. Like four eejits we were asked to pick an envelope and one by one we opened each envelope. Frankie Campbell was the lucky one, the rest us were genuinely disappointed. It was only then that we discovered that Frankie's wife Rose and Michael had set the whole charade up.

Against all odds Sean Coyle and Eamon McCourt played Kevin Barrett and Frankie Campbell in the Club Foursomes Final. This was a big deal between Michael and ourselves as to who was going to win. He actually took time out to video the final which went to the 20th hole. We were then invited down to Buncrana for the première. Once again his artistic editing was the highlight of the night.

Thanks for the turnip

Another highlight was his annual prize-giving and dinner to us in The Lake of Shadows, which took place just after Christmas. We would think nothing of posting Veronica and himself a Christmas Hamper - when opened they would discover maybe a turnip, a bicycle tube or possibly garden gloves.

Love affair with Spain

We used to read about this great golf competition in Spain, never thinking that we were good enough to play in it. (editor's note – you weren't). However Michael had other ideas and totally convinced us that we would be a great addition to the Tour.

Little did we know along with Sean Barrett, Paddy Cunningham and others, it would be the beginning of a great love affair with golf in Spain. It was a remarkable piece of organisation, pulling together people from all over the world to compete and making many friends in the process.

Michael retired from City of Derry to Buncrana with a number of health issues. We had some wonderful visits to Michael and his wife, the funny and mischievous Veronica. We continued our trips to the Nazareth House in Fahan and had many a pleasant and funny afternoon in the company of Veronica, Michael and the great Denis (Ginger).

There will be many tributes to Michael is this publication - he was an iconic golfing figure throughout Ireland but to us he was a most fun loving friend and companion. Thanks to Veronica and the family for making us so welcome.

Eamon Mc Court, Kevin Barrett, Willie Barrett, Sean Coyle, Sean Barrett

Regular visitors to Michael's home in Buncrana were Kevin and Willie Barrett and Eamon McCourt. From what I have heard, the craic was mighty.

A great picture — James 'the Miller', Michael's father, sitting outside Michael's shop at North-West.

Do you recognise these two gorgeous little children — none other than 'Ginger' and Michael.

Rosena and James Doherty, proud parents of Michael, Denis 'Ginger' and Rosamund.

Wonderful co-ordination

A reflection about Michael Doherty brings back the memory of him playing tennis with wonderful co-ordination – the same hand to eye co-ordination that is a requisite of the competent golfer. Had he not become a professional golfer he may well have been a professional tennis player.

Michael's father, the late James (the Miller) Doherty, on retiring from his normal work became the superintendent of the sports complex at the Buncrana shore front which consisted of a tennis court and putting green. The putting green was well laid out over 18 holes, beautifully maintained and equipped with full flood-lighting which enabled play to continue late into the evenings.

A mecca

Used as a tourist attraction during the day with James' encouragement and enthusiasm it became a mecca for the men of the town who came in large numbers in the evenings to play putting (for small wages) and so joyfully pass away the time healthily in the open air. There was no T.V. in those days and the weather was much better than it is nowadays but it was the personality, enthusiasm and good humour of James that kept the crowds coming. Even the late Major Hime could be seen walking from his nearby home to take part in the putting using his putter as a walking stick on the way.

Vincent Grant

This iconic photograph was taken by Derry Journal photographer Lorcan Doherty on the occasion of Junior Crossan's Captain's Drive-In at North-West in 2004. The golf ball in the foreground was heading directly at Lorcan at approximately 190 miles per hour. Half-a-second later it hit Lorcan on the arm, smashing his elbow joint. A visit to Altnagelvin Hospital followed. Look at your man three from the right, Colin Barlow. Does he look concerned? When asked to comment Junior stated that if the photographer had not got in his way, it would have been a perfectly good shot.

Dopey visits his 'muckers'

Originally written by Michael* and heavily sub-edited by the author.
*The majestically written parts of this unique story were penned by Michael – the more cynical by Colm McCarroll, a poor sinner whose one time gentle soul was corrupted by his proximity to the ruthless 'hacks' who poisoned his mind.

The story goes – "My shop door burst open one November 1977 morning and a breathless Con McClay announced that he had seen something huge in the Foyle. Even as he spoke a massive shape rose from the smooth water and then curved downwards into the river depths.

"That's a great white" - I spoke with knowledge of the subject as I had just recently seen a film called 'Jaws' in which Robert Shaw had scraped his nails across the school blackboard.

This incredible happening had to be recorded. I phoned the 'Journal' and some fifteen minutes later Colm McCarroll and photographer Larry Doherty arrived.

I did the driving and we parked opposite the spot where the 'Carcharodon carcharias' was last sighted. Silently they studied the placid water. The

demeanour of the 'Journal' men betrayed more than a little scepticism.

"What are ye on about", sneered Larry

After what seemed a lifetime it broke the surface directly opposite to where we were standing. It was breathtaking. "What are ye on about," sneered Larry, "that's not a 'great white', it's an Orca, a killer whale – you might have seen 'Jaws' but me and Lorcan went to see 'Orca'.

After a series of fabulous images were recorded, the newspapermen high tailed it back to break the most unlikely story in their newspaper's history. News and big news, it would certainly prove to be.

It didn't know 'its arse from its elbow'

There was all kinds of speculation as to why this monster of the oceans made its way up the Foyle – chasing a 'bird', a well-known past-time in Derry, was one suggestion or was it just a magnificent marine mammal whose GPS was up the left. The answer lay in the sobriquet appended to the stunning giant – 'Dopey Dick'. Derry people came to a logical conclusion – the thing didn't know' its arse from its elbow' and was fundamentally stupid. And of course the Buncrana 'wans' got in on the act straight away - 'Dopey' knew exactly where he was going – up to Derry to visit his stupid "muckers'.

Immensely rewarding

In 1995, I was persuaded to join the Michael Doherty Spanish Golf Tour by, amongst others John Hasson, a former Captain of the City of Derry Club who had toured from the early days. I immediately found the experience exhilarating and it opened up a whole new life for me in the golfing world, not just with the 4-day competitive edge that this already long-running and prestigious tour had already become noted for, but also finding myself amongst so many existing and new friends where the camaraderie was second to none.

After Colm Duffy rescued the 33rd Tour after Michael became ill in early 2008, I assumed the mantle of organising subsequent tours. This will be my ninth tour and despite having a few headaches along the way, I have found it immensely rewarding. I have rarely encountered problems and I cannot remember in my time of someone failing to report to the first tee on time. The Michael Doherty Tour is probably unique for it being consistently the largest and longest-running 4-day amateur golf tournament originating from anywhere in Europe. This bears great testimony to Michael Doherty's vision and to his skill in delivering such a quality product that has worked so very well over many years.

With forty years experience at the cutting edge of journalism, Colm McCarroll will produce a book on the history of the 'Tour' which will do justice to Michael's creativity. And with his vast knowledge of golf built up over a life-time both playing and at

Tour organiser, Andy Meenagh.

administrative level, he will produce a fascinating read. You can be sure of that.

All of the proceeds from the sale of the book and private donations will go to the Patients Comfort Fund at Nazareth House Fahan, the Parkinson's Association of Ireland or Arthritis Ireland.

Andy Meenagh
Michael Doherty Organiser from 2009

A pleasure to care for

Michael Doherty was our resident in Nazareth House, Fahan, from October 2014 until he passed away on 2nd December 2016. He was a pleasure to care for with a smile and gentle ways which won us over. He was a very curious and intelligent man keeping up with world affairs on the news and all kinds of sports. His main passion was watching every golf tournament he could find on TV.

At night time he liked nothing more than to settle into bed, enjoy eating chocolates and sweets left up by Veronica during her daily visits, watch a good movie and sleep late.

He was visited by family and friends very often and he loved to see them. Veronica visited Michael every day and was very particular with Michael's likes and dislikes.

On sunny days Veronica would assist Michael around the grounds

for some relaxation and fresh air. On occasion, they would meet other people on their walk but Michael didn't like to stop, and would say, "Keep going Veronica". He didn't like a group of women chattering.

We miss him.
Wilma DSouza
Head of Nursing Care,
Nazareth House,
Fahan, Co. Donegal

The Royal and Ancient Golf Club of St Andrews
Fife, Scotland, KY16 9JD

17 February 2017

Dear Colm

My year as Captain of the Royal and Ancient Golf Club, which concluded in September 2016, had so many highlights, and the occasions at City of Derry Golf Club on May 27 and North West Golf Club on August 5 were amongst the most special.

It was a wonderful feeling to return home to the two Clubs which were so instrumental in my early introduction to the great game of golf during the 1960s.

Sadly I did not have the opportunity to get to know my maternal grandfather, Gilbert Young, who was Captain of North West in 1933/34, but it was a special moment to note his name on the Captain's Board, and how he would have enjoyed knowing that I had first learnt to play at Lisfannon.

City of Derry was closer to home, and accessible by bicycle, so my time spent at Prehen was more frequent during the school holidays. Special memories abound of so many rounds with you and your brothers, and there was such enthusiastic support from the members of both Clubs – your father, the Jacksons, Micky McWilliams and Frankie Friel to mention a few. How much I enjoyed reminiscing with Frankie Friel during my August visit.

Michael Doherty was well established as the Club Professional at North West when I first became a junior member, and he was instrumental in teaching me the basics of the game. I am for ever grateful to him for the fact that I learnt to play to a reasonable, albeit now declining, standard for the next 50 years and more. Michael always had words of encouragement, and he took such a keen interest in all of us, as junior members at the Club.

I had completed my education and was living in Scotland when Michael moved to City of Derry in 1972, and my subsequent visits there were all too infrequent. But on each occasion that I returned, Michael was always there with a warm greeting, and those same words of encouragement.

I was saddened to learn, during my visits last summer, that Michael's illness was at such an advanced stage, and that I was not able to share my excitement as Captain of the Royal and Ancient Golf Club with him. How much I would have enjoyed that chat, and the opportunity to thank him for setting me on the road that took me to such a privileged position in the game.

I am delighted to have this opportunity to make a small contribution to this wonderful tribute to Michael, which is also an opportunity for me to say "thank you Michael. May you rest in peace".

Sincerely

Gavin

Gavin Caldwell

Captain, Royal and Ancient Golf Club, 2015/16

Telephone +44 (0)1334 460000 · Fax +44 (0)1334 460001
www.randa.org
Secretary - Martin Slumbers

A tribute from City of Derry's captain

Michael Doherty was an amazing golfing talent with unquestionable knowledge of the game. He was a coaching phenomenon having an unshakable temperament and a talent to spot improvement in an instant. I first met Michael some 40 years ago, after I was given a full set of clubs and trolley by my father-in-law. I decided to go for lessons with Michael. He eyed my swing (or lack of it) up and down, but strangely he seemed equally interested in my clubs and trolley. At the end of the lesson Michael said he recognised the clubs used by Victor Campbell . He was spot on, even though Victor had not played for several years. Such was Michael's memory for those connected to golf.

Some 20 years later when I joined City of Derry again and went back to Michael, he still remembered me (I had new clubs at this stage). After a few years I decided, after hearing so much about the Spanish tour, to give it a try. I was a bit hesitant - would I embarrass myself or finish in the dreaded dawn patrol on the last day.

Your fears soon disappear when you arrive at the airport check-in. Michael is there taking control, ensuring everyone has made it and distributing the trophies to those with the least amount of luggage – nobody refused. From arriving at the airport in Majorca to checking into the hotel Michael was there, ensuring it all went smoothly.

The respect given to him

You couldn't help noticing the respect given to him; he never raised his voice but got the job done quietly and efficiently. Even the hotel staff and golf course staff paid him the same respect, obviously a man worth listening to.

When I think back on the tour there were around 70 golfers at that time, all out to compete and enjoy themselves in the sun. I knew few golfers personally at the start, but by the end of the week you knew everyone on tour. It was a credit to the camaraderie amongst all the golfers.

Michael Doherty will be remembered by the golfing community across Ireland for many years to come. It is a fitting tribute to a great man that this book has been compiled by Colm McCarroll, highlighting some of the many pleasurable experiences enjoyed over the years. They are a direct result of **Michael Doherty's** dedication and enthusiasm, not just for the game, but for the players themselves.

Michael Carroll
Captain, City of Derry Golf Club - 2017

Loss to our profession

I LOVED COMING up to Derry to play in the City of Derry Pro-Ams and meeting my dear old friend, Michael Doherty. He was the ultimate gentleman, nothing was too much for him, a loss to our profession and City of Derry Golf Club. I was so sorry to learn that he had passed away. To his wife Veronica and family I send my sincerest condolences.

Philip Walton (Former Ryder Cup player 1995, Walker Cup 1981 & 1983 and winner of seven European Tour events).

Wizard and spiritual guide

June 15, 1997

Michael,

Congratulations on your twenty-five years at City of Derry. The members of that fine club have truly been fortunate to have you as their Wizard and spiritual guide to the game of golf throughout the past quarter century. I envy them. My association with you has been far shorter and from a greater distance than your club members but from my own perspective, no less valuable. I have had the privilege to play at City of Derry and to participate in your Spanish tour group on several occasions, enabling me to see at first-hand the great admiration and respect in which you are held by all who know you. You can count me in that number. Among the many fine personal attributes you bring to your work I will single out two... Wisdom and Wit. I know I can always depend on getting a priceless philosophical view from you on the subject of golf or life; and to see you conduct the presentation of prizes at the end of the Spanish tour event would be instructive to the likes of John Cleese. It is the hottest ticket in town!

Again, my congratulations and best wishes for the future. See you in Spain next May!

Geneva, Switzerland

Rabon Wilkins, a very popular addition to the Tour

A picture from 1980 when the party was based in Fuengirola. From left, Peter Quigley, Vincent Armstrong, Michael Doherty, Denis Nicholl and Christie McWilliams

Tribute from PGA Ireland secretary

We lost a great friend when Michael Doherty, the long-time professional at City of Derry Golf Club, passed away on 2nd December 2016, aged 77. He dedicated a lot of his time to the PGA in Ireland, serving on committee for many years, representing Ireland on the National Executive and holding the role as Captain in 1976. He was also one of the driving forces behind the hugely popular City of Derry Pro-Am which ran for 20 years from 1992.

Michael was held in great esteem amongst his peers and in 2001, as part of the PGA Centenary celebrations, he was accorded the distinction of 'Best Club Professional'.

PGA in Ireland secretary, Michael McCumiskey, stated: "Michael was highly respected by all he met through the game of golf. He epitomised all that is good in the profession and was noted for his honesty and integrity.

I enjoyed a great rapport with him because of his ability to carry out whatever was required in the context of what he was responsible for, or mandated to execute in his role as a PGA Professional."

Michael McCumiskey,
Secretary PGA in Ireland.

Michael McCumiskey

Acknowledged 'Rules' expert

Calm and relaxed, Michael had a way about him that endeared him to everyone he met. He could so easily have been lost to golf as he was both an exceptional tennis player and an expert with a cue. We were lucky he opted for golf.

He was extremely well-versed in the 'Rules of Golf' and I remember on one occasion when a youthful, inexperienced GUI Official at a Jimmy Bruen match at City of Derry had to avail of his expertise. There was a query regarding a rule about the correct way to take relief and I was confused about the proper procedure.

However I was not that confused - I decided to go to the club house to check with Michael, an acknowledged expert who had refereed in the 1977 Ryder Cup at Lytham and St. Anne's. Needless to state I returned with the correct ruling.

He was the consummate professional and a splendid teacher. I went to him for lessons and he achieved the hitherto impossible – he had me playing regularly to my handicap. He explained things in such a simple manner, giving me just the one swing thought each time which is truly the secret of tuition at the highest level. I was so privileged to call him my friend.

Barry Ramsay GUI official.

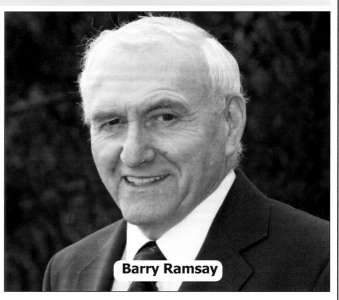
Barry Ramsay

Barry was recently nominated on the OGB (One Governing Body), a work group which will review the current range of golf club management structures throughout Ireland. This important group will involve the all-important consultation process which will greatly assist the newly agreed amalgamation of the GUI and the ILGU.

Pictured as they arrived at Mijas in 1980 are, from left, Hugh Quigley, Peter McCready, Norman Kane, Vincent Armstrong, Peter Quigley, Denis Nicholl, Leonard Finn, Hugh Cooley, Frank McCarroll jun, Tommy Daly, Patrick Doherty, Billy McElhinney, Brian Duffy, Leo Hickey, Sam Anthony, Fred Aicken, Billy Elliott, Dan Campbell and Cahir McGeady.

A little gibe backfires

I have a serious flaw in my DNA. Occasionally I say things I shouldn't say and write things I shouldn't write. As I hurtle towards my 70th birthday, it seems to be getting worse. I just can't help myself. You can be forgiven for uttering an inappropriate comment but when it is written and pondered over before it is sent, that's a different kettle of fish.

John Hasson and the Hasson family have looked after my legal affairs for a lifetime so we communicate on a fairly regular basis. I sent an e-mail to John looking for a bit of advice but unfortunately I didn't leave it there - I threw a little gibe in at the end about his superb 38 pts off 21 in the third round at Poniente in 2016. I posed what I thought was a pertinent question - "By the way, how many holes did you actually play last year when you scored 38 pts at Poniente? Speculation has it that you got confused with the new layout and played four holes twice".

Nuclear response

The response has been nuclear, a 50 megaton dirty bomb which has stripped me of my confidence, has me questioning my judgment and wondering should I apologise. Not likely, not this century anyway. Here goes the withering response from Mr. Hasson:

Hi Colm,

I refer to the last paragraph of your email 7th April. I respectfully note your comments re my winning score of 38pts at Poniente on Wednesday, 16th May, 2016.

Your jealousy was understandable but forgiveness is not within my alter ego. I applaud and admire your uncharacteristic wit which you obviously got from Cahir. Unlike yourself, 38 points was a new number for me. My victory was not really a reflection on me per se but a testimony to the drivel played by

my fellow competitors.

But as you are obviously intrigued as to how I managed to achieve 38 points; the turning point in my round came at the par 5 11th hole. My approach shot veered well to the right of the green (a cross between a slice and a push) and landed at the foothills of the 12th tee box where the hens and cockerels feed (you will remember a small crofters cottage nearby from which there is a constant smell of burning onions). My ball came to rest in the middle of the hen-run on a bare patch.

I carefully considered my options but was interrupted by shouts from the green saying "Are you playing that?!?!" There was only one answer, "But of course I am gentlemen! Fortune favours the brave". The gentlemen I refer to were Sam Smallwoods (my marker) and Tommy O'Neill.

Anyway I looked ahead and saw a medium sized hill beyond which there was a deep cavernous bunker full of sand and tucked in behind was the green. (Editor's question -

what else would a bunker be full of?) From where I was standing I only had a rough idea of where the green actually was but I was helped when I heard Sammy shout: "Tommy, keep your head down for God's sake this ball could go anywhere". With a 50 degree lob wedge I hit the ball as hard as I could (to the accompaniment of a cock-a-doodle do noise behind me) and the next thing the aforesaid gentlemen came to the summit of the small hill and shouted in tones reminiscent of the scene in Vatican Square upon the election of a new Pope.

Upon deeper enquiry it emerged that my ball hit the middle of the green from a great height and spun back 20 feet to one inch of the hole. Sammy said it was the greatest shot he had ever seen in his life and Tommy concurred. (Editor's note:- Sammy told me afterwards that it was the biggest 'fluke' he had seen in his life)

My inspiration was 10 years previously playing with Colm McCarroll at the par three 12 hole (the one after the aforementioned 11th hole). Colm's tee shot landed in the water near the edge. He took off his shoes and socks and waded in. I watched in disbelief when C.A. hit the ball (water and mud flying everywhere) and landed it on the green. He sank the putt (not normal) and claimed a spectacular par 3 (almost on a par with my achievement).

The moral of the story:- "Greatness comes to those who wait" and don't mention the fat lady!

Regards
John

(Editor's note:- I feel that I have been well and truly 'put in my box'. The moral of the story is, never lock horns with a solicitor, especially one whose DNA is as flawed as your own).

Jack Nicklaus

May 1, 2007

Dear Michael:

Please allow me to add my voice to the many who will congratulate you on your 50 years of dedication to the City of Derry Golf Club.

I hope the years ahead will be filled with good health, happiness, and plenty of time for all the things you enjoy. Finally, let me thank you for the enthusiasm you have expressed for both the game of golf and my career over the years. I am honored to have had your support.

Good luck, Michael. Enjoy your retirement and best wishes for many years of good golfing.

Sincerely,

Mr. Michael Doherty
C/o City of Derry Golf Club

11780 U. S. Highway # 1, Suite 500, North Palm Beach, Florida 33408

A gentleman and a gentle man

I first met Michael in the early 1960's when he and Veronica McConalogue became friends and I was a guest at their wedding in 1964, the ceremony performed by Fr Denis, Veronicas's brother.

I can best describe Michael as a gentleman and a gentle man. In all the years that I knew him I have never heard him speak badly about anyone and I don't know anyone who had a bad word to say about him. No wonder that he had so many friends from all walks of life. Dealing with Michael was never routine – there was always the latest story about the exploits of club members and the escapades on his golf trips.

Care for the 'handicapped'

One such story comes to mind – in Spain, himself and John O'Brien went out for a few drinks one evening and got talking to some Canadians. They enquired what kind of a holiday the Canadians were on and they explained that they had taken a number of handicapped people on holiday. They had about fifteen with them and fifteen carers. Michael informed them that he had seventy-two handicapped people with him with only himself and John looking after them. How's that for a one-liner.

Can they float?

Michael's pro-shop was always a pleasure to visit. The 'craic' was so good that quite often you left forgetting what you came in for. One particular client will never be forgotten. He explained to Michael that he lost two sets of clubs, courtesy of an irate spouse, who fired them into the 'Foyle' in a fit of rage and he needed another set. "What kind of clubs would you like"? asked Michael diplomatically. "I couldn't care less was the reply, as long as they can float".

I am delighted to claim Michael as a life-long friend, and visiting him in his twilight years was always a joy. Whenever PC's name came up, his face lit up and hosts of memories came flooding back.

Michael and Veronica celebrated their golden jubilee in 2014, a quiet family Mass marked the occasion. Despite having difficulty speaking he summed up his life with Veronica, Jim, Kevin, Mary and Patricia in three words - "I've been lucky".

By Fr. Jim McGonagle

A few memories of Michael

Like hundreds of other golfers through this region I bought my first set of golf clubs from Michael in 1970 when he was Pro at North West Golf Club. Little did I know at that time how golf would become such an important part of my life. When he was appointed professional at City of Derry in 1972 we were all so delighted to have such an outstanding player and coach as our Pro.

I had the privilege of playing with Michael on a regular basis when he came to Derry and I learned so much about the game particularly the short game where he was a genius. I also accompanied him on many Pro Ams throughout the country with much success.

We had many great times together and none more than the many golfing trips he arranged over the years highlighted by the famous Spanish Tour which is still going strong today. They are priceless memories. He was a master at observing situations as they happened and then turning them into some of the most hilarious moments in his famous presentation speeches.

The wrong profession

Michael was also a great story teller and if you went out for dinner with him you were almost unable to finish your meal because his humour was so infectious. I often thought he took up the wrong profession.

There are many many more memories about Michael to be

Cahir McGeady

told and even in his later years of ill health he never lost his wonderful sense of humour.

We have lost a great friend and he is sorely missed by us all.

Cahir McGeady

Paddy loves the Irish

The Honourable Company
Of Edinburgh Golfers
Telegrams: Muirfield Club, Gullane
East Lothian EH31 2EG

20th December 1976

Dear Mr. Doherty,

Thank you for your letter of 10th December about a party visiting Muirfield next April.

I am assuming you will be staying close to Gullane and not in Edinburgh. I believe I could take your whole party on Tuesday, 12th April, provided you played to the following format.

Morning . Medal round playing in 3's starting at the 1st and 15th tees. Ten 3's to play off the 1st starting at 08:45 at 8 minute intervals. Five 3's to play off the 15th starting at 09:20 at 8 minute intervals. If eventual numbers are not divisible by 3, one or two pairs start first off the 1st.

Luncheon will be available in the Clubhouse. If you wished to play a second round it would have to be as foursomes playing off the 1st and 10th tees - no start times in the afternoon.

I have had a word with Mr. Balfour Melville - the Secretary of Gullane Golf Club - and he tells me he could take your party on either 13th or 14th.

Green fees are currently £ 4 a round, £ 6 per day. The full luncheon is £2.50, which is usually the highlight of most visitations.

As you will see from the enclosed score card, it doesn't help the medal player much as we virtually play nothing but foursomes. To help visitors playing their own competition I enclose a copy of a stroke index I advise them to follow.

If you decide to come I would send you a supply of cards in advance.

Yours truly,
Paddy Hamner esq.
Secretary

All systems go...
By Michael Doherty

Muirfield is regarded by many as the greatest of Scotland's championship courses, At the time of the fifteenth tour it was, and probably still is, the most difficult to get on.

Secretary/Manager of Muirfield was the famous or infamous Group Captain Paddy Hanmer, to whom visiting Dukes and Millionaires paid court in the hope of getting a tee-off time.

On a visit to Glasgow I asked a leading Scottish golf organiser if he could arrange for our group to play. His reply: "I have just been trying without success to get a party of eight wealthy Americans on to Muirfield, and you want me to ask Captain Hanmer to take a bus load of 53 Irishmen. There's a phone, ask him yourself, I could do with a laugh.

I decided I would not give him his laugh. Later, I had second thoughts and decided to write to the feared captain in the knowledge that the most he could do would be to say no, or perhaps not to bother to reply all.

The reply I did receive is one I shall always treasure. (see letter left). The good captain (it is only as such that I can now refer to him) not only offered the group the courtesy of Muirfield, he suggested that we play 18 holes in the morning, have lunch in the clubhouse, then play a further 18 holes foursomes in the afternoon.

If that was not enough, Captain Hanmer then wrote that, as we would be playing Muirfield on the Tuesday, he thought we might play neighbouring Gullane on the Wednesday. So he took the liberty of arranging for us to do so.

(see pages 42 & 43)

Yanks go home

Tom Watson and Ben Crenshaw fell foul of Captain Hanmer after Watson won the 1980 Open at Muirfield. Late on the Sunday night, the two Americans had taken it upon themselves to tackle a couple of holes with hickory clubs. They played up the 10th and down the 18th.

Captain Hanmer was having a relaxing end-of-championship drink in Bissets Hotel down the road when word came that there were folk dancing on the last green. He rushed to the scene.

"What the hell are you doing?" he roared to the revellers, never mind that they included the new Open champion and his wife. The wives, incidentally, had had the good sense to remove their shoes, though Captain Hanmer was in no mood to be appreciative of such niceties. He ordered them off the course.

A very persuasive man

I first heard of Michael, and indeed City of Derry Golf Club, when I received a call out of the blue from him. The idea of playing in the City of Derry Scratch Cup was introduced and it was of particular interest to me as my father's maternal side came from Donegal. That was all Michael needed to get us all to make the trip.

I have a strange memory of the first time I played (I played on three consecutive years) I hit a wood on to the par 5 11th that had a very narrow entrance through trees. The shot was successful but stupid given the risk. I took it on through frustration at missing a few putts or hitting a bad shot or whatever.

How astute he was

It was only in the clubhouse that Michael brought it up saying he was surprised I took it on. He was right, of course. However I remember thinking how astute he was to notice. Others just thought it was a good shot. He knew it was a stupid one.

I was starting a business at the time and had little spare time. I was therefore pretty convinced in my own mind I would not return to play a second time. Ten minutes on the phone to Michael changed my mind. He was quietly and yet fiercely persuasive.

I bumped into him from time to time at places like the Belfry, where he held PGA positions. He was always charming. I remember him as a man who would have been a success at whatever he had chosen to be - it just happened to be golf.

I have enduring memories of Prehen and the members' plaque is proudly on the wall at home.

Peter McEvoy O.B.E.
Winner of the British Amateur Championship in 1977 and 1978.

On his appointment to North-West Golf Club in 1958 Michael is welcomed to the club by, on left, Dr. James McCormick, captain in 1926 and Canon R.E. Devlin who was the current captain at the time.

Proper pro

DAVID JONES
PGA 'MASTER' PROFESSIONAL

5th March 2017

Michael Doherty.

I've heard phrases like 'gentleman'... 'master professional'.. bandied about quite a bit in my time in professional golf.   Among my group of friends we have a simple term for people like Michael Doherty... a 'Proper' pro.

If ever anyone epitomised all that was good about being a club professional, Michael was that person.

I had the privilege to know him since I came back to Ireland in 1972.

He was wise.

He was incorruptible.

He was selfless.

He was forward thinking and innovative in an era when it was easier in our game to accept the status quo.

His door was always open and he was ready to help anyone who came through it.

With a few... very few... of his contemporaries he made it his mission to improve the lot of the Irish Professional Golfer.

All the young professionals who had the good fortune to train under him at City of Derry came out fully fledged and ready to make their way in the world of professional golf, and they have all gone on to successful careers of their own.

On a personal level, Michael and I became good friends as we collaborated on a few golf design projects over the years. He introduced me to Greencastle, where I later was asked to help with some course revisions. We pitched for Ballyliffin but lost out to the great Pat Ruddy design on that one, although we had some great times walking the course and thinking about it.

Our most ridiculous assignment came at Gweedore, when a business friend of his came up with the off-beat idea of doing a course on some wild exposed hills in remotest Donegal.

Michael and I went up there to walk some the hundreds of acres that we had to work with.

Unfortunately for us, just about every one of the sheep who graze on those hills were so intrigued by us, probably NOT the design and took the opportunity to follow us.

Finally we got into a little dell and found ourselves completely trapped by about a thousand sheep packed tight around us, right up against our legs.

That was before mobile phones, so we just had to wait there in the middle of baa-ing chaos till a farmer came looking for us and got us out.

Needless to say there is still no golf course there.

Golf is a great game to overcome notions of class, culture or background but it takes the occasional visionary to help golfers and people appreciate the common thread of honesty and decency that so binds the lovely Game of Golf to the Game of Life.

Our friend Michael was one of those.

"Do it!"

Michael gave me my first job as a 16-year-old trainee on a government YTP scheme. There were two other trainees, Seamus Duffy and Eamon Logue, both of whom went on to develop successful careers in golf. We had so much fun in that old portacabin. Putting competitions around the shop, chipping balls out the front door and tea with toasted banana sandwiches were all part of a normal day.

I left the proshop and spent some time trying to play full time, spent some time overseas and even had a short stint working in a shirt factory. Things weren't exactly going to plan. Once again Michael had the answers. He sat me down in his little over crowded office and suggested that I start a PGA traineeship under his tutelage at City of Derry Golf Club. In the 3 years that followed it was just Michael, myself and sometimes his son Jim who were looking after the pro shop. This is when I really got to know Michael.

He had the answer

Michael was the "Yoda" of all things golf as far as I was concerned. Whatever I wanted to know in whatever area of the business Michael had the answer. He also seemed to know someone in every part of business from all around the world. When I was considering moving overseas Michael simply told me "Do it!"

He told me that at a young age he had the opportunity to go to the US and that he regretted not trying it. Michael was of great assistance to me when I eventually did move to Australia. His letters of reference were just fantastic, sometimes I thought he was speaking about someone else they were so good.

Although I put in a serious number of hours over a year with Michael I realise now how important that was. It also made me realise that I never wanted to run a pro shop and I never have. I am sure that I was not the easiest trainee that Michael guided to full membership of The PGA.

Wasn't drama free

Although I was loyal and reliable I certainly wasn't drama free. The motorcycle crash that I had after the first round of the pro-am in the early nineties was probably the biggest drama. I was supposed to be coming back into work in the shop that afternoon but ended up in Altnagelvin Hospital. But despite all the drama, in all the years, I worked with Michael I never saw him lose his temper.

Michael was seriously witty. Once when I told him I

Kieran McLaughlin

was going to do a training course on bio mechanics he replied "Does that mean you will then be able to service our cars?" He had a very simplistic view on the golf swing which I still incorporate into my coaching. He told me that he had declined the offer to write an instructional book on the golf swing as no one would buy a 10-page book.

I feel so lucky to have trained under the great golf professional and there is no doubt that it is due to Michael's training and guidance that I have had the success I have had here in Australia as a teaching golf professional.

I probably didn't fully appreciate Michael at the time but I certainly do now.

You are badly missed Michael

Kieran McLaughlin
PGA Golf Professional
Eastern Golf Club
Melbourne Australia.

Knowledge he gave so freely

My first encounter with Michael was as a 10 year old entering the Pro shop to purchase my very first set of clubs. Little did I know some 18 years later, I would be beginning my PGA apprenticeship under his tutorship and then succeed him has the Head Professional at City of Derry Golf Club.

He was a great boss and his knowledge of the game of golf was second to none, knowledge he gave so freely when asked. One of the best lessons I learnt from Michael was, to succeed at a golf club, you must treat everyone as equals and something I still try and do every day at the club.

Michael's shop was a real Aladdin's cave and on a visit to the club, Peter Alliss described it as the best stocked Pro Shop in Europe.

Even in a busy shop there were still plenty of quiet times and Michael had a tried and tested technique for drumming up business in such an instance. When the shop was quiet Michael simply made a cup of tea knowing that he wouldn't get to drink it, because all of a sudden the door would open an in walked a customer. I can say that, mad as it sounds, Michael made more tea than he drank.

As his last trainee I can only hope I can have half the impact on golf in the North West as Michael did.

Sammy Smallwoods, Head Professional at City of Derry Golf Club — "As his last trainee, I can only hope I can half the impact Michael had."

Sammy Smallwoods
Head Professional
City of Derry Golf Club

My old boss

Michael Doherty has given me so much joy and happiness in my job. I really don't think I would have become a golf professional if it was not for his help and advice which was to stand me in such good stead over the years. I learned so much from him and have tried to emulate him.

After I left Michael I enjoyed many visits back to see him in the shop – he seemed to live on sandwiches and rich tea biscuits. So when I came to visit him I bought the biscuits to ensure that I always got invited back.

Finally, I think that when most people look back over their lives they will reflect on someone who made a profound difference to who they have become. Michael Doherty was that person for me.

Leslie Robinson
Head Professional
Donegal Golf Club, Murvagh

Leslie Robinson

He was great as a mentor

I started with Michael in January 1984 in the middle of an extended frosty period. Very few members were about but I had the advantage of familiarising myself with members by reading the club magazine "Fore", published by him and the McCarroll family. It was then that I first became aware of Michael's ability as a writer.

My abiding memory of one bitter winter day was a difference of opinion Michael had with a blanket he had put over the engine to avoid the frost. I received a distress call to say that he had forgotten about the blanket and the car had caught fire before he reached Lisfannon.

Any success that came my way was due to Michael's encouragement and wonderful ability to coach. Even today, as I coach the game myself, I am only starting to realise the value of the information he was passing on. He was a wonderful pitcher of the ball and it was clear to be seen why he was so proficient as a player in his early years. Michael was always keen to recall stories from his playing days and tales of Christy O'Connor Snr and his legendary ball striking. A session with Michael was always encouraging and gave me great belief in my ability.

He was great as a mentor, always pointing you in the right direction, giving sound advice and helping especially during my PGA exams. His knowledge and expertise was wide and varied, from club repairs to rules and course design. He took a lot of pride in club repairs and the finishing of the old wooden heads. And it was the back of the old shop we started to assemble the first "Criterion" clubs, another first for Michael.

When I set down roots in Derry in '92 it gave me an excuse to visit Michael on a regular basis. Even as I

Apart from a great all round knowledge of the golf swing and its components, Seamus Duffy is renowned for his teaching of short game skills. Here he is imparting some of his golfing knowledge to Ballybofey's Darren Crawford, who is currently at college in Florida. It's nice for some.

spent time with him in his later years his passion for the game did not diminish. I visited him last year in the Nazareth House and brought him a programme from the 2013 US Open at Merrion. On the front cover was the famous approach from Ben Hogan to the 18th hole - he proceeded to fill me in with all sorts of facts about this iconic image including some of the playing pros who were in the crowd watching. He had an absolute encyclopaedic knowledge about the game.

It was an honour and privilege to serve under Michael and I hope that just a little bit of his knowledge and passion has rubbed off on me.

Seamus Duffy
PGA Assistant to Michael Doherty 1984-1990 at City of Derry Golf Club

Special guests at Lynn McCool's wedding were Michael, Willie Barrett, Stephen Watson, sports presenter with BBC and Ed Toovey.

Memory Lane – from left are Dominic Quinn, Hugh Quigley, Jimmy McCloskey, Bill Canning, Cathal McKeever, Maurice Allen, the top of Christie McWilliams' head (the best part), Pat Ellis and Peter Quigley.

When Maurice Brennan was captain of City of Derry Golf Club in 2004, Michael invited him to attend the annual PGA dinner in the Grosvenor Hotel where he was a guest at the Irish PGA table. They are pictured with Colin Montgomerie, rated the best player in the world not to have won a Major.

Michael (The "Miller") Doherty

It was only when I turned professional back in 1986 at North-West Golf Club and met the famous member called "Mickety" Doherty that I learned all Buncrana born Dohertys required an extra name to distinguish each other. It was explained to me that the "Miller"Doherty was a reference to either Michael's father or grandfather being a hat maker thus, the "Miller".

My very first memories of Michael were at the City Of Derry when I became a junior member in the early 70's. The Pro Shop was located next to the then 1st tee where many a spectacle was witnessed from Kingsley Magowan famously snapping the 1st ever graphite shaft seen over his shoulder, the prodigious power of Jimmy Clinch and schoolboy prodigy Ronan Rafferty all being topped by the duel between Peter McEvoy and Colm McCarroll during the renowned Desmond Scratch Cup in 1981.

I was very fortunate in later years to become one of Michael's long list of assistants, joining Seamus Duffy and Kieran McLaughlin for a few months before moving to Belfast. The Pro Shop now faced towards the River Foyle, which became ideal for the lunchtime challenge game when "The Boss" wasn't around.

Michael at that time had joined a buying group of PGA Professionals called Elite Pro and, as a member, you were contracted to take an absurd amount of clubs each year to keep supplier prices down. There was

Eamon Logue

an absolute mountain of clubs to negotiate trying to reach the kettle, never mind any other stock in the various rooms located in the wooden framed building.

On the odd occasion when a message needed to be delivered we could visit his little office adjacent to the steps leading up to the shop. The first thing you heard on approach were the dulcet tones of Placido Domingo wafting out through the thin walls. Placido had no idea whose company he was in.

Before long, my short time in Derry was up, and it was only during the annual Pro-Am's did I get the opportunity to spend short bursts of time in his company.

Rest in peace Pro, you will be missed by all.

Eamon Logue
PGA Professional
Golf Operations Manager
Hilton Templepatrick Golf & Country Club

Two great friends Bob Coull and Bill Bratton with Rory O'Hare in the background.

It is little wonder that 80 years young Brendan Burke is still a formidable competitor. Eamonn Logue, who learned all of his teaching skills from his mentor, Michael Doherty, has his pupil in the perfect position at the top of his back swing.

Michael with Val Doonican outside North-West Golf Club.

We shared so many laughs

Not a day goes past where I am not thankful to have worked for the great Michael Doherty. Without his guidance and mentoring I would not be enjoying a wonderful career as a PGA professional. He was my mentor, my coach and most of all, my friend. He was a person with integrity in whom I could confide and he would never hesitate to offer his guidance. And we shared so many laughs.

One day while having a cup of tea he told me he had written a play when he was 16 years old which had been performed in St. Mary's Hall, Buncrana. I was gobsmacked. When he told me the gist of it, I just collapsed in laughter as did he.

Many years later I went to visit Michael in his home where we shared the usual laughs with Veronica. I enquired about this famous play and lo and behold, Veronica produced the masterpiece. It was on an old jotter written in the finest handwriting I have ever seen. I started to read it and as the story unfolded, I laughed till I cried. I can still picture his big grin as he watched my reaction. What an extraordinary man! I feel so lucky to have been his friend.

Lynn McCool

A Gentleman

Frank McCarroll senior

A tribute to the late Frank McCarroll senior by Michael Doherty, published in the "Derry Journal" in January 1994. Frank McCarroll passed away on 9th January of that year.

As a very young boy certain names, often mentioned in conversation by my father and his friends, became indelibly imprinted in my memory. Most of these were connected with one of two sports, golf or billiards, with both of which my father had a lifetime involvement. The name, Frank McCarroll, was mentioned more often than most, as it frequently came up in discussions of both sports.

So from an early age he was known to me as a keen golfer and billiards player - what he did for a living I did not discover until years later, as such matters were obviously considered of little importance by the sporting types who frequented our household.

I finally met the man in person when I joined the North West Golf Club as assistant professional at the age of fifteen. It was still the era of "Upstairs Downstairs" where golf clubs were concerned. Fairly rigid protocols existed governing the relationship of the professional with club members who were, by and large, of the awe inspiring variety - solicitors, bankers, doctors, army officers, clergy and particularly so to a young assistant pro.

No barriers existed

Where Frank McCarroll was concerned, however, no barriers existed, a fact he demonstrated from the outset by always taking the time for a few minutes conversation with the young assistant on his frequent visits to Lisfannon.

In succeeding years there would be countless such conversations, which on his part, whatever their duration, invariably contained some observation or anecdote that for the recipient, added to his knowledge, or broadened his perspective on a particular subject. To be in his company was almost always a learning experience. Looking back over a long span of years, Frank McCarroll's contribution to the life of his city and its environs has been immense - where the game of golf is concerned it is impossible to quantify.

A unique catalogue of honours

Captain and president of North West, captain and trustee of City of Derry, captain of Greencastle and Ballyliffin - this unique catalogue of honours is testimony not only to the esteem in which he was held, but also to his willingness to give generously of his time and energy to a game from which he himself so obviously derived much pleasure.

But to simply list the offices he held, important as they were, would be to only scratch the surface of his involvement with golf through the years. To these would have to be added the committees, sponsorships, his very active participation in events throughout the area, and his propagation of the game through the golf column of the "Journal".

It was undoubtedly pre-ordained that he would also introduce his sons to the game at an early age, and soon the exploits of Frank, Colm, Brendan and Brian, made the McCarroll name synonymous with golf right around the country.

It was about friendship

There is little doubt, however, that what gave their father most pleasure was the fact that his sons'

Passed By

enjoyment of, and rapport with the game, so closely mirrored his own.

While he was himself a doughty competitor on the golf course, for Frank McCarroll the game was about much more than competing. It was about friendship, about stories - almost always humorous. It was about the appreciation of a sweetly struck golf shot.

It was this appreciation of the beauty of sport, especially when exhibited by masters of their craft which invariably found him a totally absorbed spectator at numerous great sporting occasions.

Thus when the incomparable Mohammed Ali came to Dublin, at the height of his powers, to take on one Al "Blue" Lewis, there is no way that Frank McCarroll would not have been there. For Ali embodied all the attributes required to win a special place of affection in the McCarroll sporting hierarchy - great skill, fortitude, and just as important, he was a true "character".

The great Fred Daly

Another to whom these criteria applied and who in turn had the warmest regard for F.E. was the late, great Fred Daly. In his day Fred, like Ali, had no doubt that he was the greatest. Judging by the stories of Fred he so enjoyed recounting - F.E. was a superb storyteller - this is an assessment with which Frank McCarroll did not disagree.

That evening in Fuengirola I will never forget

Through the years I have been privileged to share Frank McCarroll's company on numerous occasions. Many of these were truly memorable, such as nights on golfing trips to Spain and Scotland when often in the company of his great friend Frank Guckian, the wine and stories flowed in equal measure. And a particular magical evening on a St. Patrick's Day in Fuengirola, when our party was joined by the most charismatic personality that Derry has ever produced and long time friend of F.E., the inimitable Josef Locke.

As his friends will know there is nothing Frank McCarroll enjoyed more than a sing-song. He had an encyclopaedic knowledge of Irish songs and ballads (of all persuasions) and had a particular affinity with the works of Percy French. That evening in Fuengirola, with F.E. and Joe Locke leading 'the entire company,' is one I shall never forget.

A prized possession

One of the most prized possessions in our family is the North-West Golf Club Captain's Prize. It was won on Frank McCarroll's captain's day in 1962 by my father. I´m still not sure who on the day was the more pleased,

my father on receiving the prize or Frank McCarroll on presenting it to his old billiards and golfing adversary. My last memory of this fine man is of an occasion a few short weeks ago in a hostelry next to the "Derry Journal", where he was quietly relaxing after work. I happened to mention that I had come across a verse of a Percy French ballad that I never knew existed. Trying to recall the words, I had barely uttered the first syllable when his hand came up, fore-finger outstretched, in that familiar F.E. gesture and he completed the verse without a single hesitation.

He enriched the lives of many

Frank McCarroll was a man of great accomplishment who by his involvement in a wide variety of activities enriched the lives of many. The game of golf, to which he gave so much, is immeasurably the poorer for his passing.

Through-out the North-West, the entire golfing fraternity will be as one with the McCarroll family in their bereavement.

We have all lost a true and irreplaceable friend.

MICHAEL DOHERTY,
City of Derry Golf Club

Gentle charm

My father, Frank McCarroll senior was a delightful man, so intelligent, so witty, so humble and so understanding. I should know – when I started working with him in the 'Journal' I was to be by his side for 40 years. I had been so lucky. When he passed away on 9th January 1994, it was the saddest day of my life.

He had a gentle charm, modest, treated everyone as an equal, generous to a fault and a great listener who respected other people's opinions. I knew his every thought, his opinions and his principles – follow them and you wouldn't go too far wrong.

Huge regard

He detested the snobbery that existed in golf clubs in years gone by, people looking down on those not quite as lucky as themselves. He had a huge regard for people from disadvantaged backgrounds who made their way in life taking advantage, for example, of the Education Act of 1947. It was to prove life-changing for so many people.

Not a great fan of established religions per se, he believed that the many different interpretations of the same fundamental belief had caused untold problems in the past and would do so in the future. Sadly he has been proved so right.

Stood me in good stead

He was a 'Jerkyl and Hyde' when it came to sport – winning was the object of the exercise as I was to find out at an informative age. I was seventeen years old when I learned a lesson that was to stand me in good stead for the rest of my golfing days. Simultaneously that lesson created more enemies than Genghis Khan had in his prime.

It was on the old par three 5th at City of Derry in the club fourball. Jim Hegarty and myself had been drawn against my father and Frank junior. All was going amicably until I putted up to three inches from the hole and picked the ball up.

I teed up on the 6th, content that I had just halved the 5th. "What did you have at that hole"? my father asked. "I had a three, Dad" said I confidently. "No you didn't", says he, "you had nothing, you lifted the ball when it hadn't been conceded". The more indignant I became, the more they laughed. It was a lesson well learnt.

Little pause

James 'the Miller' told me a story about him many years ago. He recounted that he was locked in a great battle with my father in the Debonair Cup but he had got the upper hand, walking off the 10th tee 2 up. Walking down the fairway my father commented how much he admired the little pause at the top of the "Miller's" swing.

According to James, the effect was immediate. He told me that he will never forget seeing his second shot going right at an angle of 60 degrees, hitting the top rung of barbed wired on the out of bounds fence and toppling out onto the railway line.

Great advice

One night after a publication was 'put to bed', we were sitting having a pint in the Delacroix. In the immediate vicinity were a group of people in full flow with the 'F' word flying left right and centre. He turned to me said, "You know, that is such a waste of such a great word. Used sparingly, it is a powerful way of expressing a point of view". I didn't use it much after that.

Cahir McGeady has a story that sums him up. Cahir had just joined City of Derry and had arrived out at Prehen in the hope of getting 'fixed up'. Two men were standing on the 1st tee (now the 17th), waiting to

tee off. The elder of the two asked Cahir, "are you on your own, young fella, would you like to join us?" That was the day Cahir met Frank senior and Frank junior for the first time. And Cahir recalls that the younger Frank went round in 68 gross that evening.

Great company

There was nothing the 'old man' liked better than a sing-song. At the drop of a hat, particularly after a few bottles of Guinness and a few halves of Crested Ten, he would regale the company with an endless variety of songs. He was great company, the life and soul of the party.

Don O'Doherty had some interesting words to say about him – "Frank was the great patriarch of his company. In the council chamber he had the wisdom of Solomon. I recall one particular observation enunciated by Frank. 'No rule should ever be made that doesn't have a better than even chance of being kept'. How often we do witness this simple rule being broken?

Won at Carnoustie

"On the course he was as enthusiastic as a rookie and followed all the City of Derry teams with infectious enthusiasm. In the clubhouse there was no finer raconteur, regaling us with his home spun reminiscences. Indeed one of Frank's typical cameo achievements was on the inaugural tour in 1976 at Carnoustie in his late fifties and having spent 19 hours the previous day on a tedious bus journey, he eclipsed the entire field of 54 to win on a course he had never seen".

Such were his many talents, I could spend all day writing about the 'old man'. But if I want to meet my target of getting this book published before the 2017 Michael Doherty Tour, I will need to move on. It would suffice to say he was my hero and always will be.

Introduction to golf

The McCarroll family were introduced to golf in 1929 when my grandfather, J.J McCarroll, the then Nationalist MP for Foyle and Managing Editor of the 'Derry Journal' was invited to join North-West. He was happy to join, but because of work commitments he played just a few times before his premature death in 1937. My father remembered his "swashbuckling swing".

But my father loved the game from the first time he struck a ball and a life-time's association with golf had begun. My old partner in crime, Don O'Doherty, who has been such a help over the past few months, takes up the story:- Frank McCarroll joined City of Derry Golf Club in the late 1930's and being an all round sportsman he excelled at tennis, football and billiards and was at pains to accommodate all three.

Plumped for golf

Perhaps the longevity of the golf career allied to the demise of the billiard code persuaded the young McCarroll to plump for the golfing option. His decision was soon vindicated when, in the 1941 Foyle Cup, he tied for first place and not only lost the play-off but 2 shots to boot to reduce his handicap from 18 to 16. Further success followed with victory in the 1942 Horace Bayer Cup which he won by 6 clear shots incurring a further 2 shot drop to 14.

In June of the same year a qualifying total of 143 for 36 holes again accelerated a further 2 shot reduction to 12. And in the Foyle Cup, also in 1942, he was pipped by a shot and, you've guessed it a handicap reduction from 12 to 10. April and May 1943 produced the same stories and the McCarroll handicap was now 7.

11 shots

To summarise the situation inside the space of 2 years, August 1941 to May 1943 Frank McCarroll had his handicap reduced by a massive 11 shorts, won three Open Club competitions and was beaten in a play-off for a fourth. A fine start by any standard. Thank you Don, Derry's walking encyclopaedia.

My father's love of the game was passed on to his family and here we are today, with one foot in the grave, still trying to find that little secret which will provide that all important breakthrough.

Another great past time of Frank McCarroll senior was bridge which he played for most of his adult life. This picture was taken in the 1980's when himself and Fr. Eamon Tierney won the Neil Kelly Cup. Also pictured in the front row, from left, are Sally Shortt, daughter of Neil Kelly, Teddy Caldwell, father of immediate past captain of the R and A Gavin Caldwell and Neil McMahon. Standing, from left, are Fr. Jim McGonagle, Pat Bergin, Harold McCartney, Pat Fitzharris, Cathal Harvey and Michael McLaughlin.

"What about a song Joe?"

When Joe Locke came back to Ireland he ended up living outside Burnfoot, so quite naturally he joined North-West. He was always a great friend of my father's as they went to primary school together and that friendship was renewed when he came home. My recollections of him are very fond – he was a bit of a 'wild man', sometimes fiery and unpredictable, but never dull.

What an addition

When he was on the run from Her Majesty's Inland Revenue, he lived in a villa in Benalmadena, right beside Fuengirola, the venue for Michael's 1980 trip. Of course, when he found out we were in town he made it his mission to join up with us. What an addition He pulled out all the stops, providing all of us with unforgettable moments.

On one particular night he joined my father, brother Frank, and Brian Duffy at La Mancha Restaurant for a meal. Afterwards he would entertain Derry man owner Eric Mullan's clientele with a selection of his great old 'rousers'. Eric, by the way, was a member of the family who owned the big oil company, McMullan Oils. I remember Eric giving out stink one evening about the allowance he received - £400 per week. It was a fortune in 1980, but not nearly enough for the portly Eric.

Your choice

That evening, walking along a very busy little alleyway, my father turned to Joe – "What about a song, Joe". The big man responded "of course Frank, what would you like to hear?" To which my father responded – "Joe, your choice".

Famous 'pipes'

What happened next will live with me till my dying day. (Just before I continue I need to explain Joe's physique – he had a massive upper body frame, needed to house the famous 'pipes', and spindly wee legs, not unlike one of Pearson's turkeys). Anyway he sucked in enough air to cause a vortex and let fly.

It was an Italian opera song, performed to perfection. He stopped the street, nobody moved - wee Spanish women were hanging out their windows to see what the hell was going on. Arms outstretched, looking for all intents and purposes like the 'big yin' had returned for a second visit, he gave it everything and when he finished, the packed alley erupted into rapturous applause. What a moment. I will never forget it!

In the flesh

And that wasn't the end of it. From out of the crowd came this stunner who came up to him and said "you sound just like Josef Locke". To which he replied – "in the flesh ma'am, in the flesh". Less than ten minutes later, she was sitting on Joe's knee in a pub just down the street.

Hatched a plan

Frank and myself had been in the company of Joe, my father and Brian Duffy for four consecutive nights and we were dying to see what the nightlife was like. We hatched a plan – I said to Dad that Frank and myself were feeling knackered and were going to have an early one.

"I'm feeling a bit tired myself, so I'll go to the hotel with you". So much for that plan. As it so happened Michael put Frank and myself in Room 621 and my father in 623, right beside each other. Frank and myself lay on our beds, winkle pickers pointing North, for a full twenty minutes until we could near nothing from next door.

Such precision

I have never opened a door so quietly, or placed a key in a lock with such precision in all my life. When we got far enough away from the rooms, the two of us broke down laughing inconsolably. Going down in the lift, we figured the fastest way to the London Bar was through the hotel bar.

Enjoy the 'craic'

We walked in to the bar and there he was at the counter with a pint in his hand. Jesus, my worst nightmare had just begun. But my father was so different to anybody I have ever met in my life. He nudged his glasses in his normal fashion and said "boys, enjoy the craic and don't be too late".

Canmore lady president!

This special photo of my sister Suzanne and my dad was taken during their regular visits to Donegal in the 1980's. Golf wasn't the exclusive preserve of the male members of the McCarroll family. When she emigrated t o Canada, Susie joined Canmore Golf Club in Banff where she quickly made an impression. So much so that after just a few short years, she was elected president of the ladies branch. On the last occasion I spoke to her, she made the so true observation that Dad would have been very proud of her.

With the 'Rockies' as a backdrop, Canmore is a magnificent setting for a golf club. Interestingly enough its season lasts from April to October and that's not hard to figure why – snow, bloody great masses of it. But that does not deter the big sister – she joins a group known as the 'snow-birds' in Palm Springs to spend the winter there. As my father used to say: "how the other half live".

This wonderful photo, taken by Michael, shows the party in full flow at the La Mancha Restaurant, Fuengirola in 1980. From left to right are Leo Hickey, John Hannigan, Mick Gallagher, Frank McCarroll senior, Aenas McBride, Ted Graham, Hugh Quigley, Tommy Daly, Peter McCready, Josef Locke, Liam McCaul, Peter Quigley, Eric McMullan, Eddie McCauley, Vincent Armstrong, Denis Nicholl and Cahir Fitzpatrick.

ALL SYSTEMS GO

This was the leading article, written by Michael, and published in the special "Fore" magazine, Spanish Edition which was published in May 1990. It is reproduced in its entirety for the benefit of those who would not have seen it before.

THIS YEAR'S "Spanish Tour" will be the fifteenth in a series which began in Easter 1976. The first two tours were in Scotland, both at Easter, and so what was clearly becoming an annual event became known as the "Easter Tour." Any thoughts of a long running series would, however, have been far from the minds of the members of the first tour, writes tournament organiser Michael Doherty, as they sat, cold and hungry in their coach at midnight, on a Scottish motorway.

The coach which had been limping along for some hours, finally gave up the ghost some fifteen miles short of our destination – Dundee. It was only with the help of police (none too pleased at having to leave a late-night Clint Eastwood film) and a mechanic who had to leave the comfort of his bed, that we at last reached the haven of our hotel at 2 a.m. and early next morning we had to face Carnoustie!

I most wanted Muirfield

Having on the first tour played Carnoustie and St. Andrews, the course I most wanted to include the following year was Muirfield. Muirfield is regarded by many as the greatest of Scotland's championship courses. At that time it was, and probably still is, the most difficult to get on. Secretary/Manager of Muirfield was the famous or infamous, Group Captain Paddy Hamner, to whom visiting Dukes and Millionaires paid court in the hope of getting a tee-off time.

On a visit to Glasgow I asked a leading Scottish golf organiser if he could arrange for our group to play Muirfield. His reply was: "I have just been trying without success to get a party of eight wealthy Americans on to Muirfield, and you want me to ask Captain Hamner to take a bus load of 53 Irishmen. There's a phone, ask him yourself, I could do with a laugh."

I decided not to give him his laugh. Later, I had second thoughts and decided to write to the feared captain in the knowledge that the most he could do would be to say no, or perhaps not bother to reply at all.

The reply I did receive is one I shall always treasure (it is published elsewhere in this book). The good captain (it is only as such that I can now refer to him) not only offered

our group the courtesy of Muirfield, he suggested that we play eighteen holes in the morning, have lunch in the clubhouse, then play a further eighteen holes foursomes in the afternoon.

If that were not enough, Captain Hamner then wrote that, as we would be playing Muirfield on the Tuesday, he thought we might like to play neighbouring Gullane on the Wednesday. So he took the liberty of arranging for us to do so. In fact I was about to contact Gullane to make this precise arrangement.

A chance to experience great clubs

The reason behind the first tours and all subsequent tours was to give members of City of Derry and friends from other clubs, the chance to play and experience at first hand the atmosphere of some of the great clubs and courses.

Of all the visits we have made since the tours began, perhaps the day at Muirfield best illustrates the tour's "raison d'etre." With our bus parked in front of the clubhouse we received the most cordial welcome from the Muirfield officials.

Apart from the course itself, the highlight of the day was the lunch in the dining hall, with its cathedral-like atmosphere. I am sure that never before, or since, has its oak panelled walls echoed to the sound of so many Derry accents.

I later took great pleasure in sending a copy of Captain Hamner's letter to the Scottish golf organiser with a one sentence note saying: "have a laugh at this."

A warmer climate

After the second Scottish tour it was decided to head for warmer climes and so the Spanish Tour was born in 1978. To mark this new phase, P.C. Duffy, a most enthusiastic supporter of the tour, donated the magnificent solid silver salver – The Travellers Trophy – which is presented each year to the winner of the individual tournament. This is a most sought after prize and has seen some great performances through the years.

As was fitting, Colm Duffy himself won in the first year. Thereafter came a period of almost domination by Liam McCaul, who won no less than five times. In doing so Liam produced some tremendous golf over courses that were far from easy. The only other players to have won more than once are Colm McCarroll and Eddie Gallagher. Both are set on adding to their totals and both are at short odds to do so.

The team event

While the individual tournament is the tour's "Blue Riband," the section of the tour that undoubtedly

FOR FIFTEENTH TOUR

gives most enjoyment is the team event. Here the higher handicap player can come into his own, after producing four and five "pointers" with the aid of his strokes allowance. There is no more pleasing sight on the tour than seeing a "Category Four" man receive his prize, knowing he has made a valuable contribution to his team´s success. It says much for the tour that some of its most cherished momentos were awarded not for golfing success, but, as they say, for something completely different.

Bottle of sand

One such award was a bottle of sand, suitably labelled from a bunker on the 8th hole at Muirfield. This was to mark the exploits of a tour member in extricating himself from this bunker. As was explained at the time, the small bottle contained all the sand left in the bunker.

Another special award went to a player for an amazing sequence of shots at the "agua" surrounding the 11th hole at Los Brisas. However, as a high ranking fire officer, the ability to find water is undoubtedly a most desirable attribute in his case.

The success of the tours throughout the years is without doubt due to the tour members themselves. They enjoy the golf, the banter and the fellowship, and a prize won is simply a bonus.

Generous sponsors

Very important to the success of the tour has been the support of such as "The Derry Journal," who have been generous sponsors through the years and take a very active interest in the event, as evidenced by the publication you are now reading.

I am also indebted to Eugene Dunbar, who travels each year from London and sponsors the team prize, to Colm Duffy, a marvellous motivating influence, and to Joe Ramsey, for his enthusiasm and help with the draw and many other odd jobs. Our honorary tour bookmaker, the inimitable Cahir Fitzpatrick, makes a contribution to the enjoyment of the tour that could not be quantified.

Special thanks

A very special word of thanks is due to Mrs. Pat Cassidy, of Gallagher Travel. Through the years I have never known Pat to be other than cheerful and patient, not easy, believe me, when dealing with the particular idiosyncrasies of the golf trip. Pat and I both work on the assumption that however many problems may arise, as they say in show-business: "it will be alright on the night." And always has been.......so far!

Sonny Jarvis is presented with a jar of water, a memento for his exploits on Las Brisas in 1978. He hit so many balls into the water, Davy Bredin was thinking of buying a wetsuit to go in after them.

Not well enough to travel

Very sadly, a great man will not be with us in May to play for his own 'Travellers Trophy'. Colm Duffy has fallen victim to Alzheimer's disease, the most cruel of illnesses. He is simply not well enough, a fact we have been aware of for several years as its dreadful fangs slowly but surely take grip.

No more will we make the trip to Leo's on a Wednesday night every May. The minute Colm walked in the door, there was instant recognition from the man who was both owner and performer and I knew exactly what the next song would be – "Seven Spanish Angels".

Life and soul

He was the life and soul of the party, in the middle of every debate, in the middle of every controversy which added so much fun to the trip. I normally played with him in special matches he would set up which, believe you me, were not for the faint-hearted. The stakes were always the same – 50 euro on the front nine, 50 on the back and 50 on the match. Added to that were "roll-over" birdies starting with 10 at the 1st and building up as the match progressed. He was the toughest task master I have ever come across and I was on the receiving end of his "razor blade" tongue on more than one occasion.

Example of his wrath

I will give you an example of his wrath. It was the semi-finals of the City of Derry foursomes and we were playing Brian Carson and Billy Johnston. At the short par four 16th, with the match delicately poised, I elected to take a three iron off the tee to leave Duffy with about ninety yards to go – a driver would have left him beside the green and I was aware of his tendency to genuflect when trying to assist a chip. It was the only time he ever got close to praying as his knees virtually touched the grass at impact (editor's note:- I know that is a slight exaggeration).

"I play off scratch"

Anyway, we made a 'balls' of it and lost the hole. He went bonkers – "why didn't you hit your driver?" I tried to defend myself and in the process made a comment that has haunted me to this day. I turned to Duffy and said "do you realise I play off scratch?". The reply was devastating – "scratch me arse ye baldy bastard, you couldn't play tig". That was it – I had had enough. I walked over to Carson and Johnson on the 17th tee, shook hands and wished them well in the final and walked off leaving PC with nobody to play with.

There was a deathly silence as I rounded the clubhouse

and headed for my car. But when they thought I was out of ear-shot it started – an ever increasing crescendo of laughter as my car exploded out of that car park. But I must admit that by the time I got to the Everglades, I saw the funny side of it and was laughing every bit as heartily – sure we hadn't killed anybody.

PC's brainchild

I had left City of Derry by the early 1990's and was somewhat hazy about what Colm had achieved for the club so I asked my old friend, Cahir McGeady, to fill me in.

"Buying the land at Dunhugh was the brainchild of PC and together with the club secretary, Billy Rodden and Sean O`Dwyer they persuaded council to make the purchase. Having finally bought the property the decision was then taken to apply for planning permission to build quality homes on designated sites. "This became a real issue with the planners as it was deemed a green belt in the area plan at that time. However Sean O`Dwyer, through his good offices, persuaded the Minister in question to grant permission and much to the club's delight it was finally granted. The rest is history".

Getting things done

Cahir continued, "when PC was captain of City of Derry in 1976 and during his time as vice-captain and past captain he was instrumental in getting things done. He managed the total refurbishment of the club house with most of the work carried out by his own company

at cost price. This was a huge saving for the club.
"His influence was enormous. He was the driving force behind everything positive which took place at Prehen and that included the famous City of Derry Pro-Am, the brainchild of Michael and funded very heavily by Colm's company. And talking of Michael, they were inseparable friends with a life-time bond".

The Dohertys' affection

And Cahir put the final touch to his tribute to his old friend whom he still meets every Friday without fail - "you could not help but notice at Michael's graveside the affection that the entire Doherty family has for Colm – it was so evident that he is a special person in their lives".

As a tax advisor he had few equals and he dabbled in a number of businesses including construction. He was the man behind both Baronscourt and Gleneagles which were among many other ventures. But it was his latest undertaking, McCambridge, Duffy and Co., where he was to have his greatest success. Now a nationally known Insolvency practice, it is one of the biggest private employers in the north-west with a staff of well in excess of 100.

Insightful approach

And back to the golfing sphere where he was owner of the Portsalon links until 1982. I was there the night he passed over the deeds to the Fanad club and I asked him on the way home why he had accepted what was a nominal sum for such a fabulous piece of golfing terrain. He told me that he had come to the conclusion that the 'locals' would never accept an 'outsider' and he had reluctantly come to terms with that. It gives some idea of his insightful approach to life.

I feel sad

I could write a hundred stories about Colm, one funnier or more interesting than the other. And I feel sad that he will not be able to fully enjoy this written appreciation of his great old friend Michael. But he is a fighter, he is in good health and is so well cared for. What a detestable illness Alzheimer's is – to rob someone of his huge intellect of his entire memory bank is profoundly disquieting.

Fierce competitive spirit

Colm Duffy joined City of Derry in 1962 after a highly successful athletics career, being in his time Ulster 1,500 and 5,000 metres champion. He also figured successfully in team events and walking races. Possessing a fierce competitive attitude, it was not long before Colm had his handicap reduced to single figures.

He played in the first Spanish tour off 7 having his handicap reduced to 6 courtesy of winning the third round with 37 points. To add to his bragging rights he can claim to be the first ever winner on the Spanish tour to be repeated in 1993.

Duncarbit Cup victory

On the home front Colm can boast a President's Prize, a Men's Fourball victory, a Club Championship and a Junior Scratch Cup... I suspect a special niche in his memory is reserved for his victory in the prestigious Duncarbit Cup, played at the famous Ballycastle Links over 36 holes, hitherto the exclusive preserve of category one golfers.

As is only to be expected he has a magnificent record in Spain - winner, runner-up and third on no fewer than four consecutive occasions. His wonderful alliance with the late Michael Doherty was truly cemented when he accepted the organising baton of the Spanish tour in 2008, which was then handed on to Andy Meenagh in 2009

Immense contribution

Once again in collaboration with Michael Doherty his contribution has been immense. In his capacity as club captain in 1976 he was unable to travel with the main party but opted to travel by car. It prompted the observation

in the 75th anniversary souvenir booklet that 'Mr Duffy displayed remarkable clairvoyance in travelling by car to Scotland'.

No doubt it was a pointed reference to the 1976 bus experience. His presentation of the Travellers Trophy was only one of the many examples of his generosity to the cause, many more examples could be found on the home front with his launching of numerous fund raising functions.

His puckish wit was never far from the surface. On one occasion he bemoaned the fate of a tourist who had the misfortune to 'blow up' after being level ochos. Ocho was, of course, the English numeral for 8. Again on the home front he gave the club the benefit of his professional excellence by acting as auditor from 1964 till 1971.

Don O'Doherty

In a relaxed mood in Magaluf are Willie Barrett, Danny McCloskey and Eamon McCourt.

It's always great to have a photographic record of a tour. From left are Mark O'Doherty, Kevin Barrett, Michael McGee and Cyril Ward.

He's 6 foot 5 and missing

In typical fashion Michael had organised yet another fabulous golfing holiday and this time the participants were PC Duffy, Billy Rodden, Sean O'Dwyer and Michael. They had travelled to Arizona for a Pro-Am in Phoenix.

They had a few days to spare so they headed into Las Vegas to sample the bright lights and the glitter of the gambling capital of the world. As soon as they got there, they hit the blackjack, pontoon, backgammon tables and whatever other gaming pastimes there were on offer. As everybody had their own plans how to spend the next two days, an arrangement was made that they would meet up at an appointed place at a given time, ready to head back to Phoenix.

In a blind panic

Billy was the first to get there, followed about an hour later by Michael who had just left PC in a casino, betting like 'there's no tomorrow' according to the 'old pro'. Five hours later and there was still no sign of Sean – Michael wasn't the slightest bit concerned but Billy was, by now, in a blind panic. He insisted that Michael and himself catch up with PC to tell him and bring him up to date with what was happening.

Sean had now been missing for six hours, a fact that didn't seem to worry PC unduly. He didn't even look up from the backgammon table. That is until Billy suggested that they should contact the LV police department to advise them that he was missing.

You'll be sectioned

"We are going to leave that one to you Billy, but I am going to offer you a piece of advice

These four evil looking murderers are still on the FBI most wanted list, thirty years after they raided three casinos in Las Vegas.

which might just come in handy. If you walk into a police station to report that a 6'5" Irishman on his holidays has gone missing in Las Vegas for six hours, they're going to call the local version of Gransha, have you sectioned and when you have been declared sane after a lengthy interrogation, they will deport you – that I can guarantee you". Needless to state Billy thought the better of it and Sean was duly found in another casino, making a healthy profit.

Wyatt Earp

If there was anything to do with Westerns it was right up P.C.'s alley because of his life-time interest in the Wild West. So when they were there, they had to visit Tombstone where the famous 'Gunfight at the O.K. Corral' took place and where Wyatt Earp was buried. A few photos beside his tombstone were taken, which reminds me of my favourite epitaph which was written on a tombstone in Utah –' here lies the body of Dentist McGill, in the biggest cavity he'll ever fill'.

Greatest shot ever?

It must be hundreds of articles I have now written by this stage but this one is going to be particularly enjoyable. On the annual Tour, I love meeting up with great old friends but I have a special affection for my secret lover, Eamon McCourt, my adversary and cash cow, or should I say turkey, George Pearson and the inimitable Davy Jones.

When I have the pleasure of having Davy beside me in the buggy, I love caddying for him. 99 times out of a hundred, he is looking to hit far too little club and I have to exert my authority to get the desired result. Not once, by the way, has he offered to pay me for my services.

The Pinnacle sang

First and foremost I am a statistician. I love figures (particularly the ones with pound notes on them) and records of past events. Having assimilated all of the great shots ever played in the 41 years of the Michael Doherty Tour, one shot stands out above all others. It was hit on the Wednesday of the 1999 tour at La Quinta. I have been told by witnesses that it was struck so sweetly, the Pinnacle started to sing as it left the club face.

The hole was the 202 yards par three 2nd on the Guadaiza nine of the La Quinta 27 holes complex, recognised as you can see from the cartoon drawn by my son Niall, as one of the most difficult holes on the planet.

Howitzer

Eamon MacManus and the McCarroll twins, Brendan and Brian were the other members of the fourball. Having seen some 'beezers' in their time, they knew a great shot when they saw one and provided the vital evidence to make my decision – from the moment the driver started on its backwards curve, Davy was in perfect harmony with his body. He reached the 90 degree turn at the precise moment of maximum power and unleashed a howitzer which was going nowhere else.

Four seconds after launch it re-entered and landed on the putting surface and two seconds later it was in the hole. The three spectators whooped with glee at their playing partner's wonderful, life changing shot. And he modestly accepted their admiration.

Rest day

But there was a slight problem. He played the shot of a lifetime on the Wednesday of the tournament – that was the 'rest day' and it didn't count. Well Davy, we are acknowledging it now – well done for playing the best shot ever that didn't count.

Davy-ana Jones and the hole of doom

"Happy Days"

Don O'Doherty was in the Crucible Theatre to see Mark Selby defeat Ronnie O'Sullivan in the final of the 2014 World Snooker Championship. He is pictured here with two fellow Irishmen, 1997 champion Ken Doherty and 1985 champion, Dennis Taylor.

Who you know in this life can often be the secret. No one knows that better than me. In the process of writing this book I needed the knowledge and dedication of someone special who could provide me with the vital background information I needed for this publication. There was only one man who do this for me – Don O'Doherty.

Over the past three months we have been in constant contact as more and more requests are piled on him. Funnily enough, he provided the same response to each of those requests – "CA, not a problem". I have used his encyclopaedic knowledge of the local history of golf to jog my memory – nothing was too much for him.

Don O'Doherty and myself go back to a time when life was not taken quite so seriously. The 'Rat Race' may have existed but we were not aware of it - all we wanted to do was get to the next round of the Senior Cup or the next round of the local snooker tournament.

Touch of an angel

As far as golf is concerned, he could best be described as eclectic. First of all he played left-handed, switched to right handed and then back to ciotog. But my abiding memory of him was his short game – he had the touch of an angel.

I could write all day about Don, his captaincy at City of Derry in 1972, his invaluable role at Faughan Valley Golf Club which included the role of president in 2010, his massive contribution to golf and snooker and the general well-being of the town he loved so well but I just don't have the space.

No mas CA

Over the past number of months Don has been invaluable. With his photographic memory, the encyclopaedia of knowledge which he has about a sport he loved is quite astonishing. Every golfer I needed information about, he had the details chapter and verse within days. Having that sort of back-up in a venture like this, produced in such a short time frame, was beyond value.

And when it came to the very final request he said to me, "CA, is that it, NO MAS"?. When I told him that that was the case he came out with a phrase I had never heard him use before – "Happy Days, CA, Happy Days".

'Close but no cigar'

I think you could describe my golfing career as 'close but no cigar'. I was a better than average player who was well capable of beating the best but a Championship win, the yardstick used to determine the men from the boys, eluded me. I think I lacked discipline – the appeal of the craic and the camaraderie associated with the great game was my downfall.

Perhaps it was my old partner in crime, P.C. Duffy, who summed it all up. Playing with him in a four ball match involving a right few shillings and up against Peter Villa and Eugene Dunbar, I made what he considered was a major faux-pas. He exploded into a rage. He blurted it out – "McCarroll, I always knew it - you're a textbook example of fur coat and no knickers".

I was very average until I was invited by the GUI Ulster Branch to take part in a golf instruction session at Royal Portrush. They had brought over the legendary John Jacobs to help us on our way. As he made his way down the line of young hopefuls he came to me. After hitting a few goods shots as far as I was concerned he asked me what I played off – I replied 2. His response was chilling – "you must have a good short game".

Practice, no play

I met him in the locker room afterwards and asked him what I needed to do. He advised me to get someone I could trust to line me up properly and after a few months of practice, no play, I should make a breakthrough. I asked my brother Brian, a player with excellent natural teaching skills, to be my mentor which he did with considerable success. Within a few months my game was transformed, now with the ability to control flight, a lot longer and rarin' to go.

I won Senior Scratch Cups at North-West, Ballybofey, Co. Sligo and Donegal and was selected to play for Ulster in 1983. I also played a role

as an Ulster selector, so I saw top amateur golf from both the playing and administrative angles.

Six down after 9

Two tournaments stand out in my amateur career. The first was the South of Ireland Championship at Lahinch in 1982. I had been playing really well and had worked my way to the quarter-finals, drawn against the rising young star from Cork, John McHenry. I was level par after nine holes and five down. I lost the 10th to go six down and all I could think about was avoiding a 'dog licence'.

Then it clicked

Then it all clicked. I holed a 30 footer for a 2 at the 11th, 40 footer at the 12th, birdied the 13th and 14th and was now just two down. I could see he was 'rattled' for the first time and I was now pressing very hard. The 15th and 16th were halved in par, and when I won the 17th with a par, I was just one down going up the last. When I hit the par five 18th in two and won it with a birdie, there was only going to be one outcome.

It was amazing!

I won the 19th with a par four and before I knew it I was lifted sky high by the huge crowd at the 19th, a treasured moment. And when Sheila, myself and the children walked into the dining room of the Aberdeen Arms Hotel that night I got a standing ovation – it was amazing!

In the semi-final I defeated Irish International Tom Cleary (Fermoy) at the third tie hole but lost by one hole in the final to Mick Morris (Portmarnock). I am not making excuses but I was suffering from sun stroke that day, the result of not wearing any headgear on a scorching Summer's day.

My highlight

But to win the City of Derry Scratch Cup in front of my fellow members in 1981 was my golfing highlight. There was a fantastic field, led by British

Amateur Champion Peter McEvoy, seeking to win the City of Derry Scratch Cup for three years in a row and Walker Cup star Ronan Rafferty who was playing his last tournament as an amateur.

There was a play-off between Peter and myself, and although I was nervous, I held it together to win with a birdie 3 at the third tie hole. And at this juncture I would like to mention my long-time friend and caddie, Patrick McGonagle, who had a big part to play in that memorable win – many's a great golfing holiday we had in our time.

My dad's reaction

But the one thing I cherished that day and will do so all my life was the reaction of my dad. The play-off was too much for him so he stayed at the clubhouse. Typical of the men of his day, a handshake was the sign of 'well done' but he couldn't help himself – he gave me a huge' bear hug', a moment of sheer joy for me.

At team level, I had considerable success with both City of Derry and North-West. With City of Derry we got to the All Ireland Finals of the Barton Shield at Lahinch in 1973 and Royal Dublin in 1974 and the Ulster finals of the Barton Shield at Belvoir Park with North-West in the 1990's.

In perspective

When I think back to Lahinch, the most significant event I can remember was poor Lexie Mitchell being hit full toss by a drive struck by my brother Frank at the 12th. Just over two years later, on 2nd December 1975 Lexie, along with Charlie McNaul, two unsuspecting, highly respected citizens of Derry were brutally murdered in the Dolphin Restaurant on the Strand Road by the INLA. It just puts life into perspective.

Just before the final of the South of Ireland Championship in Lahinch in 1982. Colm McCarroll (City of Derry) lost by one hole to former Kerry footballer, Mick Morris (Portmarnock) by one hole.

One of the highlights of my year as captain of Ballyliffin 2011 was greeting Rory McIlroy. Four days after winning the 2011 US Open Rory was contracted by 'Oakley' to have a photo-shoot in Ballyliffin. He was good to his word, arriving by helicopter

A thought from Joe Doherty

HI COLM. I must congratulate you on the work done on the history of Michael Doherty's tour. It will be a testament to the man himself and also the loyal members of his tour. It was for me an honour to be associated with him since we first met when Michael came to Cruit Island to lay out the golf course. We spent that day hitting balls from potential tee areas and it was not easy teeing up a ball without being up to your posterior in bent grass. (editor's note:- you are well used to that Joe) His layout still stands today and he always enjoyed announcing me as Mr. Joseph Doherty playing out of Cruit Island when I stood nervously on the 1st tee of his many tours.

247th captain

Every golfer in the north-west should be proud that one of their own, Gavin Caldwell, was awarded the ultimate accolade in amateur golf when he was invited to be the 247th captain of the Royal and Ancient Golf Club in 2015/16.

A charming and affable man, he readily accepted in a hectic schedule an invitation from both City of Derry and North-West to attend special functions in his honour last year. And that was during a year which saw him travel to so many parts of the world.

He was born in Clooney Park East 69 years ago and quickly took up golf as a youngster, hitting his first shots at Lisfannon. Then he moved to City of Derry where he played mostly with myself – 54 holes in a day was a regular occurrence.

"Magic weekend"

One of his prized possessions is a small scrapbook of articles which appeared in the 'Derry Journal', containing many references to his time in Derry. "My magic weekend took place in June 1966 when I went round City of Derry in 68 shots, two under par, (failed to win, but that didn't matter). And two days later I negotiated the Lisfannon links in a level par 72. Such happy memories."

When I met him last year at the Boys' Home Internationals in August at Ballyliffin he said he knew of Michael's condition and enquired if a visit was possible. I cautioned against it, and I am sorry I did now. But that's life.

In my childhood Gavin was a dear friend to me and, as we both approach 70 in a very short time, that friendship has never diminished. Well done old partner for achieving the honour of captaining the Royal and Ancient Golf Club. And more importantly, for being the same old Gavin Caldwell I met so many years ago.

The immediate past captain of the Royal and Ancient Golf Club, Gavin Caldwell, and myself were great golfing friends growing up at City of Derry and North-West. During the summer months, we played golf together nearly every day. I felt so honoured when he was made captain of the most famous club in the world and delighted that he specifically asked to meet me when he was honoured at City of Derry last year.

Stanley McDermott is not a happy man. He has just 'blanked' the last four holes at Mijas and is genuinely upset. But as you can see in the photo he was getting plenty of sympathy from Gilbert McLaughlin and Bobby Irwin.

Fat people have feelings too. Slightly overweight and not fully trained up for last year's event I thoroughly enjoyed the 'dawn patrol' and would hope I can get on it again this year. On the 1st tee last year at Poniente were John Hasson, myself, Peter Doherty and Kevin Barrett. On the 3rd day John Hasson scored a winning 38 pts – how in the name of Jaysus did he manage it!

My first job

Being managing director of the 'Derry Journal', the largest provincial newspaper in Ireland, wasn't the most straight-forward of occupations. I was 35 years there, experiencing all of the good and very troubled times we lived through. But there were more good than bad, so here goes with a few memories.

My introduction to the world of newspapers came when I was seventeen years old. My summer job was a two week stint on a "Klischograph", the latest in German technology, which made photographic plates. It had replaced the old chemical method which was considered too dangerous. Big Larry Doherty was my tutor and he couldn't be more helpful. I spent two weeks under his tutelage to ensure I was able to operate the equipment.

Pellet rifle

On the day he was heading off on holidays he turned to me and said – "it can boring here so I have a little past-time you might like to try". He brought out a pellet rifle and a small tin box full of pellets. He said "I go up to the top floor and take a few pot shots at the pigeons but, to tell you the truth, I have had little success. But have a go, you'll enjoy the craic."

He was no sooner out the door when I was on the top floor. I had a few pots with no success until I realised what the problem was – the sight was out of alignment by about ¾ inch so it was no wonder Larry thought he was blind.

What followed was a massacre. The second they landed on the roof, I was hitting them on every part of their anatomy. They were sliding down the roof, sticking in the gutter and falling into some neighbour's yard. It was senseless slaughter with no concept of a downside. And there wasn't the slightest pang of remorse. If it was nowadays the RSPCA would not approve.

Diplomacy needed

The 'Journal' banked in the Munster and Leinster next door and the manager was a charming man, Jack Costello. But Mr. Costello had a serious problem to discuss with Frank McCarroll senior and it had to be treated diplomatically. "I'll get straight to the point Frank, come with me to our back yard". Being bankers they had carried out a forensic body count and my father was told there were 28 pigeons either dead, decomposing, seriously ill or very lucky to have just minor injuries.

This is where the diplomacy came in. Without pointing a finger in any direction, he asked Mr. McCarroll to check if all was well next door. "Of course I will", said my father.

'Shooter' on the roof

The phone rang to the "Klischograph" office to say that my father wished to speak to me. I instinctively knew I was 'dead in the water'. Knocking on his door I entered, awaiting execution but what I got was a lesson in diplomacy. He said "Colm, I was talking to Mr. Costello next door and he said they think they saw a "shooter" on the top floor of our building, firing at pigeons. Will you keep an eye out for him".

In the years to follow, I was to witness so many examples of his wisdom, his enormous intellect, his humour and his modesty and when it came to diplomacy, he had no equals.

Thank you Christine

Many years ago in the Derry Journal when we had decided to install the very latest technology we needed a number of staff to train as touch-typists with shorthand skills. I asked about to find out who would be an ideal person and guess whose name came forward? – none other than this year's lady captain at City of Derry, Christine Mitchell.

I took advantage of the touch-typing lessons and here I am today, typing as fast as I can think. Thank you very much Christine – producing a book of this size without having the typing skills you taught me would be impossible.

Christine Mitchell

A moment I will never forget, holing out for a birdie at the 3rd tie hole to defeat twice winner of the British Amateur, Peter McEvoy and win the City of Derry Desmond Trophy for the first time.

Ideal example

In 2000, when I was planning to launch the 'Derry News', the now Minister for Finance, Mairtain O'Muilleoir, was Managing Editor of the Andersontown News. An affable, approachable man I asked him where I could go in Ireland to visit a provincial newspaper which had the latest in technology.

As an ideal example of a small family business, he suggested I contact Pauric Kennelly, owner of 'Kerry's Eye', the Kerry version of what I hoped the 'Derry News' would be. Sara, Niall and I did it in style – we flew from Derry to Dublin and on to Kerry to meet the Kennelly family. It was to be yet another extraordinary experience.

Plucked a pearl

We were given the welcome of welcomes by the Kennellys who couldn't do enough for us. Pauric was delightfully eccentric in the most charming of ways – when he wanted to give me some vital piece of information he told me to imagine there was a tree there. When I told him I could see it (I was lying), he raised his arm towards an imaginary branch and 'plucked a pearl from the tree of wisdom'.

His hand was empty but I had to hold out mine to receive the 'pearl'. When I got it, he told me to put it in my pocket. I thought I was going 'off me rocker'. This is not the figment of a fertile imagination, this is a true story.

In the kitchen

They took us round this treasure trove of modern technology, really cutting edge – I was fascinated. What happened next was truly unbelievable. He opened a door and suddenly we were in Kennelly's kitchen with the wife cooking up a feed for us. His home was attached to the business. I swear to God I am telling the truth.

She was a 'scream', one of the wittiest people I have ever met. "Do you see your man there", pointing to Pauric, "every time he sees the bank manager coming towards him, he crosses the street to get out of his way. He's trying to make me think he's penniless but I know he's rollin' in it".

An Irish jig

After we were fed royally, so it was back to the production department to see the paper put to 'bed'. I am so grateful that Niall and Sara were there to verify what happened when the last spread of pages went to press – the staff all lined up in a row, and led by Pauric, they started to do an Irish jig. And Pauric insisted that I join in. That was seventeen years ago but my family still 'slag' me relentlessly about it.

Eastern European ships

I have hundreds of stories I could retell about my experiences in the 'Journal' but here is another one I enjoy telling. It involves Pat McArt and myself, just after he had joined the staff in the early 1980's. A great journalist, he was up for any good story and when I told him about 23 Eastern European fishing vessels moored off Rathmullan, we had to have a run at it. Suitable arrangements were made through intermediaries based in the Pier Hotel so Pat, Larry Doherty and myself headed off to Rathmullan.

The Browns of Inch were running a regular ferry service out to the huge factory ships, so on a bitterly cold November day, we headed into the unknown. Climbing up the side of a huge ship on a rope ladder, not being able to swim, is life changing. Half way up that ladder I found religion again and quickly said what remnants of an "Act of Contrition" I could remember.

Get off my boat

We were welcomed politely by the captain. Politely that is until Larry produced his camera, an act of East-West aggression as far as the skipper was concerned. Immediately he pulled out a pistol and ordered us off

the boat. (ask Pat, he will confirm every line of this story). I glanced towards the water only to see the Browns making their way back to Rathmullan.

It was at this point that the diplomacy that I had learned from my father came into play. I told him that we were a small provincial newspaper with no political agenda whatsoever and that 23 ships landing in our back yard was very big news indeed.

You'll get a 'rooter'

To make a long story short it worked and after getting some great pictures and a great story we were back on Brown's boat on our way to the Pier Hotel. Half an hour later and five hot whiskeys each, it was big Larry who broke the silence – "I don't give two f's who you are, if you ever come up with an idea like that again I will give you a 'rooter' up the arse".

I could go on and on and on with the next story better than the last. That was the nature of the job I was in. It was so interesting and I enjoy recounting just a few memories of the more pleasant experiences I had down the years.

In the 41 year history of the Michael Doherty Tours the player who stands out above all others is Liam McCaul. His magical short game landed him five titles. He holed this putt to win by eleven points from second placed Eddie Gallagher at Poniente and Santa Ponsa.

World of politics

In the course of my role in the newspaper business I met three Taoiseachs. Garrett Fitzgerald, Brian Cowan and Albert Reynolds. They were all so committed to peace in Northern Ireland and I must say I was deeply impressed by Albert Reynolds, a very charismatic man. Pat McArt and myself greeted him when he graced our presence at the Derry Journal offices.

During my time in the newspaper industry I had the opportunity to meet some very interesting people from the world of politics. Taoiseachs Albert Reynolds and Garrett Fitzgerald were honoured guests at the 'Derry Journal', as were Sir Patrick Mayhew and Lord Kilclooney (John Taylor). John Hume and Martin McGuinness were frequent visitors, so I had the opportunity to meet many significant people. And in my time in the 'Derry News', Brian Cowen graced us with his presence.

The man who set up the visit by Albert Reynolds was local business man, Noel Gallagher. Of the great characters I have come across in my time, he is right up there in my estimation. At the appointed time for Mr. Reynold's visit we were gathered in Pat McArt's office awaiting his arrival.

Bord Na Mona fire log

After about half-an-hour, Noel's patience was exhausted, so he took a phone out of his jacket. It was the size of a Bord Na Mona fire log. He dials a number and I can clearly hear Mr. Reynold's voice on the other end of the line. "Where the hell (it was much stronger than that) are you, Albert, I have the Managing Director and Editor of the 'Derry Journal' here with their two arms the one length waiting on you". A contrite Taoiseach told him he was caught in traffic and would be there shortly.

Sir Patrick Mayhew was a gracious man and his visit was appreciated. This was at a time when the British Government realised that they needed realistic Nationalist opinion and we were in a position to provide that. Those politicians who visited us wanted to hear what we had to say. The likes of Pat McArt, Garbhan Downey and myself had our fingers on the pulse of what Derry and Donegal people thought about the political situation of the time. Hopefully our opinions were taken seriously. I am sure they were.

It was idyllic – until the sneeze

You couldn't get a more pleasant man to play golf with than George Pearson but he has this little idiosyncrasy which needs the urgent attention of a golf psychologist.

Here's my story of the day I played with him at Golf Park (Puntiro), which lies right on the flight-path into Palma. Air Berlin jets had been flying 200 feet overhead in the final run-in to landing and Georgie was blowing kisses to the 200 or so sunseekers, male or female it didn't matter to Georgie, every two minutes. He was totally oblivious to the thunderous sound of the jets and the landing gear crunching down.

It was idyllic – until a 'black cloud' descended on the 18th tee. In the middle of the left-hander's backswing I inadvertently sneezed. "Why the hell couldn't you have held your nose until I hit the ball?, he roared in his throaty Carrigans accent.

I replied rather foolishly that the jets hadn't put him off for the previous seventeen holes and he was only using me as an excuse for his shitty drive.

90,000 turkeys a year

The response was chilling – "I wring about 90,000 turkeys' necks a year and another one wouldn't matter two balls of blue to me". Thank God he salvaged 2 points at the hole and all was forgiven. But to this day he still keeps whinging about it – Georgie, please forgive me – I have since got my adenoids fixed so maybe you will play with me again.

But to tell you the truth I hope we don't. He's a grumpy wee so and so and, as I have developed 'wind' problems since I last played with him, I don't relish the prospect of trying to control my intestinal 'Beaufort scale' for Georgie's sake. Of course if I am standing downwind of him, now that's a different matter.

George Pearson - my hero

It's contestants of this quality that give the Michael Doherty Tour that added touch of class. Standing from left are Pat Mackey, Cahir McGeady, Willie Barrett (starter), Michael McCullough and Kevin Barrett.

Mad rush to the 'Piano Bar'

The minute the golf for the day is over, there is a mad rush to the 'Piano Bar' for a few pints before the evening meal. It is a tradition by this stage and I just love it – everybody is in a holiday mood and the craic is mighty. It's like an annual re-union, meeting old faces and just drinking in the atmosphere.

If you have had a good round there is no mention of it. If it has been a bad one, you'll get 'dog's abuse'. If you have just scored 20 pts, regret that you ever took up golf, and want to forget the six hour nightmare you had just experienced, you should have gone somewhere else.

His beady eye

Because Satan is waiting on you, with his beady eye honing in on you when you are still 100 yards from the bar. I love Georgie Pearson, but not after I have just disgraced myself again. He is like a rabid dog, hitching up his 'you know whats' and humiliating you in front of all and sundry. Why do I take it?

For one very simple reason – money. I'm not a wealthy turkey farmer, I am a man of modest means and I need to make a living. So when I am playing

well, I pretend to Georgie that I am not and he can't wait to get the 50 euro note out of his pocket. And I take him to the cleaners every time. Having revealed this now, I know the game is up and if I approach him in May, he will tell me where to shove my bet. But I reckon that over the years I have banked over 200 euro of Georgie's money. Or put it another way – I just look upon him as a cash cow who has paid for my alcohol intake for the past 10 years. Thank you Geogie for your kindness.

Brian makes history

I was there to witness a very big moment in the history of North-West Golf Club at Royal Birkdale in 2005. Our own Brian McElhinney had just won the British Amateur Championship, defeating John Gallagher by 5/4. I was so glad I made the decision to catch a plane from City of Derry Airport to Liverpool in the company of Frank Friel, Vincent Grant jun and James O'Donnell.

After an early three holes advantage to Brian in the morning round, Gallagher fought back and by the time it came to the 17th, it looked as if the Scot would bring it back to just one in arrears. Lying 30 yards short of the par five 17th green and 60 yards short of the flag he was to play one of the finest shots I have ever witnessed.

Pitching onto an undulating green with the flag placed on the crest of a small hill and the green sloping downwards past the flag towards a cavernous bunker, he did what I, and Brendan Edwards beside me, thought impossible. He fired the ball straight to the flag and as it bounced you would swear he had a string on it. It screeched to a halt to within four feet, he holed the putt for a winning four and steadied the ship. It was easy street after that.

Brian McElhinney's first major win, the North of Ireland Championship at Royal Portrush in 2003.

European Amateur win

Brian burst on the scene in 2003. He had already won several titles at boys' and youths' level, but now he was ready to move up a gear. He won the North of Ireland Championship at Royal Portrush, beating Ballyclare's Johnny Foster by one hole and then reached new heights when he won the European Amateur Championship.

2005 was to bring even greater glory. In the final of the Irish Close played at Donegal Golf Club, he was up against his great friend and club mate Michael McGeady. In a bruising match where no quarter was asked or given, Brian won by one hole.

Then it was on to greater things at Royal Birkdale which meant automatic entry into the British Open and the Masters at Augusta. What a surreal world to be living in! How many people have stayed in the 'Crow's Nest' at Augusta, Bobby Jones' attic in the clubhouse – a handful, and Brian is among them. His experience in 2006 will live with him forever, playing in the Masters with five times British Open champion Tom Watson and 2005 US Open champion Michael Campbell.

Huge contribution

His contribution at club level was also huge, contributing massively to the historic victory in the Irish Senior Cup at Rosslare in 2005. The former European Individual champion and current British Amateur title holder celebrated his 23rd birthday in style as North-West defeated Hermitage by 3-2 in the final. His performance at Rosslare against Greg Bowden was quite superb. Against a hapless opponent who played very well, Brian produced a flawless performance, with birdies at seven of the sixteen holes played.

Apart from playing in two British Opens in 2005 and 2006 and the Masters in 2006, he defeated US Amateur Champion, Edoardo Molinari by 3/2 to win the Georgia Cup, an annual match between the U.S. Open Amateur champion and the British Amateur Champion.

His record

Championships

1998 Donegal Boys' Champion; 2000 Connacht Boys' Champion; 2000 Tom Montgomery Boys' Order of Merit Champion; 2003 Connacht Youths Champion; 2003 North of Ireland Champion; 2003 European Amateur Champion; 2003 JB Carr Order of Merit Youth Champion; 2004 Irish Close Champion; 2004 Willie Gill Order of Merit Senior Champion; 2005 British Amateur Champion.

Representative Honours

1999 Ulster Boys (Interprovincials); 2000 Ireland Boys (Home Internationals); 2001 Ireland World Boys U-19; 2002 Ireland Youths (European Team Championship); 2002-2003 Ulster Youths (Inter-provincials); 2003-04 Ulster (Senior Interprovincials); 2003-2005 Ireland (Home Internationals); 2004 Ireland (Eisenhower Trophy

World Cup); 2004 Europe (Sir Michael Bonallack Trophy – Europe v Pacific Asia); 2003 & 2005 Ireland (European Team Championships); 2005 Great Britain and Ireland (Walker Cup); 2005 North-West (winners Irish Senior Cup).

Awards

2003 Donegal Sports Personality of the Year; 2003 Awarded Honorary Life Membership of North-West Golf Club; 2004 & 2005 Irish Golf Writers' Award for Men's Amateur of the Year; 2005 Radio Foyle Sports Personality of the Year Award; 2005 Renault Sports Award (for young up and coming golfers).

Other achievements

2004 Played in the British Open at Troon; 2005 Played in the British Open at St. Andrew's; 2006 Georgia Cup (winner of BritishAmateur v U.S Amateur Champion; 2006 Played in the U.S. Masters.

But a record which stands out for me is at local level in the annual singles match play tournament at North-West. At the age of 12, he won the Debonair Cup – very commendable. But to defend the title successfully for the following five years is astounding – what a match player, what a temperament!

Thanks to a very generous sponsorship offer, Brian will be able to concentrate on a playing professional career for the foreseeable future and he is already making his mark. We all wish him well.

On a personal level, I have had the opportunity to meet Brian on many occasions and to have met his relations. Believe you me, you would have to go a very long way to find a more modest, down to earth family. I feel privileged.

In a thrilling final against clubmate Michael McGeady, Brian won the 2004 Irish Close at Donegal Golf Club, Murvagh.

Brian McElhinney had the honour of representing Great Britain and Ireland and the USA in the 40th Walker Cup in 2005 at the Chicago Golf Club in Wheaton, Illinois. The USA team won by 12 and a half matches to 11 and a half. Seated, left to right, are Nigel Edwards, Brian McElhinney, Garth McGimpsey (captain), Richard Ramsey and Gary Wolstenholme. Standing, left to right are, Rhys Davies, Gary Lockerbie, Robert Dinwiddie, Matthew Richardson, Lloyd Saltman and Oliver Fisher.

Brian, winner of the European Individual Amateur Championship in 2003

The great man himself, Charlie McCafferty, pictured at the special Gala Dinner run in honour of Brian McElhinney winning the British Amateur Championship in 2005. Also in the picture are Bernie Coyle, Vincent Quigley, Dermott Coyle and Peter Anderson.

Lionel Munn - an amazing link

Second only to Brian McElhinney, the most successful golfer ever to grace the fairways of North-West was the legendary Lionel Munn. He won the Irish Close Championship in 1908, 1911,1913 and 1914 and was the first Irishman to win the Irish Open Amateur Championship, winning three years in succession, 1909, 1910 and 1911. For years he was a member of the Irish International team, as was his brother Ector.

Golf can be such an extraordinary game and here is a very interesting little story to prove it. Lionel Munn reached the final of the British Amateur Championship at Royal St. George's in 1937 only to be beaten by 3/2 by Robert Sweeney junior from the USA. The very same Robert Sweeney junior lost in the final of the US Amateur Championship in 1954 by one hole to the one and only Arnold Palmer. Golf can be such a small world!

Another Derry success story

City of Derry's David Jones achieved full Irish International status in 1998 following a highly successful run from 1995. His victories included the Waterford Scratch Cup, one of the biggest senior events in Ireland in 1997.

He put his name on the map when he won the Leinster Boys' Championship in 1996, was Irish Boys' Under 17 champion in 1997 and in 1988 he had a superb year, winning the Leinster Boys', Connacht Boys' and Irish Boys'.

At team level he was a Boys' International for three consecutive years, 1996, 1997 and 1998 and was the only person to have played on the Great Britain and Ireland Team for three years in a row. Appearances on the Irish Youth International team in 1997 and 1999 rounded off a very successful career in International team golf. David is now a teaching professional.

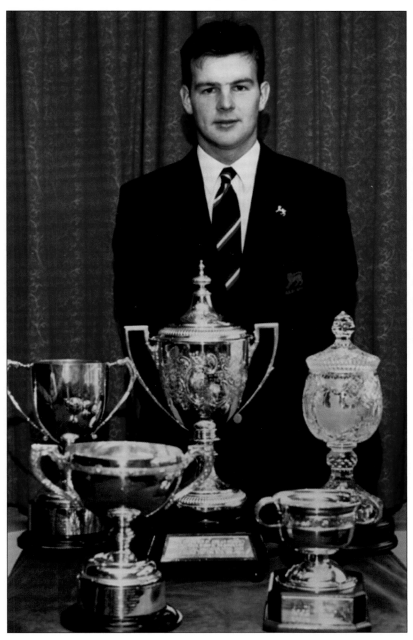

Another young Derry man who acquitted himself with distinction, David Jones. In a glittering young career, he made 1988 something special when he won the Leinster Boys', Connacht Boys' and the Irish Boys' championships.

Barney my friend

Barney McDaid

BARNEY WAS A great friend of mine. I knew him before he joined the Spanish trip to Majorca as we had played together at Prehen. He joined the tour after 2000 and was a regular until his health deteriorated. He roomed with me and was the life and soul of the party.

Filled with plenty of wit and humour he could match the younger members in the drinking stakes (as the author can confirm). A good golfer and competitor he always tried his best for the team.

On arrival Barney would head to Carlos café for his fish and chips, tea bread and butter. Many's a night was spent there enjoying the 'craic' and companionship of fellow golfers on the tour. I cherish those days and I will drink to his memory in May this year.

David Jones

Career to be proud of

I have known Michael McGeady since he was a child. I remember his first golfing days so many years ago at City of Derry and I have watched in admiration as he developed into the classy professional he is today. Along with his dad Cahir, I have travelled afar to see him play. He has had a number of great victories to which I will refer later, but Michael is someone who went so close to achieving full European Tour status, to winning the Irish Close and other significant events. In golf you must have that little added ingredient and that is luck, pure and simple.

It is hard to credit that his golfing career started way back in 1995 when he represented Ulster in the Boys' Interprovincial Championship and Ireland in the Home Internationals. Continuous representation at Boys', Youths and Senior International level, plus selection to the GB and Ireland Elite squad in 2004-05, rubber stamped his status as one of the top amateurs in the land. And for good measure he won both the Connacht and Leinster Boys' Championships in 1999.

Michael McGeady, winner of the Swalec Wales Challenge in 2008.

What a memory

I will divert for a moment to recall one of the proudest moments I have had in my life in golf and that also involved Michael. It came in 2005 when I travelled to Rosslare to see if North-West Golf Club could pull off an achievement that had eluded the Inishowen club for 110 years - winning the Irish Senior Cup. With a superb team which included Michael and recently crowned British Amateur champion, Brian McElhinney, they did just that. What a fabulous memory, what a night's celebration.

And to show you just how closely knit the world of golf can be, the golfer who finally won the day for North-West was none other than my old Barton Shield partner, Garrett Mallon. I couldn't help but think that when he partnered me in the final of the Ulster section of the Barton Shield at Malone a life-time ago, he must have thought he was playing with his grandfather.

Challenge Tour win

Back to young McGeady's exploits – he turned professional in 2005 and had his first big win three years later when he lifted the Swalec Open title, a full Challenge Tour event played in Wales. Among many fine performances, he won the IPGA Championship in 2013. Added to that portfolio were wins in the Quinn Pro-Am, Heritage Pro-Am and City of Derry Pro-Am.

So near and yet so far

The event which must have been the hardest to stomach was the final qualifying stage for the European Tour at San Roque on the Costa Del Sol. Cahir and I watched on as he played magnificent golf, only to miss out by one shot after

six rounds. It was heartbreaking, so near and yet so far. I am eternally grateful that I was never subjected to pressure at that level of golf in my life.

Like many of his contemporaries, he has a family to care for so he now mixes a more restricted playing schedule with a teaching position alongside Seamus Duffy in Strabane. You will not get a better instructor than Michael – many's a time, he has given me little tips that made all the difference. He has his father's sense of humour. One beautiful Spring day at Lisfannon, I was in the 'pits' with my chipping stroke and begged him for a solution – "ever thought of taking up table tennis?", was the cheeky brat's suggestion.

He has it all

In truth Michael has got it all. Along with his grandparents and his lovely wife Lisa, he dotes on little Molly, now six years old, who will be a name to watch out for on the European Ladies Tour a few years down the line and Jack who will win the 2040 British Open if Michael has anything to do with it. He has been a credit to City of Derry and North-West, his province, his country and most importantly, to his family. He has rightly earned the respect of those lucky enough to have crossed his path.

His record

1996 – 2005 Boys Youth & Senior Interpros
1996 – 2005 Boys Youth & Seniors Internationals
2004 – 2005 Member of GB & I Elite squad
1999 Connacht & Leinster Champion
2005 Member of North West Senior cup All Ireland winners
2005 TURNED PROFESSIONAL
2008 Winner of the SWALEC OPEN (Challenge Tour)
2009 Winner of the QUINN PRO AM
2013 Winner of the HERITAGE PRO AM
2013 PGA CHAMPION
Also winner of CITY OF DERRY PRO AM
Also Member of CITY OF DERRY all Ireland FRED DALY Team

To have two City of Derry golfers on the Irish team which played Scotland in Cork 1999 was some honour for the Derry club. Standing, from left, are Michael McGeady, Graeme McDowell, Colm Moriarty and Michael Hoey. Seated are David Jones, John Brett (captain) and Justin Keogh.

Pictured at the European Championships at Hillside in 2005 were, standing from left, Jim Carville, Michael McGeady, Seamus McTiernan and Darren Crowe. Seated are Rory McIlroy, Mark Gannon (non-playing captain) and Brian McElhinney.

Hugh's outstanding career

Hugh Brendan Smyth was born on 10th June 1950, son of Dan and Violet Smyth. Originally from Newcastle, Dan soon integrated with the City of Derry members and was outstanding in Ulster Cup games on the course and indefatigable on club affairs in the Council Chamber, being virtually single-handedly responsible for the launching of the Desmond Trophy.

Hugh first caught the media eye by opening the 72 holes 1970 British Youths' Golf Championship with a record equalling 64 at the Barton Course near Edinburgh. The fact that he equalled Ryder Cup player, Bernard Hunt's record of 1966 needs no further comment. He finished runner-up to Baldavino Dassu, a 17 year old Italian schoolboy destined later to become a successful regular on the European circuit.

Unprecedented feat

The unprecedented feat of a City of Derry member winning the 'East of Ireland Championship' at Baltray in 1974 opened all golfing doors to Hugh. He did, in fact, represent his country before his province although playing for Ulster in 'non-official' games against West of Scotland and Lancashire. Indeed, at the time of his winning the 'East' in 1974, he joined the exalted company of Billy Hume (1944) and Norman Drew (1952) as the only trio of Ulstermen to have won the 'East'.

Hugh, in fact, made his international debut in the six man European Cup Team at the Falkenstein Club, Hamburg in West Germany in July 1974, losing his foursomes partnered by Paddy Caul and winning his singles by 3 and 2.

Success in 'Internationals'

In the Home Internationals in 1974 he was unsuccessful in his morning foursomes with Mark Gannon against Michael Bonnallack and G.R.D Eyles, but opened his account with a one hole victory against Geoffrey Marks, a member of the victorious 1971 Walker Cup Team. Further success followed against Scotland, and although beaten in the foursomes, he held the tenacious Sandy Stephen to a half in the singles. The final match against Wales on the Friday saw Hugh, in partnership with Brian Kissock, complete the double winning both his foursomes by 2/1 and his singles against J.K.D Povall by 3/1 to emerge with the very satisfactory overall score of 3½ matches out of 6.

Further European Honours

June 1975 saw Hugh travel to Killarney for the European Team Golf Championship. In a very disappointing Irish team, Hugh enhanced his already growing reputation by gaining four points out of a possible six in the tournament. The respected sports correspondent, John Redmond, wrote at the time "While Ian Elliott emerged as the hero yesterday (the match to decide 7th and 8th positions), his fellow Ulsterman Hugh Smyth came through with the best record on the team. He won four of six matches to confirm his potential and my prediction is that he will make the Walker Cup Team in two years."

By the time the Home Internationals came to be played at Portmarnock in 1975, Hugh Smyth emerged as the player with the best record in the Irish side, enjoying a 62.5%

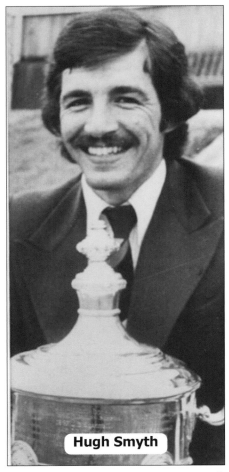

Hugh Smyth

success rate winning seven and halving one of his twelve games for Ireland. The most notable scalp was that of Walker Cup and Ryder Cup star Mark James at the 18th. He was to come 'back from the dead', being four down with six to play. In fact, a petty rules squabble probably cost Hugh a comfortable victory, James claiming that Hugh had interfered illegally with the line of his putt at the 6th hole, Hugh being one up at this stage.

Applauded off 18th

Between Killarney and Portmarnock Hugh eclipsed an international field in the Mullingar Scratch Cup, being applauded off the 18th green after a decisive three shot victory. The year was to end in further triumph when Hugh was selected as first travelling reserve to a Commonwealth Team which included two future Open Champions and three Walker Cup players, two of them members of the successful 1971 side at St. Andrews.

1976 brought further success to Hugh. The huge, tight tree lined course at Cologne proved too much for some of the Irish Team, one of the partnerships suffering the ultimate humiliation of having to borrow a golf ball from the opposition to complete their round. Hugh remained unbeaten in his singles and winning one of his foursomes, he emerged with an excellent four points out of a possible six.

In illustrious company

In the same year, in fact, Hugh had the unique distinction of being the only Irish man selected for the St. Andrew's trophy, the match between Great Britain and Ireland v Europe. Nick Faldo, Sandy Lyle, Gordon Brand and Ian Woosnam were all on that team.

Moving to Newcastle, Co. Down, in 1977, to join his father in business, Hugh played less and less serious golf and on returning from another successful continental outing in Denmark where he was selected for only one game, he decided to retire from International golf. In his one game, incidentally, Hugh, five down after six holes, recovered magnificently to win the 18th and half the match. Again the words of golf correspondent, John Redmond are worth quoting; "The selectors have certainly cause to blush as Smyth has played just one match out of a possible six."

Don O'Doherty

The Irish International Team which played at Muirfield in the Home Internationals in 1976. Standing from left are A.D. Pierce, N. Lehane, J. Harrington, B.J.S. Kissock, H.B. Smyth and Eddie Dunne. Seated from left are T. Cleary, L.M. McCarthy (non-playing captain), Declan Brannigan and D.P.W. Heather. Missing are D. O'Sullivan and M.D. O'Brien.

The Irish International Team which played in the Quadrangular Continental Matches in Cologne in 1976. From left are J.G. McErvel (president GUI), M.D. O'Brien, T. Cleary, N. Lehane, D.P.W. Heather, D. Brannigan, H.B. Smyth and L.M. McCarthy (non-playing captain).

Distinguished career

Frank McCarroll first distinguished himself in the Ulster Boys Open at Royal Belfast scorching home in 32 shots in the qualifying round before progressing to the match-play final where he lost to boy prodigy, Brian O'Brien by 2 and 1 in a memorable match. Evidence of O'Brien's undoubted ability was found in no small measure when he scored a hat trick of victories in the Connaught Boys in 1961, 1962 and 1963. He also annexed the Munster Boys' in 1962 and 1963. Turning professional and taking up a post at Shannon Golf Club, it is sad to relate that O'Brien died in London in May, 1986.

Studying dentistry at Queen's University, Frank now a 1 handicap golfer, again distinguished himself by winning the Irish Universities Stroke Play Championship twice at Baltray and Royal Portrush and the British equivalent title at Llandudno.

Holed 2nd shot at St. Andrew's

Pride of place, however, was reserved for his victory in the Boyd Quaich Trophy finishing in 'the Grand Manner' by holing his second shot at the 72nd hole at St. Andrews – what Doug Saunders would not have given for that eagle in the 1970 Open Championship.

Frank made his Ulster debut in 1965 and remained a regular until 1971, accumulating the impressive record over 49 matches of 30 wins with 4 matches halved. A gifted foursomes player Frank was the regular partner of Bertie Wilson who certainly appreciated his talent.

The 1968 Irish Close Championship has bitter-sweet memories for Frank, for while losing in a final reminiscent of the old cricket adage, "There's two teams out there, but only one playing cricket", Frank's majestic golf was overshadowed by O'Brien's miraculous scrambling; the 15th hole at Dunluce being a typical example where O'Brien halved the hole in four after being buried behind a bush on the right of the purgatory fairway.

Called up for Ireland

The happy sequel of the 'Close' was that Frank was selected to represent Ireland at Gullane in 1968, rubbing shoulders with the likes of Peter Oosterhuis and Peter Benka, daunting opposition indeed. He retained his place in 1969 at Killarney, his overall record reading, played 10, won 3, lost 7.

At provincial level, Frank has been a semi-finalist twice in the North, once in the West and was pipped by a single shot by Roddy Carr in the Baltray East of Ireland Stroke-Play event. His scratch cup performances of course, will always be overshadowed by his five Desmond Trophy Titles, although he has also annexed the 'Guinness' at Rosses Point and the 'North West' at Lisfannon.

Fighting qualities

My own enduring memory of the great fighting qualities of Frank occurred at Moyola in the quarter final of the Irish Senior Cup in 1985 when, all square with the redoubtable Peter Waddell of Knock, he emerged from the impossible situations at 3 consecutive holes to win at the 20th, putting City of Derry into the Ulster Finals for the first time.

Frank's calm temperament hides a shrewd golfing brain allied to a quiet fighting spirit. At no time does he ever give the impression that golf is anything more than a game to be played to the best of one's ability but most of all, to be enjoyed. He has made light of a painful physical condition, indeed he will probably not thank me

Frank McCarroll

for mentioning it at all.

Proof of the esteem in which Frank is held was evidenced when he was elected captain of the triumphant Ulster team, the trophy of which was destroyed in the 1982 fire at Prehen. He went on to captain Ireland and was picked as an Walker Cup selector. He is an honorary life member of City of Derry, North-West and Killarney.

Don O'Doherty

His Record

Championships – Semi-final of the North of Ireland 1961, 1963, 1968; semi-final of the West of Ireland 1969; final of the Irish Close 1968.

Representative honours – Ulster Interprovincial 1965 – 1971; Irish International 1968, 1969.

Other achievements – Ulster selector for 11 years in 1970's and 1980's including captaincy in 1980, 1981, 1982 and 1983. Irish selector for 10 years 1988 to 1997; Irish captain in 1994, 1995 and 1996; Walker Cup selector 2002 to 2005.

Won City of Derry Scratch Cup 5 times; North-West Scratch Cup; Guinness Scratch Cup at Rosses Point.

The inaugural North-West Senior Scratch Cup at Lisfannon in 1972. From left are Frank McCarroll, Joe Carr and Brendan Edwards.

Frank McCarroll being presented with the Desmonds Scratch Cup in 1970 by John Desmond. Also in the photo from left are Brendan Quigley, captain, Brian Desmond, Aubrey Thompson, honorary secretary and Jack Doherty, president.

"You need John Counihan"

During his international career, Frank McCarroll would have many interesting stories but the one that happened on Mahony's Point in Killarney in 1968 is hard to beat. It was the match against England and he had been drawn against John Davies, not renowned for his charm.

Frank's elderly caddie, John Counihan, took an immediate dislike to him and the feeling was mutual. It all came to a head at the 6th where Davies made a caustic remark to the Killarney caddie, who duly 'blew a gasket'. From out of Frank's bag came a club

and Counihan made a run at the Englishman. Davies' fleetness of foot saved the day as he made his escape from the mad Killarney man.

G.U.I officials immediately sacked the poor man and a replacement was brought in. The match continued and it duly reached crisis point at the 16th. Two up with three to play, Davies played a wonderful shot to eight feet at the par five 16th. Frank ruefully turned to his new caddie for clubbing advice and asked what he thought was needed. The caddie wasted no time – "Sir, I think you need John Counihan".

The Irish International team which competed in the European Team Championship in Belgium in 1994. Standing from left are Gary Murphy, Padraig Harrington, Frank McCarroll (non-playing captain) and John Morris. Seated from left are Garth McGimpsey, Keith Nolan and Jody Flanagan.

Lovely way about him Denis 'Ginger' Doherty

My abiding memory of 'Ginger' was him arriving up at North-West, taking a few clubs out of the boot of the car and heading out for a few holes. It was his routine but it was interrupted constantly by people who loved to hear what he had to say for himself.

Like his older brother, he was one of the old school, a true gentleman with a lovely way about him. And like Michael he was gifted with a wonderful sense of humour. He enthralled his many friends with some great stories from a life spent in the world of golf and music.

Renowned musician

Apart from being a canny golfer who knew every blade of grass at Lisfannon, he was a renowned musician, playing on the drums and singing with some of the classy old bands of yesteryear - the "Swinging Viscounts", the "Moonlight Orchestra" and Michael Galbraith. The "Plaza" in Buncrana on a Sunday night was a place not to be missed.

Stage manager

One of his passions was the annual pantomime in St. Mary's Hall, Buncrana. For many years he was the stage manager, ensuring its reputation as one of the best parochial festivals in the country.

Denis was a devoted family man whose first priority was his family. Predeceased by his wife Grace, his four children Anne Marie, Gillian, Louise and Roisin were the love of his life. What a sad time it must have been for them when he passed away in June 2015.

My strong advice to Eugene Dunbar, Frank McCarroll and Karl Doherty is to make sure you stay deadly silent when the wee man Georgie Pearson from Carrigans is teeing off.

What a typical sight. Anywhere there was golf to watch, my father Frank would be there. He was the original golf fanatic.

Impressive portfolio

Brendan Mc Carroll was born in Derry in 1985. His first swing of a golf club was at the age of two, his first clubs at six were cut down irons and by the age of eleven he was playing competitively at his home club Ballyliffin. I have only had the privilege of playing with him once and what a wonderful striker he is.

In 2001 he won the Qualifying Stage of the under 15 Irish Boys Panel and was chosen to represent Ireland on the two man team Young European Masters tournament in Augsburg, Germany, coming 5th. That was the beginning of his career proudly representing Ulster and Ireland in Boys, Youth and Senior national and international squads until 2006 when he turned pro.

Round of the day

Brendan also achieved individual amateur success. He won the Irish Boys Amateur Close Championship in 2003 by four strokes, shooting the round of the day, which earned him a place in the Faldo Junior Series final in Brocket Hall Hertfordshire, the Duke of York Young Champions Trophy in the Isle of Man and the Darren Clarke Foundation at Portmarnock. In 2004 he won the Ulster Youths Championship at Malone.

Won East in 2006

Lying seven shots behind going into the final day at a windswept Baltray course in the "East of Ireland" Championship in 2006, he made up the deficit and went on to win by two shots.

He wanted to be a professional so, in 2007, he joined the UK based Europro Tour after sailing through the qualifying stages. Looking for international competition he qualified for the Alps Tour in 2010. Here he made a huge leap forward with four notable wins in the last 3 seasons. He goes into this season with only one thought in mind - to earn his European Tour card.

AMATEUR ACHIEVEMENTS TEAM HONOURS 2006: Ireland Sherry Cup, Spain 2005: Ireland Senior Team Carey Cup (winners) 2005: Ulster Interprovincial Seniors (winners) 2005: Ireland Youths Team v Wales 2004-2005: Ulster Interprovincial Youths 2004: Ireland Boys Team v Canada 2002-2003: Ulster Interprovincial Boys 2002: Boys Home International 2001: European Young Masters two man Ireland Team

INDIVIDUAL HONOURS 2006: East of Ireland Championship Winner 2006: Rosapenna Scratch Cup Winner 2005: Ulster Youths Championship 2nd 2004: Ulster Youths Championship Winner 2003: Nissan Irish Boys Amateur Close Winner 2001: European Young Masters, Germany 5th 2001: Boyd Cup Winner

PROFESSIONAL ACHIEVEMENTS : 2014: Alps Tour Colli Berici 4th; 2014: Alps de Las Castillas 7th; 2014: Open Peugeot Winner 2014: Abruzzo Open 10th 2014: Open International de Rebetz 8th; 2013: Open de St. Francois Guadeloupe 7th; 2013: Friuli Venezia Giulia Open 5th; 2013: Gosser Open Winner.

Brendan McCarroll pictured with Nick Faldo, when he returned home from Baltray after winning the East of Ireland Championship in 2006.

Brendan McCarroll pictured with the Gosser Open Trophy which he won on the Alps Tour in 2013.

Brendan McCarroll holds aloft the East of Ireland Trophy which he won in 2006.

Brendan McCarroll got another great win under his belt when he won the Peugot Open on the Alps Tour in 2014.

One fateful night

I had never sung in public in my life and I was quite happy to keep it that way. It was all to change one fateful night in Mrs. Doyle's Bar. Myself and Barney McDaid called in about 2 am for a quiet nightcap, only to find that a Karaoke session had just begun. And who were down to sing – none other than big Willie and Captain McCourt.

Before I could utter the words "get lost", Willie had my name down for a song of my choice. I said to myself, "what the hell". When you come to think of it, the song will last only three minutes and nobody will listen anyway. The very first song that came into my head was the Ballad of Lucy Jordan by Marianne Faithfull , so I wrote it down.

Best-ever version

It was to change my life. Willie and Eamon were probably talking bull-shit but they told me it was the best-version they had ever heard of the song. To make things worse, Big Willie mentioned it on his programme on Radio Foyle.

I'm only human. Every chance I got in the car from there on I sang my heart out, perfecting the notes as I went along. Now I was ready for the big time. Over the next two years I was to sing Seven Spanish Angels in Leo's, straight over to Doyle's to treat my fans to my version of Lionel Ritchie's Hello, back to Flanagan's to sing Walk like an Egyptian and finish the night off with Teenage Kicks in Munroe's. It was like a malignant disease.

I blame Willie Barrett. He said on Radio Foyle that I was a class Karaoke singer and it went to my head. Every chance I got I had a microphone in my hand.

A mysterious shape

I did get a cure. It came in the form of a photograph I received anonymously in the post. I was told that while I was singing in Flanagan's one night, this mysterious shape appeared behind my right shoulder and he was clearly singing the lyrics – I was miming. I showed the photo to a well-known local genealogist who was able to tell me that he was a dead ringer for my great, great grandfather on my mother's side – he had just come back to give me a helping hand. It was the last time I ever sang.

Kevin – head and shoulders .....
the best ever shot

I have been asked by the editor to adjudicate on what I believed to be the best shot ever played in the 41 year history of the Michael Doherty Tour. I have pondered long and hard – I have woken in the middle of the night, panicking that I might have forgotten that 'unforgettable' shot, because I do remember vividly all the truly forgettable shots.

I remember Stephen Wray's chip shot on the 18th at Santa Ponsa, a truly classy shot which got him into a play-off. Or was it Dunbar's master stroke at the 18th, again at Santa Ponsa, where he hit an 8 iron to six inches to win in 2015.

No. Of the 797,104 shots that were struck in anger in the 41 year history of the tour, the one that is head and shoulders above the rest is North-West member Kevin Doherty's shot on the 9th at Poniente in 1989.

No Stradivarius

To describe Kevin's swing, it's no Stradivarius more like Cat Malogen. He drags the club away along the ground until his left shoulder has no option but to pick it straight up. Now that's not a good place to be – it's like being in Buncrana on a Saturday night – all dressed up and nowhere to go.

Suspended in mid-air, he spins his tiny frame with the ferocity of a light-weight boxer at the waiting chin. As he reaches impact he loses his balance and spins like a ballet dancer. He has to, because if he doesn't, it's odds on he'll end up in traction in the acute injuries ward in Altnagelvin. Every time I hear Bridie Gallagher singing "they're cutting the corn in Creeslough today", young Kevin's swing comes into my head

Back to the 9th tee at Poniente. It's a long, long par 3, playing every inch of its 190 plus yards. Using every ounce of his 7 stone 8 ounce frame, he 'bombed' his driver off the tee and pirouetted, according to witness Con Boyce, four times before his shuddering frame came to a halt. "Where am I", he asked, "am I back at Lisfannon"?

Where did it go?

"Where's me ball, where did it go"? By this time the remaining members of his fourball, Billy Rodden, Con Boyce and Maurice Brennan were in ecstasy – they were there to witness the first ever 'hole-in-one' on a Michael Doherty Tour. Champagne flowed in the bar afterwards as the former bank manager 'lost the run of himself'.

Jaysus - Where did that go?

Kevin 'Nureyev' Doherty

Seven 'aces'

Believe it or not, there have been 7 'aces' in the 41 year history of the Tour. It was reported in the 'Derry Journal in 1992 that "the shot of the tournament belonged to Joe Ramsey whose pin splitting tee shot at the 165 yards long 3rd at Santa Ponsa finished in the hole. The club used was a six iron.

In 1995 it was reported that North-West's Paul Doherty was to play a wonder shot at the 167 yards par three 4th hole at La Cala North. In 1996 it was John Moran's turn. On the first day at Son Antem, he holed his tee shot at the 16th. There were no less than three 'aces' in 1999. Both Paul O'Doherty and Eddie Gallagher holed out at the 2nd at Mijas while Davy Jones tamed the mighty second at La Quinta.

Two great old stalwarts of the Michael Doherty Tour, Walter Burnside and Mercer Shaw. They were part and parcel of every aspect of a great annual week's golf and fun.

Ready for a feast

Going to Portrush where the Irish Open was taking place in 2012 was a must. Derry was buzzing at the time with the "Clipper" festival and it was just great to be alive. We decided to watch the golf live on the opening day making the journey to Portrush by train. Cahir McGeady, PC Duffy and myself were on our way to witness a feast of golf.

Surprisingly the only person we knew on that train was former Bank of Ireland manager, Kevin Doherty. Old timers on the Michael Doherty Tour will remember the exploits of Kevin at Poniente in 1989 when he became the first-ever tour member to record a hole-in-one at the 190 yard 9th.

"Let's go to the marquee"

Once through the turnstiles at Portrush, we parted from Kevin and made our way towards an obvious vantage point – we all knew Portrush like the back of our hands and had picked our ideal spot with meticulous care. As we made our short journey to our special little place, it started to rain. Someone came up with a great idea – let's go to the tented village till the rain passes, so we headed to the huge marquee with the name BAR printed on it.

We never left it. Bar what we saw on the huge television screens, that was it. We did not witness one "live" shot, not one single one. I know it was a disgrace but it had nothing to do with me. I would have been perfectly happy to put up my umbrella but the two boyos were in form for a feast of the "devil's buttermilk".

One forward, one left

The train was heading back to Derry at 5pm so we made our way back to the station about 4.30. We had less than two miles to walk but I do know that it took me nearly three. For every step I took forward I took one to the left until at one stage I felt dizzy walking round in circles. Thankfully the older, more experienced hands were there to guide me to my destination.

Immediately back in Derry, Cahir, PC and myself headed to the "Clipper" for some more sustenance – my body was crying out for it at this stage. We were invited on to Gary McLaughlin's luxury liner, 'Southern Comfort', named after his favourite tincture, to finish off a perfect day.

I hadn't seen him

It was the following Tuesday when I met Kevin Doherty down at Lisfannon. Curious to know how he got on at Portrush, I mentioned that we hadn't seen him. "What do you mean, you didn't see me – you were sitting beside me on the way back from Portrush. And do you not remember what happened as we headed through Magilligan – you started singing Black Hills of Dakota and everybody on the carriage joined in the chorus".

I immediately went to 'Alcoholics Anonymous' to join up. They told me to "wise up" as I had already taken it seven times in the past month.

Marvellous setting in 1976

The first ever trip organised by Michael set out for Scotland in 1976. It was eventful to say the least but thoroughly enjoyed by the party of fifty-two. Two British Open Championship courses, Carnoustie and St. Andrew's, plus the picturesque Downfield and the magnificent Western Gailes on the Ayrshire coast provided a marvellous setting for the inaugural event.

The honour of winning went to City of Derry four handicapper, Gerry Coyle. A steady performer with a solid all-round game Gerry compiled a 72 holes total of 127 pts to finish three ahead of Jock Balmer (9).

Overall results

1, Gerry Coyle (4) 127 pts; 2, Jock Balmer (9) 124 pts; 3, Sean Doherty (15), North-West, 122 pts; 4, Charlie Nicell (8), North-West, 120 pts; 5, Cahir McGeady (4) 116 pts; 6, George Sweeney (10) 115 pts; 7, Jim Stewart (14) 114 pts; 8, Eamon MacManus (4) 113 pts; 9, Colm Duffy (7) 112 pts; 10, Jack Logue (10) 112 pts. Scr to 9 – 1, J.C. Cameron (5) 110 pts; 2, F.A. Hegarty (9) 103 pts; 3, James Longwill (4) North-West, 99 pts. 10 to 18 – 1, Raymond Bakewell (10), Ballycastle, 107 pts; 2, George Simms (10) 105 pts; 3, Stanley McDermott (16) 103 pts. Seniors – 1, Joe McCauley (11) 109 pts; 2, Cahir Fitzpatrick (15) 108 pts.

Team results

1, Frank McCarroll (1), Jock Balmer (9), Hugh Quigley (14) and Fred Aicken (15) 343 pts; 2, Cahir McGeady (4), Christie McWilliams (11), John Bradley (11) and Tom Crossan 339 pts; 3, Gerry Coyle (4), Ken McConomy (8), Cathal McKeever (15) and Eugene O'Doherty (16) 333 pts.

Daily results:

Carnoustie – 1, Frank McCarroll sen (14) 32 pts; 2, Gerry Coyle (4) 32 pts; 3, Sean Doherty (15) 30 pts. St. Andrews - 1, Fred Aicken (15) 38 pts; 2, Eamon McElroy (10) 36 pts; 3, Cahir McGeady (4) 36 pts. Downfield – 1, Eddie McCauley (17) 32 pts; 2, Gerry Coyle (4) 32 pts; 3, Jock Balmer (9) 31 pts. Western Gailes – 1, Gerry Coyle (4) 32 pts; 2, Billy Rodden (8) 32 pts; 3, Frank McCarroll sen (14) 31 pts.

Gerry Coyle had the honour of winning the first-ever Michael Doherty Tour.

At the presentation of prizes in the George Hotel, Stranraer, Mr. Colm Duffy, captain of City of Derry, paid tribute to the excellent manner in which the tournament had been organised by Mr. Michael Doherty and expressed the hope that this would be the first of many Michael Doherty Tours.

Just about to tee off are, from left, Bill Bratton, Brian Duffy, Stewart Canning and Hugh McQuilkin.

Group taken in the City of Derry car park before leaving on the 1976 Scottish Tour. Front Row: (left to right): James Longwill, N.W.; Danny McNally, Marvyn Gilmore, Du Pont; Hugh Quigley, N.W.; Peter McCready, Gerry Coyle, Don O'Doherty, Billy Rodden, John Bradley, Charlie Nicell, N.W.; Ted Hegarty, Sean Doherty, N.W.; Pat Doherty, Dennis Hegarty, N.W. Standing: Liam Bradley (Driver); Ken McConomy, Michael Doherty, Tom Cassidy, Eamon McElroy, John Monaghan, Joe Foley, Seamus McBriarty, Stanley McDermott, George Taylor, John McAteer, Cathal Langan, Davy Bredin, Sam Anthony, Craig Cameron, Eddie McCauley, Frank McCarroll (Jnr), Tommy Murray, Frank McCarroll (Snr), Billy Elliott, Eamon MacManus, Tom Crossan, George Simms, Joe McCauley, Raymond Bakewell (Ballycastle), Cathal McKeever, Captain Byrd (Du Pont), Roger Connor, Eamon O'Doherty, Christie McWilliams, Jack Logue, Jack Doherty, Fred Aicken, Sam Hestor (Du Pont), George Sweeney, Cahir Fitzpatrick, Jim Stewart, Jock Balmer.

Successful home coming

Normally it would have been impossible to get a large group on Muirfield, home to the Honourable Company of Edinburgh Golfers and one of the most exclusive clubs in the world of golf. But an exquisitely crafted letter from Michael to the formidable Captain Paddy Hamner, secretary manager of Muirfield, resulted in the "red carpet" being laid out for their visitors from Ireland. Not only were they invited to play singles in the morning, Captain Hamner provided a magnificent buffet lunch and invited the party to play foursomes in the afternoon. I will never know to this day how the "old pro" managed to pull that one off.

This is the same Captain Paddy Hamner who, when he heard that Tom Watson had ventured out late in the evening to re-play the 18th with hickory shafted clubs after winning the British Open at Muirfield in 1980, rushed out on the course, informed him he was trespassing and ordered him off the hollowed turf.

Jock's successful homecoming

It was back to Scotland in 1977 but, like the inaugural trip, the weather was to play a major part. It was reported at the time that "at Gullane the wind whipped in from the Firth of Forth with such force that it was not uncommon for players to arrive on the 4th tee without having registered a single stableford point". It was not surprising that the trend of thought veered towards warmer climates.

Again the quality of the courses was superb. Gullane and Longniddry were two great tests while the British Open venue at Muirfield was to prove a never to be forgotten experience.

Who better to win on Scottish soil than Jock Balmer who made a successful return to his homeland to win with 93 pts over three rounds of 11 handicap. This time he turned the tables on Gerry Coyle who had 90 pts off 5.

Overall results

1, Jock Balmer (11) 93 pts; 2, Gerry Coyle (5) 90 pts; 3, Frank McCarroll jun (2) 86 pts; 4, Brian McCarroll (4) 84 pts; 5, Jack Logue (10) 84 pts; 6, George Sweeney (10) 83 pts; 7, Cahir McGeady (4) 82 pts; 8, Danny McNally (7) 80 pts; 9, Jim Stewart (14) 78 pts; 10, Peter McCready (10) 78 pts.

Team results

1, Danny McNally, Jack Logue, Jim Stewart and Pat Loughrey 242 pts; 2, Michael Doherty, Jock Balmer and Fred Aicken 240 pts; 3, Frank McCarroll jun, Frank McCarroll sen, Christie McWilliams and Sam Anthony 236 pts.

Daily results

Muirfield – 1, George Sweeney (10) 34 pts; 2, Jock Balmer (11) 31 pts; 3, Joe McCauley (12) 31 pts. Gullane – 1, Jock Balmer (11) 32 pts; 2, Brian McCarroll (4) 31 pts; 3, Brian Duffy (14) 29 pts. Longniddry - 1, Frank Guckian (9) 34 pts; 2, Ronnie Dougherty (12) 33 pts; 3, Gerry Coyle (5) 31 pts.

A great photograph of some of the pioneers of the Michael Doherty Tours. How many can you recognise?

This was Neil McGowan's captain's day group at City of Derry in 1968. How many faces can you recognise? To Neil's right was the honorary secretary, Aubrey Thompson and to his left, the vice-captain, Kevin Hinds.

Camaderia - by John Hasson

My first tour was in 1978. The trip was to the Costa Del Sol. It took a fearful 2 days to get there as there were no direct flights with an over-night stop-over in London. I was exhausted humping clubs and cases from bus to bus and airport to airport and I said to myself – never again. I observed that the airplane had propellers and that our tour group included Frank McCarroll (senior), Frank Guckian, Bobbie Bell, Sam Anthony, Sean O'Dwyer, Billy Rodden and Don O'Doherty amongst others. I thought that if the plane went down it would have made the front page of the 'Derry Journal' at least, and I would probably get a mention.

In those early days the tour group were turned out in their Sunday best and Sam Anthony even wore a trilby hat (except when he was playing golf). It was hard to see everybody on the plane because of the cigarette smoke. The conversations were limited to questions such as "what's the Spanish for beer?" and "Is the currency fiestas or passetas?"

John Hasson

I'll show you how to fly this thing

Today: jet planes and direct flights mean that 'door to door' – the trip takes 5 ½ hours. In contrast to earlier times most passengers disregard their Sunday best and look like they have just come off a building site. Unlike our predecessors, today's tour group are confident and unafraid and not adverse to advising the pilot how to fly the plane.

The happy and animated group, now seasoned campaigners, bond with each other immediately (called camaderia): strangers become friends within minutes, stories are exchanged. The banter on the plane is juvenile like a bunch of primary school children; and this state of osmosis lasts for a week. The verbal badinage resolves around who has falsely built up his handicap prior to the tournament. The tour bookie is giving odds: I was offered 500 to 1 and was insulted (editor's note – why?)

"Come on Tommy"

We reminisce about what happened in previous years and we recall the notable events and lost opportunities. Mention is made of Tommy McBride's head to head with Paul O'Doherty on the play-off hole at Santa Ponsa: 50 people had gathered as Paul drives 280 yards down the middle. Tommy then steps up to shouts of "come on Tommy". He addresses the ball, makes a beautiful swing and skitters the ball as far as the ladies tee (in golfing terms known as a 'fanny') and the whispering spectators knew that Tommy had 'cacked'. The rest is history. Paul went on to win and dedicated his victory to Tommy's driver. Paul confided in me afterwards that – "watching your opponent play a bad shot is the most fun you can have without laughing".

"Hopefully the last"

We recall the epic efforts of Paul Brennan who snatched defeat from the jaws of victory. Coming to the 17th hole in Santa Ponsa on the last day: his drive landed 80 yards from his hole. The crowd had gathered in anticipation. We could see Paul was overflowing with adrenaline. He takes out his favourite club, a 60 degree lob wedge, and violently thins the ball 200 yards into a distant swamp where no-one had ever been before: Stevie Wray went on to claim victory that year and made history by being the first Portadown Protestant to win the Traveller's trophy (and as some would say "hopefully the last").

It hasn't been all plain sailing as there was a catalogue of memorable mishaps and injuries on the tour:-

• The broken leg of Brian ('Golden Boy') Doherty courtesy of Frankie Campbell and others attempting to play football.

• The broken leg of Brian Long courtesy of a slippery bathroom floor.

• The broken ankle of Eugene Dunbar courtesy of Andy Meenagh's reckless buggy driving (or was it intentional??).

• The head wound suffered by Patrick Doherty courtesy of a Tommy McBride hook.

• Peter Villa watching his buggy slowly disappear into a deep ravine as he made his way to the green for a crucial putt (which he missed).

• Dunbar and Furnival being locked inside San Termens Golf Course in the middle of the night which required them to climb over a high wall and then walk 3 miles to Palma (we really laughed at that).

• Larry Hasson and Cahir Fitzpatrick who fell out and abandoned their buggy just before it was about to take off over the edge of a precipice.

• Paul Brennan saving a woman's life in Palma airport.

On that happy note the 42nd Tour will see another reunion of old friends bonded together by a love of the greatest game of all - Golf.

This photo was taken by Michael in the La Mancha Restaurant in Fuengirola in 1980. Having a sing-song are, from left, Aenas McBride, Peter McCready, Eddie McCauley, Tommy Daly, Mick Gallagher, John Hannigan and Norman Bruce.

"Everything falls to the sea"

A renowned putter and dab hand at reading putts is North-West's Brendan Coyle. But he was pulling his hair out one year during the first round at Poniente. It started at the par 3 sixth. Convinced his putt would go left to right after he had completed his reconnoitre, it went the opposite way. He smiled ruefully and observed that it was a lovely day to be out and, if you miss a putt now and again, so what.

Once bitten

Next up is the par 3 ninth – "I'll not make that mistake again", said young Coyle. Again he sees it left to right and confidently makes a stroke. Identical to the sixth, I went the opposite way again. Brendan Coyle is not the sort of person to complain but on the roadway to the 10th he made the observation that Poniente was a stupid course and the greens should be dug up.

Ask the guru

The last par three, the 15th at the time, has a vicious slope from back to front and is notoriously hard to read at the best of times. Confidence shattered, he turned to the elderly guru, Larry Hasson. Right throughout the round Larry had been displaying the touch of surgeon and greens surveying skills way beyond his years – his advice "Brendan, remember one thing – everything falls to the sea". Why hadn't he asked Larry before, because on the opening team day you can seek third party advice. He looked up, spotted waves in the far off distance, calculated his line and made the stroke. To his horror his ball takes on a life of its own, going in exactly the opposite direction to what he assumed the "guru" had suggested.

"Everything falls to the sea"

Infuriated, exasperated and indignant at what had just befallen him, he turns on Larry – "Larry, I thought you said everything falls to the sea". The reply will be written in the golfing annals to be forever remembered – "But Brendan, Majorca is an island, everything falls to the sea". Now that's just another example of why I thought Larry Hasson was a genius.

P.C. is first Spanish winner

The first tournament in Spain in 1978 was a splendid occasion, played on two of the finest courses on the Costa Del Sol – Los Naranjos and Las Brisas. Well out of contention at the half-way stage, Colm Duffy (7) came from fifteen points behind to lead by one going into the final day at Las Brisas. In typical fashion he held on bravely, holing a four footer on the last to avoid a play-off with Cahir McGeady and Liam McCaul.

Overall results

1, Colm Duffy (7) 123 pts (28,28,37,30); 2, Cahir McGeady (4) 122 pts (34,29,26,33); 3, Liam McCaul (7) 122 pts (39,34,19,30); 4, Hugh McQuilkin (11) 118 pts (30,33,29,26); 5, Peter McCready (9) 117 pts (33,25,,27,32); 6, John Love (5) 116 pts (26,26,34,30); 7, Frank Guckian (8) 112 pts (31,25,30,26); 8, Frank McCarroll (1) 110 pts (25,31,25,29); 9, Craig Cameron (6) 106 pts (24,28,27,27); 10, Patsy Fagan (6) 106 pts (28,26,26,26).

Daily results

Los Naranjos – 1, Liam McCaul (7) 39 pts; 2, Cahir McGeady (4) 34 pts; 3, Peter McCready (9) 33 pts. Las Brisas – 1, Kingsley McGowan (17) 37 pts; 2, Liam McCaul (7) 34 pts; 3, Hugh McQuilkin (11) 33 pts. Los Naranjos – 1, Colm Duffy (7) 37 pts; 2, John Love (5) 34 pts; 3, D.W. McKerr (8) 31 pts. Las Brisas – 1, Cahir McGeady (4) 33 pts; 2, Peter McCready (9) 32 pts; 3, Liam McCaul (7) 30 pts. There were no team results recorded in 1978.

Another glimpse at the past – from left, Patrick Doherty, Colm Duffy, Pat Morrison and Dixon Ward.

1978 Las Brisas
Front: Frank Guckian, George Sweeney, Liam McCaul, Oliver Campbell, Declan Hasson, Larry Hasson, Eddie McCauley, Cahir McGeady, Hugh McQuilkin, Billy Rodden, Peter McCready, Teddy Stewart, Patsy Fagan, Frank Campbell, Jock Balmer, A.N. Other, Cahir Fitzpatrick, Billy McElhinney, Michael Doherty
Middle: Davy Pollock, Kingsley McGowan, Donald McKerr, George Taylor, Brian Duddy, Ian Doherty, Bill Bratton, A.N. Other, Wilf Abel, John Hannigan, Bobby Bell, Hugh Quigley, Raymond Bakewell, Norman McMorran, Eanas McBride, Mick Gallagher, Joe Taylor, Don O'Doherty, Billy Elliott, Leonard Finn, Joe Ramsey, Dan Campbell, Sam Anthony, Davy Bredin, Cathal McKeever, John Hasson, Christie McWilliams.
Back: Hector Simpson, Cathal Langan, Frank McCarroll, Norman Bruce, Ken Sharpe, Seamus Hannigan, Craig Cameron, John Love, Eugene O'Doherty, Frank McCarroll (Jnr.), Eamon MacManus, Colm Duffy, Michael McCann, Sean O'Dwyer, Joe Foley, Brian Duffy, Fred Aicken, Stanley McDermott, David Black.

Start of remarkable run

For the second continental trip the party moved off shore to the island of Majorca in 1979. It was to be a very popular venue for many years to come. Santa Ponsa was the venue for all four rounds and it proved a demanding test with an average of less than 32 pts needed for victory. It was the start of a remarkable run of success for five handicapper Liam McCaul whose ability to run three shots into two around the greens was the perfect formula for continental golf.

Considerable merit was added to his victory by virtue of the fact that both the heads of his driver and three wood became loose and he was not able to use either in his final round.

Liam McCaul shows the perfect position through impact. Looking on is Sean O'Dwyer.

Overall results

1, Liam McCaul (5) 126 pts (30,28,37,31); 2, Jimmy McGlinchey (3), Ballybofey, 124 pts (32,30,30,32); 3, Frank McCarroll jun (2) 124 pts (33,28,32,31); 4, Norman McMorran, Strabane, (11) 124 pts (27,32,34,31); 5, Hugh McQuilkin (9) 123 pts (29,34,30,30); 6, Sean O'Dwyer (11) 121 pts (30,28,36,27); 7, Joe McMenamin (5), Ballybofey, 116 pts (29,33,23,31); 8, Frank Guckian (9) 115 pts (33,32,24,26); 9, Cahir McGeady (4) 114 pts (34,27,26,27); 10, Jim Doherty (11) 114 pts (33,27,27,27).

Team results

1, Frank McCarroll (2), B. Duddy (14), Billy McElhinney (20) and Pat Doherty (18) 174 pts; 2, Peter McCready (7), Sean O'Dwyer (11), Cahir Fitzpatrick (15) and Bill Bratton (18) 167 pts; 3, Jimmy McGlinchey (3), Fred Aicken (14), Kingsley McGowan (14) and Gilbert McLaughlin (18) 166 pts.

Daily results

1st day – 1, Cahir McGeady (4) 34 pts; 2, Frank McCarroll jun (2) 33 pts; 3, Jim Doherty (11) 33 pts. 2nd day – 1, Hugh McQuilkin (9) 34 pts; 2, Stanley McDermott (15) 33 pts; 3, Joe McMenamin (5) 33 pts; 3rd day – 1, Liam McCaul (5) 37 pts; 2, Sean O'Dwyer (11) 36 pts; 3, Norman McNorman (11) 35 pts, 4th day – 1, Billy McElhinney (20) 33 pts; 2, Jimmy McGlinchey (3) 32 pts; 3, Sam Anthony (22) 32 pts.

Wrong way round Bill

THE LATE Bill Sharkey, a school teacher from Derry, told a great story about going out for a lesson with Fred Daly, former professional at City of Derry. By his own admission he had developed an extraordinary fault, brought about by two unstoppable forces - he was a big man and had a backswing which went straight up with no take-away. The nett result was that, more often than not, he came down right on top of his balata ball, cut it to shreds and more importantly, imparted a ferocious back spin which made the ball shoot backwards.

Fred asked him to hit a few shots to get a picture of what was going on – true to form, and under even more pressure than normal, Bill was coming down on top of the ball with even more ferocity and now importing even more back spin as the errant balls shot backwards.

Fred, as funny and cynical a man as you could ever meet, had the answer to Bill's dilemma. "Bill" he says, "it's simple – you're playing the wrong way round". Sharkey dined out on that one for many years after.

Walking up the steps of the Santa Ponsa clubhouse are Kingsley McGowan, Jim Doherty and Billy Elliott.

What a duo — Leo Hickey and Josef Locke in full flow at the La Mancha Restaurant, Fuengirola.

Derry man Eric McMullan (of the famous McMullan Oils family) strains his vocal chords along with Peter McCready and Tommy Daly. I don't know who the 'looker' is but to quote Raymond Chandler — "she'd make a bishop kick a hole in a stained glass window".

Poniente is stunning

In my reckoning, and I have been lucky enough to play most of the finest courses in Europe, Poniente is right up there as the ultimate in golfing architecture. Designed by renowned golf architect, John Harris, it is stunning – there is little point looking for a "feature" hole because there are so many of them. My own personal favourite is the 16th. I hate it with a passion, but when I occasionally hit that elusive fairway and find the green sward with my 2nd, it's just like when I've sampled one of Tom Gallagher's 30 years old Scotch whiskeys – a treat to die for.

Golf is a very small world - John Harris had been brought in by Real Club Puerto De Hierro in Upper Madrid to make a number of alterations to the Madrid course. By a coincidence the same Real Club Puerto De Hierro was originally designed by the legendary Harry Colt, architect and designer of both the Royal Portrush and Royal Co. Down links.

Peter Quigley takes on the drive at Poniente's famous 16th hole. Looking on are Jimmy McCloskey and Liam McCaul.

Planning permission refused

I know little of Poniente's original history but I remember Michael telling me that the previous owner had hoped to get the requisite planning permission to build luxury villas on the surrounds of the course. Disastrously for him, planning permission was refused but, to his eternal credit, he kept his dream alive by financing the upkeep of his marvellous creation.

The new manager, Borja Ochoa, is as clued in as they come. A top executive brought in by the new German owner, he organised the background music for Phil Coulter's Irish Rugby anthem last year plus "Danny Boy" and the rafters shook at Poniente like never before. Andy has made the clever decision to play at Poniente on the final day which should result in a truly grandstand finale. And two afternoons that Poniente won't forget in a hurry.

Michael with his dear old friend Zisca, better known to us as "Francisca".

One of the most pleasant aspects of playing Poniente is the opportunity to renew the acquaintance of Zisca Tugores, Poniente's Club Administration Manager. Michael was very fond of her and I know that she had the same affection for him. He called her "Francisca", a name he used for convenience for those of us not quite familiar with Spanish names. When you met Zisca there was always a welcoming smile and she just couldn't do enough to make you feel welcome. We very much look forward to meeting up with her again in May.

About to tee off are Eddie Gallagher, Eugene O'Doherty, Don O'Doherty and Leonard Finn.

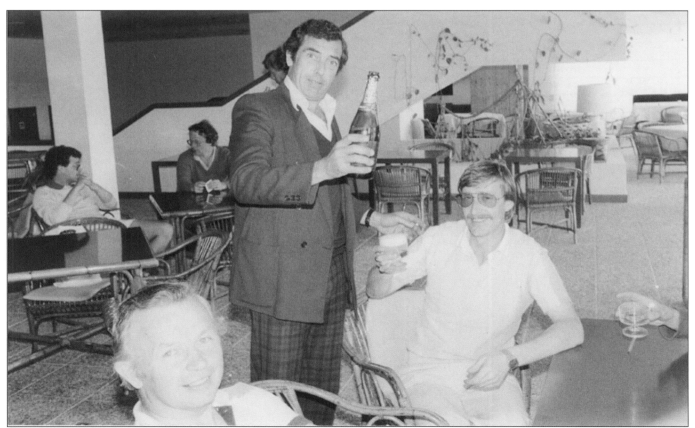

When Australia's Leo Hickey was being served, he liked to be served by the best of the best. He is pictured here getting a glass of champagne from former Spanish Amateur champion, Pepe Gancedo, course designer of the superb Torrequebrada and one of the architects involved in Santa Ponsa. In the foreground is John Bradley.

First win for McCarroll

On his first trip on the Michael Doherty Tour in 1980, Colm McCarroll (1) came out on top with a four round total of 137 pts on the Los Lagos course at Mijas, venue for all four rounds on the Costa Del Sol. That year will be remembered for the Irish style weather which was so wet that one of the rounds had to be postponed.

Welcome guests at Mijas were twice winner of the British Amateur championship, Peter McEvoy and international singing star, Josef Locke who played in the third round.

Overall results

1, Colm McCarroll (1) 137 pts; 2, Norman McMorran (8), Strabane, 134 pts; 3, Eanas McBride (5), Letterkenny, 133 pts; 4, Joe McMenamin (4), Ballybofey, 130 pts; 5, Enda McMenamin (2), Ballybofey, 129 pts; 6, John Hannigan (5), Letterkenny, 122 pts; 7, Cahir McGeady (3) 122 pts; 8, Hugh Cooley (8) 120 pts; 9, Ronnie Hill (9), Strabane), 120 pts; 10, Don Quinn (16) 119 pts; scr to 9, Frank McCarroll (2) 116 pts; 10 and upwards, Fred Aicken (15) 110 pts; veterans' prize, Sam Anthony.

Team results

1, Peter McCready (5), Norman McNorman (8), Brian Duffy (17) and Pat Ellis (18) 175 pts; 2, Mick Gallagher (5), Sean O'Dwyer (9), Ed Stewart (18) and Norman Bruce (18) 169 pts; 3, Jimmy McGlinchey (3), Hugh Cooley (12) and Leo Hickey (18) 167 pts.

Daily results

Round 1 – 1, Colm McCarroll (1) 37 pts; 2, Joe McMenamin (5), 37 pts; 3, Sean O'Dwyer (9) 35 pts; Round 2 – 1, Liam McCaul (6) 34 pts; 2, Ronnie Hill (11) 33 pts; 3, Joe McMenamin (5) 32 pts. Round 3 – 1, Norman McMorran (10) 40 pts; 2, Hugh Cooley (15) 40 pts; 3, Eanas McBride (6) 38 pts. Round 4 – 1, John Hannigan (5) 37 pts; 2, Colm McCarroll (1) 36 pts; 3, Enda McMenamin (2) 35 pts.

Sean O'Dwyer handing over the prizes for the 1980 team event to Pat Ellis, Peter McCready, Norman McMorran and Brian Duffy.

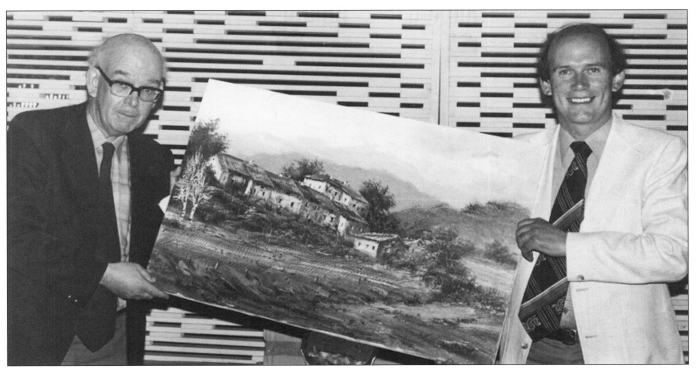

Frank McCarroll senior, on behalf of the 'Derry Journal', sponsors, handing over a superb painting to the 1980 winner, Colm McCarroll.

A very welcome visitor for one of the days during the 1980 Tour was twice British Amateur champion Peter McEvoy who played with Colm McCarroll, Cahir McGeady and Sean O'Dwyer.

Landslide victory

Such was the domination of the 1981 tournament at Poniente in Majorca by Liam McCaul that he could have walked in after nine holes in the fourth round and still won. That was the statistic that emerged when the cards where checked on the final day. He had just eleven points on the back nine of his final round but still won by the huge margin of thirteen points.

Pictured before teeing off at Poniente are, from left, Eddie Gallagher, Liam McCaul, Frank Guckian and Sean O'Dwyer.

Overall results

1, Liam McCaul (5)136 pts; 2, Peter McCready (5) 123 pts; 3, Colm McCarroll (scr) 118 pts; 4, Eanas McBride (6) 118 pts; 5, Bob Coull (13) 117 pts; 6, Frank Guckian (7) 114 pts; 7, Cahir McGeady (2) 114 pts; 8, Hugh Quigley (13) 112 pts; 9, Noel O'Donnell (15) 111 pts; 10, John Hannigan (4) 110 pts.

Team results

1, John Hannigan, Dominic Quinn, Les Carruthers and Bill Bratton 171 pts; 2, Hugh McQuilkin, Bob Coull, Brian Duffy and Sidney Canning 170 pts; 3, Norman McMorran, Brendan Burke, Michael McCann and Maurice Allen 168 pts.

Daily results

1st day – 1, Liam McCaul (5) 35 pts; 2, Peter McCready (5) 33 pts; 3, Cathal McKeever (20) 33 pts. 2nd day – 1, Cahir McGeady (2) 35 pts; 2, Liam McCaul (5) 33 pts; 3, Frank Guckian (7) 31 pts; 3rd day – 1, Liam McCaul (5) 37 pts; 2, Peter McCready (5) 33 pts; 3, Eanas McBride (6) 31 pts. 4th day – 1, Colm McCarroll (scr) 34 pts; 2, John Hannigan (4) 33 pts; 3, Brendan Coyle (8)32 pts.

1982 winner Liam McCaul receives the Travellers Trophy and a beautiful piece of Lladro from Frank McCarroll, sponsor.

797,104 SHOTS

I RECKON SINCE Michael's Tour started in 1976 that 797,104 shots have been struck by a broad spectrum of golfers whose abilities range from the sublime to the ridiculous. I have based this carefully worked out figure on the assumption that an average of 52 competitors took part each year and that a triple bogey is recorded for every "blank".

I particularly invite accountants to use their considerable brainpower to make a reasoned analysis of how I came to this very accurate figure. Why I specifically mention accountants is the fact that this is what they do for a living and are paid bloody fortunes for it.

This great photograph was taken outside the clubhouse at Poniente where all four rounds were played in 1981. The leader of the pack – out in front is Michael, a picture of sartorial elegance. Kneeling, from left, are Tommy Daly, Norman Bruce, Dan Campbell, Hugh Cooley, Patrick Doherty, Peter McCready, Dominic Quinn, Ted Stewart, Maurice Allen, John Bradley, Mick Gallagher and Hugh Quigley. Second row, from left, are Denis Hegarty, Colm McCarroll, Hugh McQuilkin, Frank McCarroll senior, Norman McMorran, Gordon Mills, Aenas McBride, Sam Anthony, Brian Duffy, Leonard Finn, David Liston, Eamon MacManus, Gordon Manchini, Des Ferry, Brendan Burke, John Hasson, Stewart Canning, Les Carruthers, Frank Guckian, Don O'Doherty, Cathal McKeever, Bob Coull, Cahir McGeady, Walter Brady, Cahir Fitzpatrick, Ted Graham, Gilbert McLaughlin, Michael McCann, Dixon Ward and Norman Bruce. At the very back are Maurice Quigg, Liam McCaul, Leo Hickey and John Hannigan.

Hickey 'flashed the cash'

Just before heading off to Silks Restaurant, Puerto Banus for one hell of a night are Leo Hickey, Terry McCullough, Maurice Quigg, Michael and Cahir McGeady.

Big Cahir McGeady tells a great story about the night that Terry McCullough, Maurice Quigg and Leo Hickey invited Michael and himself to the flashy 'Silks' restaurant in Puerto Banus. It was a "thank you" to Michael and Cahir for their part in making the trip that year so successful.

They hadn't booked so when they arrived they were informed by the Maitre D that the restaurant was completely booked out with no chance of a table. Calm as you like, Hickey produced a load of pesetas, and within minutes they were seated, ready for a sumptuous meal.

It must have been some feed

And that's what they got. According to McGeady, he was suitably replete, full of food, the best of wine and ready for the night to come. (editor's note: if Cahir was "suitably replete" it must have been some feed. His reputation that he could eat you out of house and home was not earned on a wet afternoon).

Michael had an 'eagle eye' for everything and everybody – he was a walking encyclopaedia. He spots a big deal figure up at the bar with a huge cigar "stickin' out of his ja'bone" as they say in Derry. He was clearly the owner on the nightly 'meet and greet' trail. "I know that man", said the old pro, "I have seen his face before".

Are you 'Tashy'

As he came up to the boys' table to ask them if they had enjoyed their meal, Michael asked if, by any chance, he was Gareth 'Tashy' Jones who had fought Doak, Co. Antrim's Henry Turkington, in an eliminator for the British Super Welterweight title in Wales in 1977. Turkington had stopped him that night and effectively finished his career.

According to Cahir, 'Tashy' looked as if he had taken another straight to the chin by another Irishman and was mesmerized by the extraordinary detail that Michael went into.

Stan Baldwin puts on a show

'Tashy' was truly impressed by this unique diner in his restaurant and invited the boys to stay on for a bit of entertainment – Liverpool comedian Stan Baldwin had dined in Silks that night and had happily agreed to put on a show for the clientele.

Also there that night was entertainer, Lionel Blair, which gives some idea of just how exclusive a place it was. McCullough, Hickey and Quigg were high fliers – nothing but the best. The likes of us plebs were more than happy with a Big Kahuna Burger, a really tasty burger which had the same outcome as Silks fine dining but about a 100 times cheaper. Some people have more money than sense.

It is now 5am as the boys say "goodnight" to 'Tashy'. They had been relieved of about 100,000 pesetas but what the hell, McCullough will just charge more when he gets back to Derry.

Off to Gibraltar

What happened next has baffled me to this day and I have not been able to get an explanation from McGeady – he said he was that "full", he couldn't remember his Christian name, never mind the extraordinary decision as to what they did next.

With tee-totaller Michael on hand to drive, they decided to go to Gibraltar for breakfast. When McGeady woke up after demonstrating his famous death snore to the unfortunate threesome in the car, the first thing he remembered was seeing a "bobby" in a full English policeman's uniform.

"At that very moment I took a mental pledge, swearing I would never, ever, not ever let alcohol pass my lips again. So what does McCullough do? The so-and-so ordered a bottle of Dom Perignon and we were on the road to perdition again". As Don O'Doherty so often says – "Happy Days".

An interested group of Tour members watching the drama unfold at Son Vida in 1997. It was won by Dave Trickett from Canada, a sure indicator of the international appeal of the Michael Doherty Tour.

Four great old pals together — from left are Charlie Stafford, Sonny Jarvis, Joe Ramsey and Billy Rodden.

Triumphant procession

The bright lights of Majorca proved irresistible so it was back to Majorca for the 1982 tourament. It was to prove another triumphant procession as far as Liam McCaul was concerned. Making light of the fact that his handicap was reduced from 7 to 5 for the final two rounds on the Poniente and Santa Ponsa courses, Liam ran out a winner by a massive fifteen point margin.

Overall results

1, Liam McCaul (5) 138 pts; 2, Frank Guckian (7) 123 pts; 3, Christie McWilliams (13) 120 pts; 4, Ted Graham (18) 118 pts; 5, Eddie Gallagher (4), Ballybofey, 117 pts; 6, Cahir McGeady (2) 116 pts; 7, Sean O'Dwyer (12) 116 pts; 8, Willie Dunlop (10) 115 pts; 9, Dermott McGale (7), Omagh, 115 pts; 10, Billy Elliott (5) 113 pts; scr to 10, Eanas McBride (6), Letterkenny, 113 pts; 11 to 22, Eugene O'Doherty (17) 106 pts.

Team results

1, Liam McCaul, Cahir Fitzpatrick, Bertie Long and Walter Burnside 176 pts; 2, Dermott McGale, Denis Hegarty, Norman Kane and Pat Morrison 175 pts; 3, Frank Guckian, Christie McWilliams, John Bradley and John Gormley 168 pts.

The results of the first and second day's play are not available. Apologies to those who starred on those two occasions

Third day

1, Cathal McKeever (18) 36 pts; 2, Norman McMorran (10) 34 pts; 3, Sean O'Dwyer (12) 33 pts.

Fourth day

1, Ted Graham (20) 37 pts; 2, Leo Hickey (15) 36 pts; 3, Christie McWilliams (13) 34 pts.

In the days when men were men and buggies a thing of the distant future. From left are Liam McCaul, Archie Grey and Willie Dunlop.

Up at Mijas in 1980 Seated, from left, are Ted McQuilkin, Hugh Quigley, Leo Hickey, Ted Graham, Mick Gallagher, Liam McCaul, Vincent Armstrong, Norman Bruce, Hugh Cooley, Ted Stewart and Cathal McKeever. Standing, left to right, are Michael McCann, Sean O'Dwyer, Joe McMenamin, Patrick Doherty, Gilbert McLaughlin, Norman Kane, Dan Campbell, Maurice Allen, Brian Duffy, Sam Anthony, Frank McCarroll senior, Billy McElhinney, A.N. Other, Billy Elliott, John Hannigan, Leonard Finn, Pat Ellis, Christie McWilliams, Aenas McBride, Norman McMorran, Tommy Daly, Dominic Quinn and Denis Nicholl.

McCaul again

Liam McCaul's mastery of continental golf courses continued on the Costa Del Sol in 1983 with another fine four round total of 147 pts off 6. He was chased all the way by Omagh's Dominic McGale (8) on the final day until the 14th at Torrequebrada which Liam birdied and Dominic ran up an ugly double bogey 7.

Overall results

Liam McCaul (6) 147 pts (40,39,40,28); 2, Dominic McGale (8), Omagh, 143 pts (41,37,32,33); 3, Colm Duffy (9) 136 pts (36,33,34,33); 4, Billy Elliott (7) 130 pts (32,28,36,34); 5, Ken McConomy (9) 127 pts (30,27,36,34); 6, Brendan McLaughlin (13), Ballyliffin, 124 pts (40,27,30,27); 7, Sean O'Dwyer (12) 123 pts; 8, 8, Eugene O'Doherty (18) 122 pts; 9, Eneas McBride (8), Letterkenny, 119 pts; 10, Danny McNally (9) 119 pts.

Team results

1, Brian Doherty, Cliftonville, Harry McNulty, Christie McWilliams and Brendan McLaughlin 187 pts; 2, Colm Duffy, Les Carruthers, Pat Doherty and Eugene Dunbar 185 pts; 3, Billy Elliott, Joe Foley, Pat Ellis and Eugene O'Doherty 182 pts.

Daily results

Mijas – 1, Dermott McGale (9) 41 pts; 2, Brendan McLaughlin (13) 40 pts; 3, Liam McCaul (8) 40 pts. Torrequebrada – 1, Liam McCaul (7) 39 pts; 2, Dermott McGale (8) 37 pts; 3, Stanley McDermott (14) 35 pts. Parador – 1, Liam McCaul (7) 40 pts; 2, Sean O'Dwyer (11) 37 pts; 3, Billy Elliott (7) 34 pts. Torrequebrada – 1, Ken McConomy (9) 34 pts; 2, Billy Elliott (7) 34 pts; 3, Colm Duffy (9) 33 pts.

Norman McMorran gets a new head of hair during the 'knees-up' at La Mancha Restaurant, Fuengirola. Also in the picture are Aenas McBride, Liam McCaul and in the background Cathal McKeever and Josef Locke.

This spritely group arriving at the Barbados Hotel in 2000.Left to right are Davy Jones, John Bradley, Eugene Dunbar, Ernie Heywood, Charlie McCafferty, Pascal Harpur, Denis Doherty, Bert Whoriskey, Gilbert Dougherty, Pat Swain, Billy McElhinney, Jess Furnival, Terry Phillips, Gary Leckey, Barney McDaid and Brendan Coyle.

Who will win?

Who do you think will win the 2017 Michael Doherty Tour? If I have been asked this question once, I have been asked it a hundred times over the past few weeks. I have suggested that Brian McClure might well repeat his splendid win of last year, Tommy McBride might get his just reward or maybe Georgie Pearson will spring a surprise – that really will be a surprise.

But I have had a good look at this year's entry list, and to tell you the god's truth, I am underwhelmed. There isn't a "class act" in the field apart from just one person – me. I truly believe I am going to make the biggest comeback since Lazarus. My name is scheduled to go onto that trophy for the fourth time on Friday 19th May 2017.

Best books

I have been reading four of the best books ever written about the mental side of golf – Dr. Bob Rotella's The Golfer's Mind, John Richardson's 50 Greatest Golf Tips, Harvey Penick's Little Red Golf Book and John Daly's My Life In And Out Of The Rough.

Of the four, John Daly's is by far the most profound because his primary tip is that if you don't have a good day on the course, you can make up for it by having "one hell of a night on the town". That's the best golf tip I have ever read in my life.

So it's going to be "all duck or no dinner" – either I'll be a nervous wreck in that horror of horrors, the final fourball on the last day, or out in the "dawn patrol", having a ball with Bob Smyth, Oliver Logue and John Bradley.

The "singing coalman"

Since the word got out that a book about Michael and golf in the north-west is due to be published, I have come across some great characters with their story to tell of their annual trip to destinations far and near. George McIntyre, known as George the singing coalman told me of his trip to the August Masters, an annual event run by Terry Phillips. The destination that particular year was Sligo.

George takes up his story – "I was playing with Jackie Johnston who was great to play with - encouraging me as I holed putt after putt. Off a handicap of 35, I did the impossible – I won with 41 pts".

Stupid enough

But George was soon to discover that winning has its downside. Questions were asked how this beginner could produce the goods at the perfect moment. George had the answer – if they were stupid enough to give him 35 shots, they deserved what they got.

George told me that a special quiz had been organised as one of the night's entertainment highlights – yes, you read it right, a quiz. But George wasn't having it. With guitar in hand, he sneaked off with Charlie McCafferty for a night's sing-song. Any Howard Keel song you like to hear, George will give you a classy rendition. When Charlie and himself re-joined the group he said they were given a 'yellow card' for not adhering to the week's itinerary. Now that's the sort of discipline we need for Michael's tour.

Wrong foot

GOLF FANS WILL never forget the fate of Jean Van de Velde who got the head staggers in the British Open at Carnoustie in 1999 when he attempted to play out of the notorious Barrie Burn at the final hole with disastrous results.

The world famous Carnoustie was one of the venues for the inaugural tour in 1976. There were stories aplenty about mishaps galore, but the one I enjoyed most involved the inimitable Cahir "Fitzy" Fitzpatrick. And it happened at the Barrie Burn, this time at the 17th where it also interferes with play.

After landing in the water, "Fitzy" decided to play it out – he had seen it done before on TV so why not. Slowly but surely he took off his right shoe and sock and headed into the burn without a moment's hesitation. But he had made a fundamental miscalculation – it should have been his left shoe and sock. It was a chastened "Fitzy" who squelched his way up the 18th.

MICHAEL DOHERTY TOUR INDIVIDUAL WINNERS

1976	Gerry Coyle (4) (32,31,32,32) 127 pts - Carnoustie, St. Andrew's, Downfield, Western Gailes.
1977	Jock Balmer (11) (31,32,30) 93 pts - Muirfield, Gullane, Longniddry.
1978	Colm Duffy (7) (28,28,37,30) 123 pts, - Los Naranjos, Las Brisas.
1979	Liam McCaul (5) (30,28,37,31) 126 pts - Santa Ponsa.
1980	Colm McCarroll (1) 137 pts - Los Lagos.
1981	Liam McCaul (5) (35,33,37,31) 136 pts - Poniente.
1982	Liam McCaul (5) 138 pts - Poniente, Santa Ponsa.
1983	Liam McCaul (6) (40,39,40,28) 147 pts - Mijas, Torrequebrada, Parador.
1984	Liam McCaul (7) (38,40,36,31) 145 pts - Poniente, Santa Ponsa.
1985	Dermott Gallagher (7) (32,33,29,33) 127 pts - El Paraiso, Atalaya Park, Los Naranjos, Sotogrande.
1986	Eddie Gallagher (6) (31,40,35,39) 145 pts - Poniente, Santa Ponsa.
1987	Eddie Gallagher 131 pts - Santa Ponsa.
1988	Colm McCarroll (2) (31,32,38,32) 133 pts - Los Olivos, Parador, Los Lagos, Las Brisas.
1989	Brian Doherty (18) (34,37,35,29) 135 pts - Poniente, Santa Ponca, Son Vida.
1990	Brian Doherty (12) (42,33,29,36) 140 pts - Los Olivos, Los Lagos, Parador, Torrequebrada.
1991	Phil McLaughlin (10) (33,36,33,40) 142 pts - Poniente, Son Vida.
1992	Christie McWilliams (11) (36,32,33,36) 137 pts - Poniente, Santa Ponsa.
1993	P.C. Duffy (10) (34,33,30,38) 135 pts - Poniente, Santa Ponsa 1 & 2.
1994	Eugene Dunbar (11) (40,34,35,39) 148 pts - Santa Ponsa 1 & 2.
1995	Maurice Brennan (7) (35,34,35,32) 136 pts - La Cala North and South, Los Olivos, Torrequebrada.
1996	Eddie Gallagher (8) 141 pts - Son Antem, Son Vida, Santa Ponsa.
1997	Dave Trickett (15) (31,34,37,37) 139 pts - Poniente, Son Antem, Son Vida.
1998	Maurice Brennan (5) 140 pts - Son Antem, Son Vida, Santa Ponsa.
1999	Maurice Brennan (6) 135 pts - La Cala North, Mijas, Parador, La Quinta.
2000	Peter Villa (12) (32,36,33,32) 133 pts - Santa Ponsa, Poniente.
2001	Frank Campbell (11) 130 pts - Poniente, Santa Ponsa.
2002	Paul O´Doherty (10) (37,33,35,29) 134 pts - Poniente, Santa Ponsa.
2003	Stephen Wray (9) Portadown, (36, 32, 34, 33) 135 pts - Poniente, Santa Ponsa.
2004	Cyril Ward (15) (34,38,37) 109 pts - Poniente, Santa Ponsa.
2005	Ernie Heywood (1) (32,35,39,32) 138 pts - Poniente, Santa Ponsa.
2006	Ciaran O'Neill (9) (38,32,36,39) 145 pts - Poniente, Santa Ponsa.
2007	John Chambers (15), 143 pts - Poniente, Santa Ponsa.
2008	Mark O´Doherty (6) (37,31,41,40) 149 pts - Poniente, Golf Park, Santa Ponsa.
2009	Ciaran O'Neill (8) (31,34,37,35) 137 pts - Son Antem, Golf Park, Son Quint, Santa Ponsa.
2010	Colm McCarroll (8) (33,33,40,37) 143 pts - Poniente, Son Vida, Son Quint, Santa Ponsa.
2011	Brian Long (6) (37,32,38,38) 145 pts - Poniente, Santa Ponsa.
2012	Sean Doyle (15) Arklow (44,40,38,34) 156 pts - Poniente, Santa Ponsa.
2013	Maurice Quigg (18) (36,36,33,37) 142 pts - Poniente, Santa Ponsa.
2014	Eamon McCourt (11) (39,39,39,40) 157 pts - Poniente, Santa Ponsa.
2015	Eugene Dunbar (14) (36,34,40,33) 143 pts - Poniente, Santa Ponsa.
2016	Brian McClure (8) (37,37,33,39) 146 pts – Poniente, Santa Ponsa.

We are all the better for it

Cahir McGeady can look back on his life in golf with great pride. Father of Michael, who has been the most outstanding player Derry has ever produced, Cahir has given so freely of his time and expertise to further the cause of golf.

Formerly a footballer, and a very dirty one at that if stories are to believed, he was a very successful slow left hand bowler for City of Derry. Then he found out about golf and we are all the better for it. He joined City of Derry in 1970, was captain in 1980, president in 2000/2001 and a trustee until 2001. He is also a life member. He is also a long-time member of North-West Golf Club.

Over the past few years he has played no more than twice which is a terrible shame. A severe back problem has put paid to a great career but we are still hopeful that he will make a comeback for this year's tournament. He still hasn't played in 2017 and hasn't yet entered this year's Tour but Andy will leave a space for him, I'm sure of that.

Fabulous touch

For such a big man he had a fabulous touch around the greens . Combined with that was effortless power which saw him eventually play off 2 handicap. He won the Magee Scratch Cup at Murvagh, numerous trophies at City of Derry and throughout the North-West and represented City of Derry both as a player and team captain for the Senior Cup, Barton Shield and Junior Cup.

But his proudest moment came in 1976 when he won his old pal Colm Duffy's captain's prize. It is a magnificent grandfather clock which has pride of place in the McGeady household.

He has a downside, but so do we all. In his case it's a lack of generosity, particularly when it comes to giving short putts and I mean short putts – under 12 inches. How miserable can you get.

Cahir McGeady, Davy Jones and John Bradley ready for action

I'm having difficulty pinning down the year for this particular photo but I would bet that, based on the youthful looks of this group it was taken in the 1990s. If I'm wrong, so what, I'm not perfect. Front, left to right, are Kevin Doherty, Bert Whoriskey, Eugene Dunbar, Sonny Jarvis, Pat Morrison, Mark O'Doherty and John O'Brien. Back, left to right, Brian Doherty, Eddie McCauley, Colm Duffy, Paddy Cunningham, Paul O'Doherty, Dermod Rooney, Walter Burnside, Tommy Daly, Charlie McCafferty, Raybon Wilkins and Jimmy McGee.

Gentlemen to the core

I had ten minutes or so to spare a few months ago before collecting the grandchildren from school, so I called in to the palatial offices of North-West Tyres, owned by City of Derry member, Dan McAnulla. The great man was there in person so I had the opportunity to find out if he would be the first president of a new golf society we were setting up.

I have to say he was delighted and when I advised him that there was no work involved from his point of view, he was a very happy man. Eventually he became curious – "What is the Society about and where do we play".

I told him that no golf was involved, but when he is playing in Ireland the newly formed Derry branch of the Darren Clarke Appreciation Society would go along to see the great man from Dungannon.

Get out of my car park

I know Dan has a short fuse, but I just didn't know how short – "if you haven't got your car out of my car park in 20 seconds, I'm going to get my mechanics to remove all your tyres and wrap the spare round your neck."

What did I say wrong? I knew exactly what I said – I knew that Dan had politely asked him for his autograph after Clarke had finished a round at Valderamma and had received a most abrupt, negative response.

I had previous experience of Clarke. I played him in the quarter-finals of the Irish Close at Royal Portrush in 1988 and would have described him as somewhat precocious. We were to meet again at Belfast International Airport not so long ago and when I greeted him, his demeanour was less than courteous. A little lesson in manners wouldn't go amiss.

Wonderful ambassadors

Why can't they make them all like Paul McGinley, Graeme McDowell and Rory McIlroy, all gentlemen to the core. And Padraig Harrington, another wonderful ambassador for Ireland.

The last time I was talking to Paul was in the Victoria clubhouse in Vilamoura along with his dad Mick – in the run-up to the Ryder Cup, his schedule was crazy. Having just completed his final round in the Portuguese Open he was heading to Faro for a 2.30pm flight to Heathrow. Then it was on to New York where he had been invited to "ring the bell" to open the New York Stock Exchange the following day. The moral of the story is – it takes all kinds to make a world.

Out for a dander in Magaluf are Jackie Smith, Bert Whoriskey, Joe Ramsey and Sonny Jarvis.

I am nearly sure this is the balcony at La Cala. Seated from left are Maurice Brennan, Cahir McGeady, Bob Coull, Cyril Ward and Eugene O'Doherty.

A hand of cards was a popular past time in the good old days. The man with the film star looks in the middle is Brendan Burke with Hugh Quigley (left). Cahir Fitzpatrick is calculating the odds while an obscured Eamon MacManus and Rory O'Hare look on.

Dying for a drink

We were staying in Santa Ponsa and it was 2am. My geriatric partners had "crashed" and I was dying for a good drink. I was long since out of the tournament so it was time to go on my holidays. I spotted an Irish pub and wandered in for a pint of Guinness and who did I see but Captain McCourt and his merry men.

Being someone who was always a little bit shy and backward, I really didn't know Eamon all that well but he immediately made me feel like part of the family. And it was that very night that I discovered something I never knew before – I was as good a dancer as Michael Flatley.

Asked me out to dance

As soon as the diddly-dee music started McCourt asked me out to dance. He is a good looking boy so I asked myself the obvious question – was he "throwing a shape?" I was mortified. I thought I had walked into the only Irish gay bar in Majorca. We hit the floor with a vigour only reserved for those tanked to the eye-balls in liquor. I got the timing straight away. I could tell McCourt was very experienced with his little pistons prancing up and down in perfect rhythm.

It was beautiful

Inhibitions banished forever, I was in heaven. Hands down by my side, knees bouncing in the air, I knew I was awesome. Then we went for a spin, holding hands and acting as one. It was beautiful. The audience bawled out for more – "Encore, encore". Had that dance lasted another five seconds, I would have ended up in the Hospiten in Palma. There was no encore and no sympathy from my wee dancing partner the next day when I posted 22 pts round Poniente.

Oh Lord but it's hard to be humble, when you're perfect in every way — Two handsome specimens, John Moran and Mark O'Doherty, and Eamon McCourt.

Eureka

AFTER PLAYING GOLF for more than sixty years I have finally found the secret. I picked up a medical journal recently which had a fascinating article about the intricacies of the brain. I never knew that if you are right-handed, it is the left side of your brain which controls your actions and vice-versa.

Applied to golf this means that if you are right-handed, the left side of your brain contains all the relevant information regarding your golf swing, your technique and, particularly, your thoughts. Obviously the right side is the other way round.

Eureka. I quickly came to the conclusion that if I chipped and putted left-handed, the right side of my brain would have no idea how bloody awful a chipper and putter I am. And that is exactly what is happening as I pen this article. My velvet touch around the greens has returned, I am a new man. Always someone who plans ahead, I have written a lovely winner's speech which I will deliver in the Poniente clubhouse on Friday 19th May around 5pm.

I didn't realise McCourt was so tiny. From left are Eamon McCourt, George Pearson, Eugene Dunbar and Gary Leckey.

The early days

City of Derry was a wonderful place to be in the 1950's and 60's. Members were so friendly and supportive and young age was not considered an obstacle in any way. I played nearly every day with my old friend Gavin Caldwell, immediate past captain of the Royal and Ancient Golf Club. During the summer we would play as many as 45 holes a day on a regular basis and occasionally 54.

'Nancy boys'

Getting to Prehen was a different 'kettle of fish'. It was considered an exclusive game played by the well-off middle-aged and not a game for teenagers. Carrying golf clubs from West End Park to Great James Street each morning during the summer months was a challenge. I couldn't count the number of times

we were called 'nancy boys' – come to think of it, maybe we were.

When we got there it was a haven. Ted Pope, the professional and his wife were very kindly people as was Freda Craig, the ladies branch secretary, who looked after us like a favourite aunt.

Timebomb

I have so many stories, but one I enjoy recounting involves my twin siblings, Brendan and Brian. Genetically they might have been twins, but they were complete opposites. Both fine players to this day, Brian was a placid and easy going while the older of the two, born nine minutes before him, was a timebomb.

Now serene in his twilight years, Brendie had the most ferocious temper I had ever witnessed. Any errant shot he played would result

in clubs flying in all directions, leaving the twin brother the task of collecting the dispatched clubs. He would then make his way to the clubhouse awaiting the balance of his set.

Where are they?

It came to a head one fine summer morning in or around 1960. Brendie cleaned out his bag , then threw the bag away and headed for the clubhouse. When Brian arrived, Brendie asked him had he collected his clubs and bag and where were they. Brian told him that he collected all of his clubs plus his bag. "Where are they"? asked an indignant older twin.

"I fired them into the drain at the 6th"(present par five 3rd). Apparently it did the trick.

Another peerless performance

For the fourth time in five years, Liam McCaul stepped up to receive the "Travellers Trophy" when he produced another peerless performance in Majorca in 1984. In a class of his own, he returned 145 pts over Poniente and Santa Ponsa to win by another huge margin, this time 11 points.

Overall results

1, Liam McCaul (7) 145 pts; 2, Eddie Gallagher (7), Ballybofey, 134 pts; 3, Colm Duffy (10) 133 pts; 4, Dominic McGale (7), Omagh, 129 pts; 5, Billy McElhinney (12) 125 pts; 6, Davy Bredin (20) 123 pts; 7, Christie McWilliams (11) 121 pts; 8, Mercer Shaw (18) 120 pts; 9, Cahir McGeady (5) 119 pts; 10, Don O'Doherty (13) 118 pts.

Team results

1, Eddie Gallagher, Don O'Doherty, Eugene O'Doherty and Leonard Finn 181 pts; 2, Frank McCarroll jun, Eugene

Frank McCarroll junior, on behalf of the 'Derry Journal' presents the Travellers Trophy to Liam McCaul who won for the fourth time.

Dunbar, Willie Dunlop and Sonny Jarvis 181 pts; 3, Liam McCaul, Leslie Carruthers, John Gallagher and J. Hegarty 181 pts.

Daily results

Poniente – 1, Liam McCaul (7) 38 pts; 2, John Gormley (19) 37 pts; 3, Billy Elliott (8) 36 pts. Santa

Ponsa – 1, Liam McCaul (7) 40 pts; 2, Dermott McGale (7) 38 pts; 3, Davy Bredin (20) 35 pts. Poniente – 1, Hugh Cooley (10) 38 pts; 2, Mercer Shaw (18) 37 pts; 3, Liam McCaul (7) 36 pts. Santa Ponsa – 1, Don O'Doherty (13) 37 pts; 2, Eddie Gallagher (7) 36 pts; 3, Colm Duffy (10) 36 pts.

Winners of the team event in 1984 were, from left, Eugene O'Doherty, Eddie Gallagher, Don O'Doherty and Leonard Finn.

Frank McCarroll senior, Bill Canning and Eamon MacManus pictured outside the Barbados Hotel, Magaluf in 1981.

Pictured at Mijas in 1980 were, from left, Hugh Cooley, Jimmy McGlinchey and Leo Hickey.

My father and myself pictured with Eamon MacManus outside the Barbados Hotel in 1981.

He nicked my suite

As organiser of the 2009 'Carrycullion Classic' I arrived at the luxurious Andalucia Palace Hotel a day early to make sure everything was ready. I showed my passport as requested at reception and awaited the card for the Presidential Suite which had been promised to me as the organiser. "Mr. McCarroll, we are very sorry. Someone from your party arrived an hour ago and we thought it was you, so we gave it to him".

So for the next eight days I stayed in this piddly wee single room on the 9th floor while Phelim O'Neill indulged himself in the lap of luxury in my Presidential Suite. When he realised what had happened he immediately insisted on changing but I wouldn't have it - I really enjoyed the fact that he was having a ball.

What a character

I was to spend quite a bit of time with Phelim that week and I found out what a great character he is. Full of fun, he just wanted to be where the craic was and that was Joy's Piano Bar, right down at the port and teeming with life. The highlight for me came on the Friday night – the tournament was over so we felt we could stay out late.

Before I could tell him to sit down and behave himself, he got up on a stool and led the chorus of Whiskey in the Jar. And he got such a reception he was asked to do an encore. It was yet another brilliant night – sure isn't that the point of having these annual get togethers. They're priceless.

Teenage victory in '85

Ballybofey teenager Dermott Gallagher, son of Eddie, made his debut in 1985 a winning one in Spain. With a total of 127 pts the Donegal seven handicapper pipped the experienced old warhorse Cahir McGeady (4) by a point. The winning score reflected the playing difficulty of the four courses chosen for the 1985 trip – El Paraiso, Atalaya Park, Los Naranjos and Sotogrande.

Overall results

1, Dermott Gallagher (7), Ballybofey, 127 pts (32,33,29,33); 2, Cahir McGeady (4) 126 pts (32,29,35,30); 3, Colm Duffy (6) 125 pts (33,30,30,32); 4, Liam McCaul (7) 125 pts (28,39,32,26); 5, Dermott McGale (6) 121 pts (33,35,28,25); 6, Eddie Gallagher (7) 118 pts (28,28,32,30); 7, Norman McMorran (10), Strabane, 112 pts; 8, J. Copas (10), Clones, 112 pts; 9, Derek McLaughlin (10), Clones, 112 pts; 10, Stanley McDermott (12) 109 pts.

Team results

1, Dermott McGale (6), Joe Foley (13), Les Carruthers (13) and Pat Morrison (17) 178 pts; 2, Cahir McGeady (4), Norman McMorran (10), Bob Coull (14) and Bill Bratton (20) 175 pts; 3, Colm Duffy (6), Derek McLaughlin (10), Walter Burnside (15) and Norman Bruce (20) 174 pts.

Daily results

El Paraiso – 1, J. Copas (10), Clones, 36 pts; 2, Les Carruthers (13) 35 pts; 3, Jock Balmer (13) 33 pts. Atalaya Park – 1, Liam McCaul (7) 39 pts; 2, Eddie McCauley (13) 37 pts; 3, Dominic McGale (6) 35 pts. Los Naranjos – 1, Cahir McGeady (4) 35 pts; 2, Patrick Doherty (13), Gweedore, 33 pts; 3, Eddie Gallagher (7) 32 pts. Sotogrande – 1, Stanley McDermott (12) 33 pts; 2, Dermott Gallagher (7) 33 pts; 3, Colm Duffy (6) 32 pts.

Pictured on the 1st tee at Poniente are, from left, Bill Bratton, Les Carruthers, Dominic Quinn and John Hannigan.

Cathal McKeever (left) and Sam Anthony show the younger generation how to dress properly as they do a bit of window shopping in Magaluf.

We had a special guest in 1985 when scratch golfer, Gilberto Malaughlioni flew in from Sicily to take part. He said in broken English that he had heard that the general standard of play was 'total crap' and he had a good chance of winning something for the first time in his life.

Pictured at Poniente are, from left, Raymond Nash, Norman McMorran, Eugene O'Doherty and Davy Bratton.

The offending bread roll

We were all out for a meal in 'Fish Alley' in Fuengirola, a great little area for good restaurants. After an excellent meal, we asked for the bill. Just as were about to divide the figure by seven, one of our party, none other than Carndonagh vet Phil McLaughlin, asks to have a look at the bill.

We were all in shock. Was big Phil, the wealthiest vet in Western Europe, going to pick up the tab. Sadly we were all a bit previous – from out of his pocket comes a calculator and he quickly gets to work. When it came down to the nitty gritty, the only discount he was seeking apart from what he ate was for a bread roll he said he hadn't ordered.

Slight error of judgment

Bill paid, we head off to a pub for a few drinks. We were less than enamoured and we let him know that producing a calculator was probably a slight error of judgment. There was a bit of 'slagging' about the bread roll but nothing that the big Yank couldn't handle. Unknown to us, the older brother Frank had taken the bread roll out of the restaurant with him.

On the way back to the hotel, Frank was to display a skill which I never knew he was capable of. Suffering from all sorts of arthritic problems from an early age, he would readily admit that he was never athletic. But when the drink is in, the arthritis is out.

From out of his pocket comes the bap, and stepping back in true David Beckham style, he booted the offending object about half a mile into the Mediterranean – "Big Phil, that's what I think of you and your bread roll".

If at first

If there is one place you should avoid it's the greenside bunker on the left of the 13th green at Muirfield. The man who would have been able to vouch for that was the late Cahir "Fitzy" Fitzpatrick. With its revetted face, the pot bunker was the average golfer's idea of hell.

If at first you don't succeed, try, try again. Nine attempts he made according to playing partner, Cahir McGeady who made what I thought was a cynical, unnecessary remark – "all that was missing was a bucket and spade".

The word got back to Michael who marked the occasion with a special gift for "Fitzy" – a little bottle of sand, taken from that very same bunker. Renowned for his razor sharp wit, Michael observed that it was "the last grains of sand left after Mr. Fitzpatrick was finished with it.

Some familiar faces from days gone by. From left are Jim McWilliams, Karl Doherty, Mercer Shaw, Maurice Temple, Dixon Ward and Walter 'the Brad' Brady.

It's time to relax after a long day on the course. Some look content, one looks distressed, three couldn't care less and the rest are at peace with the world. Front are Bobby Irwin, Eddie Gallagher and Gilbert McLaughlin. Standing from left are Joe Ramsey, Pat Morrison, Sonny Jarvis, Patrick Doherty and Stanley McDermott.

Enjoying a pint at Poniente are Willie Barrett, Artie Philips, Captain McCourt and John Chambers.

Eddie was unstoppable

Hot on the heels of the victory by his son, Eddie Gallagher was unstoppable in Majorca in 1986 where Poniente and Santa Ponsa were the chosen venues. With a superb total of 145 pts off 6, he finished nine points ahead of the former East of Ireland champion, Hugh Smyth (2).

Overall results

1, Eddie Gallagher (6) 145 pts (31,40,35,39); 2, Hugh Smyth (2) 136 pts (37,34,31,34); 3, Colm Duffy (7) 129 pts (34,32,35,28); 4, Brendan McCarroll (5) 127 pts; 5, Brendan Coyle (9) 126 pts; 6, Billy Rodden (13) 125 pts; 7, Frank McCarroll (2) 124 pts; 8, Dermott Gallagher (7) 122 pts; 8, Con Boyce (5) 121 pts; 10, Christie McWilliams (11) 121 pts.

Team results

1, Frank McCarroll jun, Eddie Gallagher, Charlie Stafford and Eugene Dunbar 178 pts; 2, Brendan McCarroll, Joe Ramsey and Eugene O'Doherty 175 pts; 3, Colm Duffy, Dermott Gallagher, Noel Connolly and Sonny Jarvis 175 pts.

Daily results

Poniente – 1, Hugh Smyth (2) 37 pts; 2, John Hassay (9), Lurgan, 36 pts; 3, Billy Rodden (13) 35 pts. Santa Ponsa – 1, Eddie Gallagher (7) 40 pts; 2, Con Boyce (5) 35 pts; 3, Hugh Smyth (2) 34 pts. Poniente – 1, Christie McWilliams (11) 37 pts; 2, Colm Duffy (7) 35 pts; 3, Eddie Gallagher (7) 35 pts; Santa Ponsa – 1, Eddie Gallagher (6) 39 pts; 2, Denis Doherty (6) 36 pts; 3, Brendan Coyle (9) 35 pts.

Eddie Gallagher receiving the winner's prize in 1986 from Colm McCarroll, representing the 'Derry Journal', sponsors of the Tour.

No details

I MAKE A PLEA to all Tour travellers I will meet this year and hopefully for many years to come. Please don't go into detail of how you accomplished your miserable score of 29 pts or whatever. Don't tell me how many 'blanks' you had, don't tell me what you think your score should have been. I DON'T care. I will still be trying to keep the contents of my pint in the glass, still physically shaking after taking 50 putts, still trying to erase from my memory, the past six horrendous hours of my life. Phone the wife, phone the girlfriend, phone your mother, phone the boyfriend, phone someone who cares, but please leave me in peace until I get at least half a gallon of San Miguel into the system.

Senility prayer

THIS LITTLE PRAYER was sent to Fr. Jim McGonagle on the occasion of a special birthday – Grant me the senility to forget the people I never liked anyway, the good fortune to run into the ones I do, and the eyesight to tell the difference.

Ready for action in the first round of the Michael Doherty Tour are, from left, Stewart Canning, Norman Bruce, Bill Bratton and Cahir McGeady.

Five contestants who were legends in their own minds. From left are John Gormley, Sonny Jarvis, Joe Ramsey, Maurice Quigg and Charlie McCafferty.

Eddie repeats winning formula

For the second year in succession, Eddie Gallagher won the individual event with a total of 131 pts on the Santa Ponsa course. Conditions were very tough, thanks to a combination of strong winds and inferior greens which did not live up to their reputation of previous years.

Overall results

1, Eddie Gallagher 131 pts; 2, Colm Duffy 127 pts; 3, Dougie Irwin 127 pts; 4, Brendan McCarroll 126 pts; 5, John O'Brien 123 pts; 6, Colm McCarroll 122 pts; 7, Dermott Gallagher 122 pts; 8, Billy Elliott 122 pts; 9, Christie McWilliams 120 pts; 10, Joe Ramsey 120 pts.

Team results

1, Con Boyce, Joe Ramsey, Dougie Irwin and John Gormley 177 pts; 2, Eddie Gallagher, Christie McWilliams, Pat Ferry and Kevin Doherty 174 pts; 3, Frank McCarroll jun, Eamon Grant, Charlie McCafferty and Charlie Mullan 171 pts.

Daily results

1st day – 1, Dougie Irwin (16) 35 pts; 2, Joe Ramsey (11) 34 pts; 3, Colm Duffy (7) 33 pts. 2nd day – 1, Eddie Gallagher (5) 36 pts; 2, Walter Burnside (13) 34 pts; 3, Kevin Doherty (16) 33 pts. 3rd day – 1, Brendan McCarroll (5) 35 pts; 2, Eddie Gallagher (5) 34 pts; 3, Dermott Gallagher (5) 34 pts. 4th day – 1, Denis Doherty (7) 34 pts; 2, Eamon Grant (10), Portsalon, 33 pts; 3, Colm Duffy (7) 33 pts.

Lisfannon – never looked better

It is hard to believe that Damian Doherty first started with North-West in 1993. It only seems like yesterday since the affable Head Greenkeeper graced us with his presence at Lisfannon. He started his career in 1993 under the guidance of Plunkett Duffy, a name synonymous with the Inishowen club.

In his time working at North-West he gained his NVQ Level 2 and Level 3 and was selected from the regional finals to represent Ireland in the Toro Student Greenkeeper awards.

Did his tutor proud

In June 2000, Damien took a position at Malone Golf Club as an Assistant Greenkeeper and in his time there he furthered his education in Elmwood College, Cupar, Scotland gaining a HND in Golf Course Management. Damien was also promoted to Deputy Golf Course Manager.

In January 2008, he returned to North-West to take up the reins of his now retired former boss, Plunkett. And he has done his tutor proud, bringing the Inishowen links to the very peak of condition. I have played on the fairways of Lisfannon for sixty years and I can honestly say that it has never looked better. Young Doherty, take a bow.

What odds

In his career Damien has been involved in the course preparation for lots of major golfing tournaments, the British Open, British Seniors and the Irish Open to name but a few! What odds he will be involved in both the Irish Open at Ballyliffin in 2019 and the British Open just two weeks later at Royal Portrush. Exciting times lie ahead.

Won't be beaten

The best ever score in the 41 year history of the Tour came in 2014 when Eamon McCourt put in a truly wonderful performance round Poniente and Santa Ponsa. Rounds of 39,39,39 and 40 pts were put together for a total of 157 pts off 11. If you know the Poniente and Santa Ponsa courses, you will have some idea of how he performed. It was spectacular and I don't expect it will ever be beaten.

In the tribute to Michael in this special book, Eamon, Willie Barrett, Kevin Barrett and Sean Coyle stated that they didn't feel they were good enough to take part in the Michael Doherty Tour when Michael first suggested it to them many years ago. I believe they were right. I have trawled through the records and, despite McCourt's aberration in 2014, it has been a pretty dismal showing from the four of them. So there you are.

Another fine photo from the dim and distant past. From left are Declan Campbell, Larry Hasson, Jim Hutton, Charlie McCafferty, Pascal Harpur and Eugene O'Doherty.

Brian Budd downloading his score to Michael Cunningham. But is he really all that interested?

What a privilege!

It has been a privilege and a joy to act as starter and photographer for the past ten years of the Michael Doherty Tour. So many new friends have I met, friends that I cherish and look forward to meeting every May. From all over Ireland, England, Australia, America and everywhere in between they will land on the first tee at Santa Ponsa on Monday 15th May and I will be there to greet them.

When Michael took ill in 2008, he asked me to take over the task he had carried out with such grace and charm for a lifetime. I did so willingly and, armed with a new camera, Lord Lichfield was re-born, recording for posterity the superb annual golfing extravaganza. When I brought my collection to Colm McCarroll's house a few months ago we had great 'craic' browsing through 100's of photos. Still to come were contributions from Karl Doherty and Davy Jones, so I have no idea how the author will come to his final decisions – rather him than me.

For me the big change has been the introduction of a computer system devised by North-West member, Sam Condit. What used to take many hours can now be completed no more than fifteen minutes after the last cards are returned. The Tour is indebted to Brian Long and Michael McCullough for their expert input. Roll on **MAAAY!**   **Willie Barrett**

What a warbler! Willie Barrett in full swing in Munroe's.

It's not all serious just in case you think we are a bunch of golfing fanatics, unable to have a bit of fun. This bunch of rowdies, led by Brendan Coyle, are having a ball.

Jimmy McGee, John McDermott and Jimmy Ryan epitomise what the Tour is all about – a chance to relax and renew acquaintances with old friends.

After working long hours for fifty-one weeks of the year, Karl Doherty and Gilbert McLaughlin looking forward to getting to Majorca for a well-earned battery charger.

Brendan Coyle and John Hassay giving their rendition of 'Have you ever thrown your granny off a bus'.

It's a dog's life

THE LATE CATHAL McKeever, a member at both North-West and Greencastle, was a quirky character with an impish sense of humour. An early participant on Michael's tours, he loved the "craic". He had a little Jack Russell whom he called "Jack" and he was his constant companion. So much so, that when Cathal headed into the Men's Bar at North-West, he always brought Jack with him.

Nothing stays the same in golf clubs – a new house convenor, Dr. Paddy O'Leary, had been appointed and Dr. O'Leary was not going to countenance dogs in the men's bar.

On seeing Jack on the stool beside Cathal, the doc issued a stern directive that pets were not permitted in the holy of holies.

"Groundhog Day" – four weeks later to the day, Paddy walks into the bar only to see Jack on his favourite stool. "Mr. McKeever, I thought I had made it abundantly clear that pets were not permitted in the bar." Not unlike the final iconic scene in Shane, Cathal drew up to his full height and said – "Paddy, do you remember seconding an application for house membership I put before you in this very bar two weeks ago". Paddy acknowledged that he did. "Paddy, that was for Jack and he is now a house member."

To his eternal credit, Paddy got the message straight away and immediately offered to buy Jack a pint.

Second win for McCarroll

It was back to the Costa Del Sol for the 11th Spanish Tour in 1988. The two Mijas courses, Parador and the superb Las Brisas were the venues. Winner for a second time was 2 handicapper Colm McCarroll who played steadily thoughout the week for a total 133 pts.

Perhaps the outstanding performance of that year came from 10 handicapper, Charlie Stafford. The 68 years old turned back the clock with a vintage display which saw him finish in third place.

Overall results

1, Colm McCarroll (2) 133 pts (31,32,38,32); 2, Cahir McGeady (4) 129 pts (26,29,38,36); 3, Charlie Stafford (10) 129 pts (29,32,35,33); 4, Colm Duffy (7) 127 pts (29,26,36,36); 5, Brendan McCarroll (5) 126 pts (27,29,35,35); 6, Con Boyce (4) 126 pts (29,30,33,34); 7, Kevin Doherty (17) 125 pts; 8, Bobby Irwin (13) 124 pts; 9, Phil McLaughlin (9) 124 pts; 10, Christie McWilliams (11) 122 pts.

Team results

1, Colm Duffy, Derek McLaughlin, Walter Burnside and Bill Bratton 183 pts; 2, Noel Connolly (Clones), Charlie Stafford, Leo Hickey and Pat Morrison 179 pts; 3, Kevin Hinds, Bobby Irwin, Danny Cooley and Kevin Doherty 177 pts.

Daily results

Los Olivos – 1, Phil McLaughlin (9) 36 pts; 2, Kevin Doherty (17) 35 pts; 3, John O'Brien (7) 33 pts. Parador – 1, Eugene O'Doherty (18) 38 pts; 2, Bobby Irwin (13) 34 pts; 3, Paddy Morrison (19) 33 pts. Los Lagos – 1, Christie McWilliams (11) 40 pts; 2, Phil McLaughlin (9) 40 pts; 3, Colm McCarroll (2) 38 pts. Las Brisas – 1, Cahir McGeady (4) 36 pts; 2, Colm Duffy (7) 36 pts; 3, John Hasson (14) 35 pts.

Taken in Silks Restaurant in Puerto Banus after Colm McCarroll won the 1988 Tour. From left are Brendan McCarroll, P.C. Duffy, Joe McElroy, Colm McCarroll, Phil McLaughlin, Kevin Doherty and Brian McCarroll. Big Phil picked up the tab.

Disaster struck

AS ALWAYS EACH day is not without its humorous incidents. One long handicapper (we won't name you Eugene) was struggling to cope with a very windy Gullane in 1977. And to make things worse, he was feeling under pressure as he was playing with, in his eyes, the exalted company of Frank McCarroll senior and Frank Guckian. Disaster was to strike – somehow or other, and no-one knows how to this day, he succeeded in playing all of the three balls of his partners at the same hole. **Don O'Doherty**

Relaxing after a round in Santa Ponsa are international traveller Peter Doherty, all the way from Perth, Australia, John Hasson and Sean McKane.

Four players hoping to make their presence felt at Poniente are John O'Brien, Jim McWilliams, Ken McConomy and Norman Bruce.

Brian breaks the mould

The domination of single figure golfers came to an end in Majorca in 1989 when 18 handicapper Brian Doherty became the first category three golfer to win the coveted trophy. Right from the start Brian was among the leaders and was never really troubled after establishing a seven point lead going into the final day's play at Santa Ponsa. The courses played were Poniente (twice), Santa Ponca and Son Vida.

A talking point again in 1989 was the condition of the courses which, with the exception of Son Vida, were in very poor shape. Poniente as usual was hit or miss while Santa Ponsa fell victim to a breakdown of their desalination plant which led to thousands of gallons of salt water sprayed on their greens with disastrous consequences.

Overall results

1, Brian Doherty (18) 135 pts (34,37,35,29); 2, Con Boyce (3), Rosapenna, 131 pts (35,32,32,32); 3, Kevin Doherty (17), North-West, 128 pts (33,36,32,27); 4, Cahir McGeady (4) 126 pts; 5, Christie Williams (10) 126 pts; 6, Brendan McCarroll (4), North-West, 125 pts; 7, Maurice Brennan (9), Downpatrick, 124 pts; 8, Brian McKee (10), Strabane, 124 pts; 9, Brendan Coyle (7) 124 pts; 10, Eugene Dunbar (24), Highgate, 121 pts; Category 1, Colm McCarroll 121 pts; Category 2, Bud Hamilton 115 pts; Category 3, Leo Hickey 111 pts; Category 4, Len Finn 102 pts.

Team results

1, Con Boyce, Maurice Brennan, Billy Rodden and Kevin Doherty 191 pts; 2, Colm Duffy, Stanley McDermott, Sidney Canning and Bill Bratton 183 pts; 3, John O'Brien, Walter Burnside, Brian Doherty and Eugene Dunbar 183 pts.

Daily results

Poniente – 1, Con Boyce (3) 35 pts; 2, Brian Doherty (18)

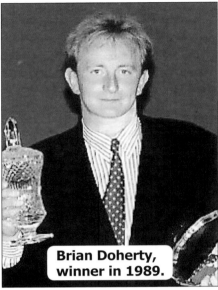

Brian Doherty, winner in 1989.

34 pts; 3, Kevin Doherty (17) 33 pts. (Poniente) – 1, Brian Doherty (18) 37 pts; 2, Kevin Doherty (17) 36 pts; 3, Brendan McCarroll (4) 34 pts. (Son Vida) – 1, Christie McWilliams (10) 37 pts; 2, Bert Whoriskey (14) 36 pts;; 3, Brian McKee (10) 35 pts. (Santa Ponsa) – 1, Bob Coull (14) 42 pts; 2, Noel Hynes (8) 37 pts; 3, Eugene Dunbar (24) 35 pts.

Winners of the team event in 1989. From left are Kevin Doherty, Billy Rodden, Eugene Dunbar (sponsor), Con Boyce and Maurice Brennan.

Bob Coull was captain of City of Derry in 1989 and as was tradition, he had the honour of presenting the prizes. Second in the team event were, from left, Bill Bratton, Colm Duffy, Stanley McDermott and Stewart Canning.

Bobby Irwin, North-West, and Gilbert McLaughlin, City of Derry, were delighted to learn that they were headline news in the Daily Mirror. The two boys played 18 holes the previous day and then took part in the annual Majorca triathlon.

A great little story from Seamus

I WAS AT work in Roe Park the day after the 1999 Open Championship at Carnoustie writes Seamus Duffy, still trying to figure out how Jean Van De Velde had managed to lose it, still hearing Peter Alliss' brilliant commentary playing over and over in my head. As I walked into the hotel foyer who did I see but Peter Alliss himself.

He was there to commentate on the Senior Open at Royal Portrush. When I introduced myself to Mr. Alliss as the club professional, he was kind enough to talk to me about the remarkable happenings of the previous day. As we continued our conversation he found out that I had trained under Michael Doherty. To my amazement he said he knew Michael well and a sudden tone of respect came to his voice as he spoke about Michael. Later in the week I called Michael to tell him the story only to find out that Mr. Alliss had called out to City of Derry to see him. Respect indeed!

A Memory Of Michael

When asked to do a short article in memory of Michael, my mind went back to the very beginning of the Trip. I can remember the broken down bus in Scotland, memorable visits to Troon and Muirfield, wonderful evenings on the Costa del Sol with characters like my late father, Frank Guckian, Josef Locke and many others too numerous to mention. Finally we more or less settled on Majorca where everything was close at hand which made a balance between the competition and the entertainment possible.

Throughout all of these changes of venue, the one constant unflappable character was Michael Doherty. I first met Michael in the 1950s and over the years got to know him better and better. He was a very intelligent and well-read person, a skilled golfer and an able administrator. He had this wonderful ability to sort out all types of problems that naturally occurred on a trip of this size with a minimum of fuss.

Legendary speeches

He was well respected and liked by all the staff and officials of the various hotels and golf courses we visited. Michael had a wonderful sense of humour and he liked to know everything that went on during the trip so that he could come up with an amusing anecdote during his legendary speeches on prize-giving night along with a suitable booby prize.

On one occasion we were sitting at a table outside a restaurant in Majorca having had a nice meal and feeling no pain. We were indulging in that favoured pastime of watching the world go by when three elderly ladies appeared around the corner and walked past our restaurant. While doing so they started smiling and waving at our table – "see you next year", they said. Michael's curiosity was aroused and he had to know who they were. "Oh they're from the Titanic", said my brother Colm. "Well they're remarkably well preserved" replied Michael. It turned out that Colm and Cahir McGeady had been in the Titanic Bar around the corner for a quick drink and had a conversation with the ladies. Obviously the Irish charm had worked.

May he rest in peace

Frank McCarroll

Two great old friends relax on the beach, Michael and Frank McCarroll junior.

The boss in full flow, delivering yet another masterpiece of a presentation speech, the highlight of the week.

Alec Campbell, Gilbert McLaughlin and Eddie McCauley having a ball.

A talented all-rounder, James O'Carroll entertains John Hassay, Gilbert McLaughlin and a wee interloper wearing a stupid hat.

Six shot reduction

In the year following his splendid win in 1989 Brian Doherty had his handicap reduced from 18 to 12. To his great credit and with twenty-four less shots to play with, he won on the Costa Del Sol in 1990. A fantastic 42 pts on the opening day at the Los Olivos course in Mijas lay down the marker for the week. That was followed by 33 pts at Los Lagos, 29 pts on Parador and 36 pts at Torrequebrada on the final day.

Not for the first time, Sonny Jarvis showed his liking for continental golf, finishing in second place on 135 pts.

Overall results

1, Brian Doherty (12) 140 pts (42,33,29,36); 2, Sonny Jarvis (17) 135 pts; 3, Brian McKee (10) 132 pts; 4, Eddie Gallagher (6) 131 pts; 5, Con Boyce (1) 127 pts; 6, Brendan Coyle (7) 126 pts; 7, Denis Doherty (8) 125 pts; 8, Maurice Brennan (8) 124 pts; 9, Brendan McCarroll (3) 124 pts; 10, Patrick Doherty (15) 124 pts.

Team results

1, Noel Hynes, Maurice Quigg, John Gormley, Seamus Cassidy 189 pts; 2, Denis Doherty, Brian Doherty, Pat Morrison, Seamus Crumlish 186 pts; 3, Maurice Brennan, Don O'Doherty, Charlie McCafferty, Eugene Dunbar 182 pts.

Daily results

Los Olivos – 1, Brian Doherty (13) 42 pts; 2,Charlie McCafferty (16) 40 pts; 3, Patrick Doherty (16) 40 pts. Los Lagos – 1, Maurice Quigg (14) 41 pts; 2, John Hasson (12) 37 pts; 3, P.C. Duffy 7) 36 pts. Parador – 1, Maurice Brennan (8) 32 pts; 2, Joe Ramsey (11) 32 pts; 3, Eddie Gallagher (6) 32 pts. Torrequebrada – 1, Brian Doherty (12) 36 pts; 2, Brian McKee (10) 34 pts; 3, Sonny Jarvis (17) 32 pts.

A report of that year would not be complete without a mention of three tour members – Seamus McDevitt, Eamon Harkin and Brendan Coyle. Their contribution to the enjoyment of one and all could not be overstated.

Pictured with the sponsor Eugene Dunbar were the winners of the 1990 event. From left, Noel Hynes, John Gormley, Seamus Cassidy and Maurice Quigg.

When you compile a 256 page book, you can occasionally get stuck — who's your man in the red hat. I know the rest. From left are Mark O'Doherty, Suki Nagra, Eamon McCourt and Eugene Dunbar.

Just before they set off at Poniente are from left, Pat Mackey, Joe Ramsey, John Bradley and Frankie Campbell.

Wonderful shot

Thanks to a great last round of 40 pts off 10 in terrible conditions at Son Vida, Carndonagh's Phil McLaughlin leap-frogged through the field to win the 1991 tournament win a total of 142 pts. Poniente and Son Vida were the two venues chosen by Michael.

One ahead with three to play, Cahir McGeady was in the driving seat until the par three downhill 16th where he missed the green on the left. Seizing his opportunity, Phil played a wonderful shot to within two feet which he converted to go into the lead.

Overall results

1, Phil McLaughlin 142 pts (33,36,33,40); 2, Cahir McGeady 139 pts (35,39,33,32); 3, Joe Ramsey 135 pts (35,29,41,30); 4, Maurice Brennan 134 pts (28,36,34,36); 5, P.C. Duffy 131 pts (34,35,33,29); 6, Christie McWilliams 129 pts (31,32,31,35); 7, Brian McKee 127 pts (27,31,31,36); 8, Stanley McDermott 127 pts (30,30,37,30); 9, Con Boyce 125 pts (26,36,34,29); 10, John Gormley 124 pts (28,29,33,34).

Team results

1, Cahir McGeady, Joe Ramsey, Walter Burnside, Sonny Jarvis 191 pts; 2, Brendan Coyle, Christie McWilliams, Stanley McDermott, Gilbert McLaughlin 186 pts; 3, P.C. Duffy, John Haddock, Dermott Hutton, John Gormley 186 pts.

Daily results

Poniente – 1, Cahir McGeady (5) 35 pts; 2, Joe Ramsey (13) 35 pts; 3, Brian Doherty (11) 34 pts. Poniente – 1, Cahir McGeady (5) 39 pts; 2, Phil McLaughlin (10) 36 pts; 3, Maurice Brennan (9) 36 pts. Son Vida – 1, Joe Ramsey (13) 41 pts; 2, Stanley (14) 37 pts; 3, Noel Hynes (8) 35 pts. Son Vida – 1, Phil McLaughlin (10) 40 pts; 2, Kevin Doherty (14) 37 pts; 3 Brian McKee (11) 36 pts.

Phil McLaughlin receives the Travellers Trophy in 1991 from P.C. Duffy.

15 SHOTS LATER – "isn't it great to be alive".

IF YOU THINK that you have had a bad hole please read this extract from the Derry Journal which was sent to the G.U.I. newsletter in 1990 by Colm McCarroll.

There were plenty of stories of misfortune over the weekend but none could match the sad tale of Carndonagh veterinary surgeon, Phil McLaughlin.

On the first tee at North-West, he announced a new strategy for the 1990s – "carefree golf" – swinging the golf club free of any thoughts of grip, stance, posture, shoulder spin etc.

Things didn't go as planned . 1st shot – Drive off the tee; 2nd shot – one iron (ball lost); 4th shot – one iron into heavy rough; 5th shot – wedge; 6th shot – wedge; 7th shot – wedge (ball jumps up and hits him – two penalty shots); 10th shot – three wood; 11th shot – sand wedge to 10 feet; 12th shot – putt to six inches; 13th shot – ball moves as he addresses putt; 14th shot – putt just misses on the left lip; 15th shot – middle of the hole.

"Isn't it great to be alive", said Phil as he made his way to the 2nd tee.

The Barrett sisters. From left are Willie, Sean and Kevin.

Winners of the 1991 team event were Sonny Jarvis, Walter Burnside, Cahir McGeady and Joe Ramsey. They are pictured with the sponsor, Eugene Dunbar.

"Hard Rock Cafe"

In 2007 when the "Carrycullion Classic" was taking place in the Algarve, I decided for a change to fly a few days early into Lisbon, a place I wanted to see and this was my chance. It was quite magnificent, well worth the extra effort. As it so happened, I found a very nice hotel in the centre.

After a pleasant dinner with the usual consumption of far too much alcohol, I decided to go for a walk. I hadn't gone one hundred yards when I spotted it, a Hard Rock Cafe. I had read about them in numerous newspapers and magazines - the atmosphere, the fabulous music from the sixties, the decor.

I saw a "mountain"

I headed straight for it. As I approached the entrance I saw a mountain. He was at least 6ft 2in, weighed in at about 23 stones and had massive shoulders which were needed to keep his bullet shaped giant of a head on his neck. I froze – I knew I was going to be rejected because I was fast approaching the bus pass stage.

What the hell says I, I'll ask him anyway – "am I too old to go in there?". He glared at me and asked me in a strong Southern drawl – "who were the big names in your day?"

I responded, "the Beatles, Elvis, the Rolling Stones, Buddy Holly and…….". He stopped me in my tracks and said to me – "Hey buddy, you started it all. Get in there and get yourself a beer". I had one hell of a night.

Their shoes stood out

I REMEMBERED being invited to participate in the annual N.I. Press Golf Society outing which was taking place at Royal Portrush. Fred Daly was the honorary president at the time and he was there to see everyone off the 1st tee. He was a remarkable man, so intelligent and humorous and, as it so happened, a very good friend of my father when he was at City of Derry and spoke with great affection for him.

I will never forget his wonderful speech, merciless in the extreme, which raised the roof at Royal Portrush. As it was winter time and most of the entrants were from the inland courses around Belfast, it was of little surprise that their shoes weren't at their shiny best.

A bit of elbow grease

And Fred let them know it – "I watched all of the members of this prestigious society tee off the 1st today and I have to say, the thing that stood out was the filth of your shoes. Did any of you ever think of asking the wife to use a bit of elbow grease. This is Royal Portrush boys, not the "hen runs" you play on every Saturday. Brilliant stuff.

Michael and his great friend, the late George Sweeney

The legendary Fred Daly

OUTSTANDING ADMINISTRATOR - Anne Wallace

The most distinguished lady member in the history of City of Derry Golf Club is Anne Wallace. An outstanding administrator, a wonderful career reached its pinnacle in 2009 when she was elected President of the Irish Ladies Golf Union, a reward for a lifetime's contribution to the development of ladies golf. In the two years of her presidency, she witnessed Ireland winning the European Girls' Championship and Danielle McVeigh winning the British Ladies Open.

In addition to her presidency she has achieved a long list of honours, the most significant of which came in 2003 when she became only the fourth person from Ireland to be appointed Chairman of the Ladies Golf Union. She was lady captain of City of Derry in 1979.

It was another legend at City of Derry, Freda Craig, and the famous Curtis Cup captain, Zara Bolton (Royal Portrush), who asked Anne to put her name forward for election to the Northern District of the Irish Ladies Golf Union in 1983. After three years she was elected Chairman. Her skills were quickly acknowledged and she served as the Northern District delegate of the ILGU for no less than three separate terms between 1990 and 2002.

On top of that she was appointed an Ulster selector and captained the Ulster Ladies Inter-provincial team in 1998 and 1999. And if that wasn't enough, she managed to fit in the role of lady captain of Royal Portrush in 1997/98. An honorary

Anne Wallace

life member at City of Derry, she is still a handy player. City of Derry can readily salute its most outstanding member in the club's distinguished history.

Great supporters of the Michael Doherty Trip were Gabriel Dolan, Deep Sharma and James Dolan. The Dolans did things in style. They hired out an American limousine with bull's horns on the bonnet and often hired out a light aircraft for a few days. Not in one of the many trips they made did they strike a single golf ball.

A shining example of success

The story of "Foyle" is a shining example of how golf clubs should be run. A superbly organised and managed business, it is a credit to the Gallagher family, Rob, Avril and Robert junior. And what is the secret? Quite simple really – unfettered by the hundreds of different opinions which blight the structured development of many clubs, they are clever business people who know exactly what their membership wants.

And they deliver in spades – a splendid 18 holes course, designed by renowned architect Frank Ainsworth, and opened on 30th July, 1994, a gem of a par three 9 holes course, opened on 29th April 1994,

which is a great little challenge and a state-of-the-art Driving Range which attracts golfers from far and wide. The first ball was struck there on 21st October, 1994.

And typical of the whole operation, the Foyle club house is a perfect example of how a modern facility can deliver exactly what golfers need.

There is a marvellous story of historical interest attached to Foyle. That involves the legendary Amelia Earhart, the first lady to fly solo over the Atlantic, in 1932. On a fateful day on 20th May of that year, she crash landed on what is now the 6th green when she was unable to keep her single engine plane the "Little Red Bus" in the air any longer. So it is no surprise that the 6th is called

'Amelia's Landing' and the function room, 'Amelia Earhart'.

After the crash, Amelia experienced the best of Irish hospitality in Rob's father's home before setting off again on her travels.

And two golfers who thoroughly enjoyed their visit to Foyle were Mae McFetridge and the legendary Norman Wisdom.

Let's go back to the start of a great success story. Avril was sitting watching television one Sunday evening many years ago when Rob said to her "What would you think about building a golf course?" The reply was short and sweet – "are you mad?". The rest, as they say, is history.

The brains behind the magnificent Foyle Golf Centre which has added so much to Derry as a centre of golfing excellence. From left are Rob Gallagher, Avril Gallagher and Robert Gallagher, a family team with every right to feel proud of their creation

Ready for action at Poniente are Maurice Allen, Cahir Fitzpatrick, Charlie Patton and Tom Cooke.

In holiday mood are from left, Peter Harkin, Pat Mackey, John O'Brien, Walter Burnside, Kevin Doherty and Bill Bratton.

Barton Kilkoyne

One of Michael's great stories about P.C. Duffy

When I mentioned Barton Kilkoyne's name to Colm Duffy, he knew I was trying to rattle him. PC was out for his usual morning run in some far off land as a warm-up for his forthcoming daily game of golf. He chanced upon Barton Kilkoyne, a lithe little Dubliner sprinting along the dunes. They ran nose to nose but PC noticed that he just couldn't get beyond him and as they approached an agreed finishing spot Barton speeded up, his little legs going like pistons and left PC an exhausted wreck, gasping for breath in the sand.

"Would you like another little run tomorrow Colm?", asked Barton, because he loved the thought of someone running alongside him during his holidays. Never one to shirk a challenge, Colm agreed and the appointed time was 11 am when Barton would call for him.

Unprintable

What I had to listen to when PC came back was unprintable – this little underfed bastard had caught him unawares and had beaten him out on the sand-dunes. Tomorrow was going to be another story.

It was about an hour later that I first noticed that PC's primary functions were imploding – he couldn't get his heart rate down, his bodily organs were up the left and he was shaking like a leaf.

Never was the reply

"Take a piece of advice from me PC, give Barton a call and politely decline". "Never" was the reply, "that wee creep from the Ailesbury Road is going to get the lesson of his life. I am now going to my bed I'll be fit as a fiddle in the morning".

Morning came - I dreaded the fate which was about to befall my life-time friend. At exactly 11am there was a knock at the door – "is Colm in, we are due to go out for a little run". He was bouncing up and down, loosening the limbs for the forthcoming encounter.

I knocked on his door – no reply. Gingerly I opened the door and there he was (I think) - under the blankets, nowhere to be seen. I told him who was there and what should I do? I do not use bad language as a rule, but I felt obliged to inform Mr. Kilkoyne exactly what he said. I said "Mr. Kilkoyne, Mr. Duffy has asked me to tell you to "feck off and don't ever come back."

Paul O'Doherty and Peter Villa look relaxed as they wait to tee off.

You would think that Peter Doherty would be well used to having the sun in his eyes by now. On the buggy is my old buggy partner, Davy Jones.

"Spondulax" on its way to Co. Down

Make no mistake about it PC Duffy is a "wild man". On one trip he inveigled me into a match with the Trip's two hot shots, Stevie Wray and Brian McClure, playing for 50, 50 and 50 with 10 euro roll-over birdies. I had been out on the town the night before, while Stevie and Brian were quietly relaxing in the local Casino, making sure they had enough "spondulax" for the big match and all excited about the prospect of "cleaning our clocks" the next day.

All was peace and tranquillity after 9, I think we were all square and I left temporarily to attend a call of nature. When I got back it was clear that the "Good Friday Agreement" had collapsed. PC had ruled in his favour as to whether his ball was in a water hazard – I had no idea what happened but the air had turned blue – an hour earlier he was talking about how much he enjoyed playing with his old friends from Co. Down each year.

Now they were "the biggest Orange bastards" he had ever met in his life and he was going to get them banned from the tour, sine die.

I snapped

The rant was getting to me – I was nursing the mother and father of a hangover and I all wanted was peace, perfect peace. It was on the par three 15th that I snapped – with PC still ranting in the background, I hit the worst 7 iron shot in my life into the trees on the left. And my state-of-the-art Mizuno followed.

We quickly found the ball but the 7 iron was nowhere to be seen. At a feeble attempt at a joke I said to the boys that "my five minutes were up and I was retiring to sit with the chickens in the clubhouse".

I was quite prepared to leave that club permanently behind me in Poniente, along with its thirteen mates but the two Orangemen made a second search and found it well entrenched up a tree – fair play to them. I subsequently asked them would they be prepared to keep the series of unusual events a little secret among ourselves.

To this day I believe they did – but I couldn't help noticing that everytime PC and myself were spotted in the general vicinity later that day, you'd swear the boys were sucking the "Laughing Gas".

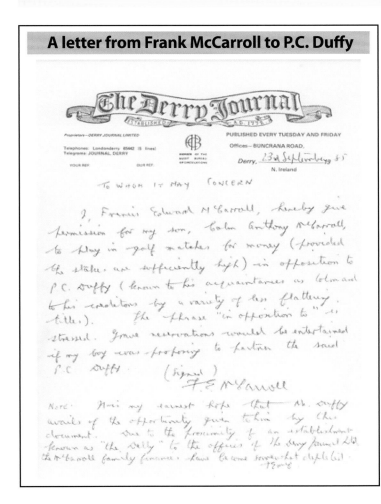

A letter from Frank McCarroll to P.C. Duffy

P.C. Duffy - Mr father once described him the bridge notes in the 'Derry Journal' as a 'silver haired Adonis'. On the strength of this photo, he should have been in the movies.

They look more like four gunfighters than golfers. From left are Christie McWilliams, Maurice Brennan, Eugene Dunbar and Cahir McGeady.

In 1994, Santa Ponsa 1 and Santa Ponsa 2 were the venues for the tournament won by Eugene Dunbar. Included in this photo is Donal Maloney, who travelled to Majorca that year despite suffering from a very serious illness. Sadly, Donal died in December 1994 RIP. Front, left to right, are Eugene Dunbar, Maurice Quigg, Eddie Leonard, Donal Maloney, Eamon McCourt, Seamus McDevitt, Paul Gallagher, Eamon Harkin and James O'Carroll. Back, left to right, are Gilbert McLaughlin, Tommy Daly, Denis 'Ginger' Doherty, Frank McCarroll jun, Pascal Harpur, Dermott Coyle, James McGeady, Seamus McBriarty, Frank Friel, Paddy Cunningham, Liam Gallagher and Leo Hickey.

A DO OR DIE SHOOT-OUT

I have so many stories about Larry Hasson I wouldn't know where to start, so I am going to have to settle for a couple of my many favourites.

He was a wonderful singer right through to his 90's, testing those powerful lungs to the hilt. My wife Sheila has a great little story about a weekly battle that Larry knew nothing about. Because of her mother's illness, Nassie (Sheila's father) and Lily had moved to our home and Sheila took Nassie to Steelstown for 12 Mass each Sunday.

A prolific singer himself, Nassie had been the doyen of St. Patrick's, Pennyburn, outgunning all challengers with his melodic tenor voice. But he became increasingly agitated at the new venue because, as far as he was concerned, he was now in a "do or die" shootout with opposition with impeccable credentials.

As Nassie's vocal chords strained to breaking point, it was also noted that the wee man had also stuck his foot on the accelerator. It was a battle to the death.

It was after the 5th week that Sheila heard the words she had prayed to St. Jude for – walking towards her car after another thunderous session Nassie turned to her and uttered the immortal words – "you know Sheila, I'll never out sing that wee bastard".

"DO I HAVE TO PLAY WITH THESE TUBES"?

Michael Doherty took hours to tell this story, and in doing so cried nearly as much as he laughed –it was his 'piece de resistance'. The old 1st tee at Santa Ponsa, sited left of the clubhouse and not right as it is now. First up is Maurice Quigg, suffering from dysentery, eye focussing disorder and alcoholic poisoning – According to Michael, his tee-shot teetered at the end of the 1st tee, sat there for a few seconds and then "vomited" over the side.

Always nervous on the 1st tee, Joe Ramsay had not been impressed by what he had just witnessed. Confidence shattered, he opted for an ugly quick hook which vanished into the boondocks.

God only knows what was going through Billy Rodden's head at this stage. Known in the trade as chronic "shoulder-spin" Billy launched his Titliest straight right, banging up against the clubhouse wall.

At this stage Larry was in the middle of his very carefully orchestrated preparation – not a muscle, not a sinew would be used until they met with his approval. The driver was stretched above his head and round his waist in a tried and tested manoeuvre. He was now ready for action – he tees his ball up and takes his stance.

About to initiate his backswing, he stops. And turns the 'old pro' and says – "Michael, do I really have to play with these three tubes?"

Two of the great ambassadors whom Michael just loved to see coming on his Tour, Larry Hasson and Cahir Fitzpatrick.

'92 was Christie's year

It was inevitable that Christie McWilliams would make his mark on the Michael Doherty Tour. 1992 was his year, winning with a four round total of 137 pts.

The only disappointment that year was the condition of the Santa Ponsa course. In great order just a week before the tournament, it fell victim to a rampant disease which all but destroyed the greens.

It was noted in the Journal report of 1992 that most of the after golf entertainment was provided by Brendan Coyle and North-West professional Seamus McBriarty whose luggage that week included guitars. Their contribution to a great week was much appreciated.

Overall results

1, Christie McWilliams (11) 137 pts (36,32,33,36); 2, Sonny Jarvis (18) 134 pts (30,32,35,37) 3, John O'Brien (6) 134 pts (31,39,39,25); 4, Stanley McDermott (13) 133 pts (38,29,33,33); 5, Phil McLaughlin (10) 132 pts (33,34,32,33); 6, Bobby Irwin (14) 128 pts (27,35,31,35); 7, P.C. Duffy (9) 127 pts (37,28,32,30); 8, Eddie Gallagher (6) 127 pts (34,35,32,26); 9, Eamon McCourt (10) 122 pts (30,31,30,27); 10, James Kelly (17) 121 pts (33,31,30,27).

Team results

1, P.C.Duffy, Paul Brennan, Maurice Quigg, Eugene Dunbar 183 pts; 2, John Hassay, Leo Hickey, Sonny Jarvis, Jimmy Ryan 182 pts; 3, Phil McLaughlin, Brian McKee, Bobby Irwin, Kevin Doherty 182 pts.
Daily results

Poniente – 1, Stanley McDermott (13) 38 pts; 2, P.C. Duffy (9) 37 pts; 3, Cyril Ward (18) 36 pts. Santa Ponca – 1, John O'Brien (8) 39 pts; 2, Sean McGrane (19) 39 pts; 3, Karl Doherty (20) 38 pts. Poniente – 1, John O'Brien (7) 39 pts; 2, Sonny Jarvis (18) 35 pts; 3, Christie McWilliams (11) 33 pts.

The shot of the tournament belonged to Joe Ramsey whose pin splitting tee shot at the 165 yards 3rd hole at Santa Ponca finished in the hole. The club used was a six iron.

In addition to the main prizes there was a special award, the "Bookies Prize", for the most improved player of the week. That went to North-West member Paul Gallagher about whom the Derry Journal golf correspondent of the time quoted – "he is a player who will surely figure in years to come". It shows you how little that correspondent knew about golf.

Mercer Shaw, Billy Elliott and Christie McWilliams on the first tee at Poniente.

The shortest round

THE SHORTEST ROUND ever played in Majorca took place a few year's ago when the "Autumn Tour" was still up and running. The fourball was Colm Duffy, Bob Smyth and two others whose names I can't recall. Bob drove off, quite a good shot for him, but it didn't quite make the end of the tee-box. Up stands P.C, swings far too quickly and loses his balance, just makes contact and no more with his split new Titliest Pro Vxi. It shoots along the tee making a full on contact with Bob's.

There was a lot of laughter. But it was at that moment that two minds became one. In a moment of collective genius they decided they had had enough. They apologised profusely to their playing partners and headed to the bar. From there they took a taxi to a renowned fish restaurant and a had day to remember.

Winner of the 1992 Tour, Christie McWilliams pictured with Colm McCarroll who presented the prizes on behalf of the sponsors, the 'Derry Journal'.

Rabbit hunt

BALLYLIFFIN IN THE good old days was a great place to be. It was full of characters who enjoyed life to the full. A man I remember with great affection is James McLaughlin, a real entrepreneur whose many projects included ownership of the Atlantic Ballroom. He was a very handy golfer, playing off around 8, and a joy to play with.

We had a night time ritual which was hilarious when I think back on it. As soon as it got dark, rabbits would appear in their hundreds on and around the 18th green, so we felt duty bound to do something about it. James was the driver, big Phil McLaughlin the co-pilot, myself and others whose names I can't remember, under the directions of the head of the rabbit assassination squad Sgt. Brian O'Reilly, headed out in James's car up the 18th fairway. As soon as we had a suitable number stunned in the headlights, we all piled out of the car, armed with golf clubs.

The rabbits had a distinct advantage which became obvious to us eventually – we were all so 'full' during our sorties, there wasn't a hope in hell of pinning one of them down. In the half a dozen or so times we ventured out, our success rate was zero. In many ways I am glad as we would have to have lived with the guilt of it.

The weather isn't always perfect. Pictured on the 1st tee in their wet gear are, from left, Davy Jones, Cahir McGeady, Willie Barrett and Dermott Coyle.

Vintage display by Duffy

On a dull overcast last day in Majorca, City of Derry ten handicapper Colm Duffy returned a terrific 38 points under pressure to win the 1993 Travellers' Trophy by three shots with a four round total of 135 points.

A former winner of the title in Spain in 1978, Colm turned the clock back with a vintage performance on two great championship courses, Poniente and Santa Ponsa 2.

Going into the final day's play, he trailed Maurice Brennan, City of Derry, and Bobby Irwin, North-West, by four points.

Nothing much happened until the final eight holes when Colm came into his own - he covered them in one under par, great golf by any standards, to cruise past the long time leaders and win by a convincing margin.

Overall results

1, P.C. Duffy (10) 135 pts (34,33,30,38); 2, Kevin Doherty (15) 132 pts (28,37,37,36); 3, Maurice Brennan (8) 132 pts (31,37,33,31); 4, Bobby Irwin (12) 131 pts (30,33,38,30); 5, Hugh Cooley (9) 130 pts (26,31,37,36); 6, John Moran (18) 130 pts (26,32,36,36); 7, Brendan McCarroll (3) 130 pts (33,27,38,32); 8, John Hassay (13) 128 pts (31,28,31,38); 9, Dermott Canning (4) 128 pts (31,31,34,32); 10, D. Douglas (15) 127 pts (29,29,32,37).

Team results

The winning team was captained by Cahir McGeady who was ably assisted by Christy McWilliams, David Douglas and John Moran. Cahir's squad won by the considerable margin of 10 points.

Daily results

Poniente – Colum Murphy (9) 34 pts; 2, P.C.Duffy (10) 34 pts; 3, Pat Morrison (15) 34 pts. Santa Ponsa 2 – 1, Phil McLaughlin (11) 38 pts; 2, Maurice Brennann (8) 37 pts; 3, Kevin Doherty (15) 37 pts. Poniente – 1, Eamon McCourt (8) 39 pts; 2, Bobby Irwin (12) 38 pts; 3, Brendan McCarroll (3) 38 pts. Santa Ponsa 2 – 1, Eanas McBride (6) 40 pts; 2, John Hassay (13) 38 pts; 3, P.C. Duffy (10) 38 pts.

The final four ball, pictured before they crossed the bridge at the 18th in the final round of the 1993 Tour at Santa Ponsa 2. From left are Brendan McCarroll, Bobby Irwin, Maurice Brennan and Colm Duffy, the eventual winner.

Frank Friel and Charlie Collins

Horrified at outburst

On hearing the news recently about the "Honourable Society of Edinburgh Golfers" decision to permit lady members to join since Muirfield was opened in 1744. I am reminded of a story written by comedian Tom O'Connor in his book "From the Wood to the Tees", published in 1992.

The story goes – At a snooty Home Counties club, a party of ladies were sitting out on the clubhouse veranda enjoying morning coffee. Below them was a male fourball just completing the 18th. One of the players, obviously heading for a good score, duffed his second shot into heather beside the green. He duly unleashed a mouthful of four letter expletives.

Official complaint

Horrified at such an outburst within earshot of the august gathering on the verandah, the lady secretary was charged with the duty of making an official complaint to the men's committee.

The committee duly met and took the incident very seriously. After due deliberation they agreed that such an occurrence should not happen again. They took the only option open to them – the ladies were banned from the verandah.

You just have no idea how much I enjoyed recalling that story. Aw come on girls, I'm only joking.

Team event sponsor Eugene Dunbar pictured with the 1993 winners. From left are John Moran, Cahir McGeady, David Douglas and Christie McWilliams.

Starter – A vital role

STARTERS of tournaments, both local and national, are and were generally distinguished people who provided the day's proceedings with that little bit of gravitas. Take City of Derry, for example - when headmaster Dermott McDermott called you to the 1st tee, you were suitably intimidated. It was hard enough trying to get that first shot off the tee with that sort of pressure.

What a gentleman Buddy Hill was. Official starter at the big events in North-West, he had a wonderful old charm about him which was so endearing. Buddy's approach was fatherly rather than officious.

Past master

Michael was the past master. Every year it was a vintage performance, giving everyone generous praise as they gingerly dipped their toes in the forthcoming nightmare of nightmares - "Now we have Joseph Doherty, playing out of Cruit Island in West Donegal, Ireland". To tell the truth Joe was more renowned for his flashy tee-shirts than his ability with the sticks. Anyway, he is a very nice source of annual income to me, so why should I rock his boat.

Enter William

Enter William Barrett C.B.E. Like Andre Rieu, he conducts his annual duties with aplomb. Civil to a fault,

he was been looking after us since poor Michael took ill. And if you fancy a Karaoke night down in Munroe's in Palm Nova, Willie is treated like a rock star when he walks through the door.

And could I mention just one more starter, Marguerita. I was the only Irish representative in the 2009 Swedish Seniors Amateur, something I always wanted to do, because I wanted to visit the beautiful city of Stockholm. And the course was situated in the grounds of the Royal House of Drottingholm – what an experience.

Bulldog

I don't think Marguerita was renowned for her female guile and charm - she was like a bulldog that licked the 'you know what' from the nettles. She immediately checked the legality of my golf ball, how many clubs I had in the bag and anything else that came into her 'scone'. This was an inquisition.

Then the miracle happened – one minute she looked like a banshee, the next like Greta Garbo. Her face lit up as she looked at the tag on my bag – Member of Ballyliffin G.C. "Oh what a beautiful place, what wonderful scenery, what friendly people. I was there last month with my husband and we had the holiday of a lifetime". From that moment on, Marguerita and I were the best of friends.

While the serious golfers retire for an early one, the reprobates hit the bottle – some things never change. Bobby Irwin makes sure Noel Hynes' glass is replenished while Brendan Coyle entertains John Hassay and Stanley McDermott.

'Ginger' leads the chorus in "I don't care if it rains or freezes", assisted not very well by Eddie McCauley and Dermott Coyle.

"Hello, is it me you're looking for, I can see it in your eyes, I can tell it by your smile".

It's all happening in room such and such. In this case the hosts were Mercer Shaw and Gilbert McLaughlin and, you know what they say, "if you want to throw something, throw a party". It's moments like this that make Michael's Tours unmissable.

Plain sailing in '94.

The new "Golden Boy" of Spanish golf emerged in 1994 when long-time Spanish Tour participant, Eugene Dunbar came of age at Santa Ponsa with a stunning win by 11 points. With a superb total of 148 pts he left the formidable Donegal pairing of Eddie Gallagher and Con Boyce trailing in his wake.

It wasn't all plain sailing for the new champion. After six holes in the final round at Santa Ponca his lead had been cut to four by the chasing Eddie Gallagher but, with the panache of a true winner, he responded with killer blows at the 7th and 8th which yielded no less than seven points. Now nine points ahead a cool, calm and collected leader stretched the winning total to 11 points. His average of 37 pts set a new 72 holes record which was to stand for quite some time.

Overall results

1, Eugene Dunbar (11) 148 pts (40,34,35,39); 2, Eddie Gallagher (8) 137 pts (36,33,34,34); 3, Con Boyce (2) 132 pts; 4, Kevin Doherty (14) 132 pts; 5, Cahir McGeady (5) 130 pts; 6, Colm Duffy (10) 127 pts; 7, Maurice Brennan (7) 126 pts; 8, Brendan Coyle (9) 125 pts; 9, Mark O'Doherty (6) 124 pts; 10, Raybon Wilkins (17) 124 pts.

Team results

1, E. McCourt, K. Doherty, J. McGee and E. Dunbar 192 pts; 2, P. O'Doherty, L. Hickey, J. McDermott and S. Jarvis 186 pts; 3, E. Gallagher, P. Cunningham, D. Douglas and W. Dunlop 181 pts.

Daily results

Santa Ponsa 1 (1st day) – 1, Eugene Dunbar (24) 40 pts; 2, Raybon Wilkins (17) 36 pts; 3, Eddie Gallagher (8) 36 pts; Santa Ponca 2 (2nd day) – 1, Kevin Doherty (14) 36 pts; 2, Cahir McGeady (5) 35 pts; 3, Kevin Barrett (11) 34 pts; Santa Ponsa (4th Day) – 1, Eugene Dunbar (22) 39 pts; 2, Eddie Gallagher (8) 34 pts; 3, Raybon Wilkins (17) 33 pts.

Long-time official at City of Derry, Billy McElhinney (centre) presented the team prize in 1994 to Kevin Doherty, Eamon McCourt, Eugene Dunbar (also the sponsor) and Jimmy McGee.

The first-ever 'ace' was recorded by Kevin Doherty who holed his tee shot at the 190 yard 9th in 1989. He is pictured here receiving a special award from the then club captain, Bob Coull.

Left-hander Eugene receives the winner's prize from John Hasson in 1994.

Knackered. While Declan Campbell and Gino Del Pinto could have happily gone on for another week, it all proved too much for Jimmy Ryan and Peter Villa. You know what they say — "when the going gets tough......".

20 minutes

IF YOU HAVE ever played Rosses Point you will be aware that, apart from the 3rd, the first ten holes go directly away from the 1st tee to the furthest point from the clubhouse, the 10th green – all the way out and then the long journey home. Depending on the tide, the Co. Sligo links could be a brutal challenge during the West of Ireland Championship which always took place at Easter.

I had a late start on the 1st day and arrived in the locker room about 1pm. Sitting in a heap with his arms wrapped round his head was Carnalea senior player Clive Robinson. I should have minded my own business. "How you did you get on?", I asked. Without raising his head he told me that he was out in 54. Now I'm not a mathematician but I could quickly work out that that was an average of 6 strokes a hole. Not good by any stretch of the imagination.

Why couldn't I have left it there. Let the poor man drown in his anguish without any further input from me. But no – the nosy journalist just had to find out how things panned out on the more difficult back nine. "What were you back in", says I to Clive. "I was back in 20 minutes" was the reply.

Quite a co-incidence

At the Barbados Hotel many years ago, Brendan Coyle, Bobby Irwin and myself were checking into the hotel and were each handed a little white card to fill in the usual details. I glanced over at Brendan's details only to notice that we had the exact same date of birth, 18th June. Lo and behold, Bobby pipes up to inform us that this birthday was too 18th June. Quite a co-incidence by any stretch of the imagination.

Start of a great run

1995 was the start of a great run for Maurice Brennan in the latter half of the 1990s. The courses chosen by Michael, La Cala North and South, Los Olivos in Mijas and finally at Torrequebrada, could not have provided a sterner test of golfing skills. To win needed an exceptional touch around the greens and in that department there was no-one more skilled than Maurice who coped best with the ferocious pace of the greens.

The shot of the tournament that year came from North-West's Paul Doherty who holed his tee-shot at the 167 yards 4th hole at La Cala North.

Entries came from far and wide in 1995. Apart from the usual suspects, the 20th annual Tour attracted entries from golfers based in New York, Wisconsin, North Carolina, Singapore, Switzerland, Aberdeen, London and Burton-on-Trent.

Overall results

1, Maurice Brennan (7) 136 pts (35,34,35,32); 2, Eddie Gallagher (8) 134 pts (37,29,36,32); 3, Colm McCarroll (4) 134 pts (37,32,33,32); 4, Brendan Coyle (9) 131 pts (27,35,41,28); 5, Kevin Doherty (13) 130 pts (37,33,32,28). Other leading scores:- 129 pts Con Boyce (2); 127 pts Danny Gallagher (12); 126 pts Dermod Rooney and Billy McElhinney; 125 pts Danny McNally (7) 124 pts P.C. Duffy (10) and Maurice Quigg (16).
Winners of the team event were Christie McWilliams, Colm Duffy, Raybon Wilkins and Tommy Daly with 191 pts.

Daily results

La Cala North — 1, Danny Gallagher (12) 35 pts; 2, Paul Doherty (19) 35 pts; 3, Kevin

Maurice Brennan

Doherty (13) 35 pts. La Cala South — 1, Danny Cooley (13) 37 pts; 2, Brendan Coyle (9) 35 pts; 3, Con Boyce (2) 35 pts. Los Olivos — 1, Brendan Coyle (9) 41 pts; 2, Danny McNally (7) 41 pts; 3, Eugene O'Doherty (24) 40 pts. Torrequebrada — 1, John O'Brien (7) 35 pts; 2, Maurice Brennan (7) 32 pts; 3, Eddie Gallagher (8) 32 pts.

The winner in 1995 with 136 pts was Maurice Brennan (7) who finished two ahead of Eddie Gallagher (8).

Two great old friends, Eamon "Lisowen" Doherty and Denis "Ginger" Doherty.

There from the very start the one and only Patrick Doherty

When I look at this photo I can observe a few things they all have in common – rugged good looks, plenty of money and a willingness to part with it – particularly the fisherman from the back end of god knows where and the wee turkey assassin from Carrigans. I look forward to relieving them of a few euro in due course. From left are Leo Hickey, Pat Mackey, Joe Doherty and George Pearson.

You won't believe this story *

* but every word of it is true

The 5th hole (461 metres) at La Cala South – the first time I had ever laid eyes on it and not a baldy notion where to go. My buggy partner Brian McCarroll teed off first, launching a howitzer into the great unknown, right down the fairway as it so happened. I followed with a low 'raker' which was heading to Mijas village until it whacked a wee tractor which came chugging out of nowhere, miraculously re-directing my shot to the correct fairway.

"Gosh, isn't this fun"

Exactly the same dilemma confronted us for the second shot on the most stupid hole I have ever played in my life. I turned to Brian and said "Gosh, isn't this fun" – that's not what I said but this is a family publication.

To the acclaim of my playing partners I hit my 'Sunday best', another rocket but this time heading for a bunker. Now you're not going to believe this, I know you won't. The same wee tractor, a 1935 John Deere, appeared from nowhere and nodded my ball in a completely different direction from its original flight path. By this stage we were looking for a defibrillator – McCarroll was rolled up in a ball on the fairway while the rest of us laughed so hard, we cried like weans.

"I'll sue that tractor driver"

But the story is only beginning – convinced I would never see my lake ball again, a Warwick I had bought at a Car Boot sale in Greysteel, a 'black cloud' descended as we made our way up the fairway – "I'm going to sue that stupid Spanish tractor driver and get back the 10p I paid for my Warwick". I was really 'raging' as they say in Derry.

We searched for several minutes in desperation until I heard the sweetest words ever uttered by another human being – "you're not playing a dirty oul Warwick by any chance?" – it was lying 3 inches from the cup for the most extraordinary 'eagle' ever recorded in the annals of golf. And for the team 5 points, the reward for a nett 'albatross'.

Typical of Michael, he found just the perfect keepsake to remember an unforgettable experience – a child's toy tractor which has pride of place in my cabinet at home.

By Dermott Hutton

Dermott Hutton receiving a memento of a truly unique achievement on Tour when he bounced off a tractor twice on his way to a miraculous 'eagle' 3 at La Cala. To this day he swears he did it deliberately. Quite frankly, while I acknowledge his integrity without question, I have my doubts.

There is nothing more enjoyable after a day's torture in the pits of hell than a quiet pint with the lads. In a very relaxed mood are Dermott Coyle, Paul O'Doherty, Eddie McCauley and Peter Harkin.

Ready for action at Santa Ponsa are Brian "Golden Boy" Doherty, Maurice Brennan, Peter Lawrence and Paul Gallagher.

Third win for Eddie

Ballybofey's Eddie Gallagher lived up to his pre-tournament favourite tag to win in 1996 for a third time. He had a comfortable margin of five points over Peter Villa (17) whose day was yet to come. Son Antem, Son Vida and Santa Ponsa were the courses chosen by Michael.

It was reported at the time that Son Antem was played for the first time and certainly not the last – the superb parkland course on the other side of Palma was in immaculate condition and a pleasure to play on. The same could be said of Son Vida, playground of Palma's rich and famous.

Shot of the tournament came from John Moran who holed his tee shot in Son Antem at the 16th.

Overall results

1, Eddie Gallagher (8) 141 pts; 2, Peter Villa (17) 136 pts; 3, Christie McWilliams (10) 136 pts; 4, Kevin (11) 135 pts; 5, Brendan Coyle (8) 133 pts; 6, Peter McCready (6) 132 pts; 7, Mark O'Doherty (7) 131 pts; 8, P.C. Duffy (8) 131 pts; 9, Eamon McCourt (9) 128 pts; 10, Dermod Rooney (7) 127 pts.

Team results

1, P.C. Duffy (8), Kevin Barrett (11), Kevin Doherty (13) and Pascal Harpur (21) 187 pts; 2, Peter McCready (6), Danny Gallagher (11), P. McDaid (10) and Peter Villa (17) 186 pts;

3, Eddie Gallagher (8), Andy Meenagh (13), Dave Trickett (14) and Charlie McCafferty (17) 181 pts.

Daily results

1st day (Son Antem) – 1, Peter McCready (6) 35 pts; 2, Denis Doherty (11) 34 pts; 3, John O'Brien (6) 34 pts. 2nd day (Santa Ponsa 1) – 1, Eamon McCourt (9) 39 pts; 2, Christie McWilliams (10) 36 pts; 3, P.C. Duffy (8) 36 pts. 3rd day (Son Vida) – 1, Brendan Coyle (8) 41 pts; 2, Eddie Gallagher (8) 39 pts; 3, Kevin Barrett (11) 38 pts. 4th day (Santa Ponsa) – 1, Eddie Gallagher (8) 37 pts; 2, Peter McCready (6) 36 pts; 3, Christie McWilliams (10) 34 pts.

Winners of the 1996 team event were, from left, Kevin Doherty, Pascal Harpur, Kevin Barrett and Colm Duffy. On the right is team event sponsor, Eugene Dunbar.

Two of the most consistent players on Tour, Eugene Dunbar and Davy Jones.

Still on the tee

The best par I have ever witnessed came at the par five 13th hole at Santa Ponsa. Knowing he needed a big tee shot to go for the green in two, Paddy Cunningham leapt six inches into the air as he attacked his ball on his downswing. He quickly discovered how that can cause problems. As he looked anxiously down the fairway to see where it landed, we could have told him straight away – it was still sitting on the tee.

I will never forget the look on his face – it was one of embarrassment, bewilderment, shock and ultimately sadness. He realised that when he got to the clubhouse and as soon as he was out of earshot, we would all be telling our mates abut the shot that never was.

But every cloud has a silver lining – fresh air can be good for you. To his eternal credit, Paddy gathered himself to such an extent that he managed to finish the hole in five shots – I removed my hat in admiration – it ain't over till the fat lady sings.

Over the years I have extracted a considerable number of euro from Dunbar and Pearson – when will they learn sense. They are pictured here with tour organiser Andy Meenagh and Pat Swain.

Canadian victory in '97

Introduced to the Tour by his colleagues in Du Pont, Canadian Dave Trickett won Majorca in 1997 in a thrilling last day encounter with Eddie Gallagher. The reception he got when he played a delightful chip to win at Son Vida bore testimony to the popularity of Dave's win.

Overall results

1, Dave Trickett 139 pts (31,34,37,37); 2, Eddie Gallagher 138 pts (39,32,32,35); 3, Peter Villa 137 pts (37,33,35,32); 4, Brian Doherty 137 pts (37,33,33,34); 5, Christie McWilliams 136 pts (32,35,33,36); 6, Eugene Dunbar 135 pts (28,36,35,36); 7, P.C. Duffy 134 pts (35,27,34,38); 8, Martin O'Kane 130 pts (25,36,31,38); 9, Cahir McGeady 130 pts (28,33,37,32; 10, Maurice Brennan 130 pts (32,34,33,31).

Team results

1, Brian McCarroll (4), Brian Doherty (11), E. McCauley (13), Eugene Dunbar (21) 348 pts; 2, Cahir McGeady (4), Danny Gallagher (10), Dave Trickett (15), N. McDermott 325 pts; 3, E. Gallagher (7), John Moran (11), Liam Tourish (14), Patrick Doherty (15) 325 pts.

Daily results

Poniente – 1, Eddie Gallagher (8) 39 pts; 2, Brian Doherty (11) 37 pts; 3, Peter Villa (18) 37 pts. Son Antem – 1, Martin O'Kane (6) 36 pts; 2, Eugene Dunbar (21) 36 pts; 3, Christie McWilliams (10) 35 pts. Poniente – 1, Liam Tourish (15) 38 pts; 2, Cahir McGeady (4) 37 pts; 3, Dave Trickett (15) 37 pts. Son Vida – 1, John O'Brien (7) 38 pts; 2, Martin O'Kane (6) 38 pts; 3, P.C. Duffy (9) 38 pts.

A very popular winner in 1997 was Canadian Dave Trickett, who heard about the Tour from fellow Du Pont colleagues. He is pictured here receiving his prize from Colm McCarroll.

You're both wrong!

ONE OF THE funniest stories I have heard about James "the Miller", Michael's father, comes courtesy of long time member of North-West, Vincent Grant. It was at an annual general meeting and two members stood up to oppose a Resolution. In response, James stood up and issued the immortal words – "It is one of the few times that I have seen you two boys agree about something and you're both wrong!"

"Parley vous Italiano"?

WITH HIS BALL lying on the right side of a line up along the 9th fairway at Los Naranjos in 1978, Larry Hasson is not sure whether he is in or out of bounds. He spots a green keeper sitting beside a tree having his lunch. "Is ballo out of boundo"? asks Mr. Hasson. And typical of his wonderful sense of humour, he continues – "parley vous Italiano"? He was a genius, no question about it.

On the first tee at Poniente are Pat Mackey, Leo Hickey, Eamon McCourt and George Pearson.

I don't question their commitment but this group have two things in common – they were all alcoholics and they have never won on Michael's trips. Seated are Paul Gallagher, Bobby Irwin, Eddie McCauley and Stanley McDermott. Standing, from left, are Alec Campbell, Noel Hynes, Mercer Shaw, John Hassay, Brendan Coyle, Karl Doherty, Pat Mackey, Frank McCarroll and Dermott Coyle.

World Travellers from Du Pont

As the 42nd Michael Doherty tour approaches, I got to thinking about the many journeys my colleagues from Du Pont made from around the world to be there. I started going in 1981 on the advice of the late Norman Bruce and Bill Bratton who told me that it would be an amazing experience for a novice golfer - boy were they right. I had the dates put in my diary early on to ensure I met up with Bill, Norman, Stewart Canning and Bob Coull plus all the regulars from the tour.

Around 1991 I met Rabon Wilkins in Luxembourg who was friendly with Bill Bratton, so we invited him to Spain and he kept coming even when he transferred to headquarters in Switzerland with me. His greatest memory was finishing in the top 10 and representing the tour versus La Cala. Sadly he passed away in 2015. (Editor's note – a letter from Rabon to Michael appears elsewhere in this book).

Whilst Rabon and I were in Switzerland we had Dave Trickett in our fourball so we invited him to join us in Majorca. After a one year apprenticeship, Dave achieved the golfing highlight of his career when he won the Travellers' Trophy in Son Vida in 1997.

Other ex pat golfers who made the long journeys were Bob Coull, past captain at City of Derry, who travelled from Singapore and the late Alex Campbell who came from Korea.

In 1998 I changed career moving to the USA. During the next ten years I managed all but one of the trips. The Mercury Marine team event played on the 3rd round proved a popular addition to the tournament with golf balls and team prizes being shipped across the pond.

As I reflect on my 36 years association with the Michael Doherty Tour, I can safely say on behalf of all of us Du Ponters that the miles travelled have proven to be a great investment in terms of great memories and great lasting friendships.

Pat Mackey

Du Pont added greatly to the prestige of the annual Tour with entrants from other countries. Along with our own Bill Bratton and Bob Coull were the most welcome of guests, Dave Trickett from Canada and Raybon Wilkins from Carolina, USA.

On the first tee at Santa Ponsa are, from left, Brendan Coyle, Steven Wray, Maurice Brennan and Brian Long.

Despite sometimes appearing to be a little grumpy, Colin Montgomerie is exactly the opposite. He is a very charming man, typical of most of the World's top professionals. This photo was taken just a few years ago in the upmarket 'Wellies' in Puerto Portals. From left are Hugh Casey, Tommy McBride, the great man himself and Maurice Brennan.

An international field

Golfers from New York, Wisconsin, North Carolina, Singapore, Switzerland, Aberdeen, London and Burton on Trent were among the starters in a truly international field in Majorca in 1998. Pre-tournament favourite, Maurice Brennan, justified the bookies tight odds winning by a runaway margin of six points

The foundation for the winner's fine score of 140 pts were his second and third rounds at Poniente and Son Antem where he had scores of 37 and 39 pts respectively. That gave him a four point cushion going into the final round and in incessant rain at Poniente he increased the margin to six.

City of Derry five handicapper, Maurice Brennan won the prestigious "Travellers' Trophy" for the second time, having first secured victory back in 1995 on the Costa Del Sol.

The competitiveness of the Spanish Tour team event continues to attract significant attention and one player regularly associated with such success is the redoubtable Eddie Gallagher (7), a member of the Ballybofey and Stranorlar Club. Eddie, who finished runner-up in the individual event, successfully guided his team, consisting of Tony Toland (13), Ballyliffin, Pat Mackey (16), U.S.A. and Pascal Harper (21), Ballyliffin to the top honours with a superb score of 333 points.

The much sought after gross prize was secured by Frank McCarroll (3), North-West, who carded a very respectable 109 points for the four rounds.

Overall results

1, Maurice Brennan (5) 140 pts; 2, Eddie Gallagher (7) 134 pts; 3, Peter Villa (14) 131 pts; 4, Paul McDaid (13) 129 pts; 5, Christie McWilliams (11) 129 pts; 6, Cyril Ward (15) 128 pts; 7, Niall McDermott (15) 126 pts; 8, Bill Bratton (20) 126 pts; 9, Brendan Coyle (9) 125 pts; 10, Dave Trickett (11) 124 pts.

Team results

1, Eddie Gallagher (7), Tony Toland (13), Pat Mackey (16), Pascal Harpur (21) 333 pts; 2, Liam Tourish (9), Dave Trickett (11), Paul McDaid (13), Bill Bratton (20) 323 pts; 3, P.C. Duffy (8), Peter Harkin (10), Eddie Leonard (15), Pat Morrison (20) 316 pts.

Daily results

Santa Ponsa - 1, Kevin Barrett (12) 36 pts; 2, Eugene Dunbar (20) 35 pts; 3, Peter Villa (14) 35 pts. Poniente – 1, Cyril Ward (16) 38 pts; 2, Maurice Brennan (6) 37 pts; 3, Paul McDaid (13) 36 pts. Son Antem – 1, Maurice Brennan (6) 39 pts; 2, Bill Bratton (20) 38 pts; 3, Dave Trickett (11) 36 pts. Poniente – 1, Paul McDaid (13) 36 pts; 2, Eddie Gallagher (7) 36 pts; 3, Eddie Leonard (15) 36 pts.

Winners of the 1998 Team event with 333 pts were Tony Toland junior, Pascal Harpur, Pat Mackey and Eddie Gallagher. They are pictured with the sponsor, Eugene Dunbar.

Pat Swain (centre) who had taken a 'sabbatical' is pictured with Tommy McBride, Maurice Brennan, Steven Wray and Sean McKane.

Chilling out at the Piano Bar are Paddy Cunningham, Eddie Leonard, Billy McElhinney, Bert Whoriskey, Joe Ramsay and Eamon McCourt

Three wins out of five

Maurice Brennan proved without doubt what a consistent performer he was in the latter half of the nineties, making it three wins out of five in the second half of the nineties. La Cala North, Mijas, Parador and La Quinta separated the men from the boys. It was around about this time that Portadown's Stephen Wray was serving notice that a win in the Travellers Trophy was on the horizon.

Overall results

1, Maurice Brennan 135 pts; 2, Stephen Wray 134 pts; 3, P.C. Duffy 133 pts; 4, John O'Brien 131 pts; 5, Jess Furnival 130 pts; 6, Christie McWilliams 129 pts; 7, Cahir McGeady 129 pts; 8, F.E. McCarroll 129 pts; 9, Brendan Coyle 127 pts; 10, Con Boyce 126 pts.

Team results

1,Frank McCarroll, Peter Villa, Ken McConomy and Eugene Dunbar 332 pts; 2nd, Cahir McGeady, Paul O'Doherty, Cyril Ward, Michael Cunningham 330 pts; 3, Michael McGee, P.C. Duffy, Stephen Wray, Seamus McGorrian 317 pts.

Daily results

La Cala North – 1, P.C.Duffy (9) 39 pts; 2, Maurice Brennan (6) 36 pts; 3, Stephen Wray (12) 36 pts. Mijas – 1, Jess Furnival (16) 41 pts; 2, Eugene Dunbar (20) 40 pts; 3, John O'Brien (7) 38 pts. Parador – 1, Frank McCarroll (3) 38 pts; 2, Gavin Killeen (19) 35 pts; 3, Maurice Brennan (6) 34 pts. La Quinta – 1, Stephen Wray (12) 34 pts; 2, Cyril Ward (16) 34 pts; 3, Brendan Coyle (9) 34 pts.

There were no less than three "aces" in 1999. Both Paul O'Doherty and Eddie Gallagher holed out at the 2nd at Mijas while Davy Jones tamed the 200 yard 2nd hole at La Quinta with the perfect stroke.

There was an innovation in 1999 when a team from the La Cala Club challenged a hand-picked squad from the Michael Doherty contingent. The visitors were more than up for the challenge, winning by 3.5 to 1.5.

Ernie Heywood, winner in 2005, Peter Harkin, Brendan Coyle and Eugene Dunbar, winner in 1994 and 2015)

Brian McClure, winner in 2016, with the official starter, Willie Barrett.

Two past winners, Maurice Brennan (1995,1998 and 1999) and Frankie Campbell (2001).

What will we give him?

P.C. Duffy was generous to the extreme, a quality he illustrated so many times. And to his friends, his giving hand was always there. This little memory involves four priests, Fr. Jim McGonagle, Fr. Ignatius McQuillan, Fr. Seamus Farrelly and Fr. Joe O'Conor.

Colm had a villa in a golf and sporting development, Peaarl Valley, just 45 minutes outside Cape Town, South Africa. From what I have been told it was magnificent, located by the 7th green of the Peaarl Valley Golf Course.

When he heard that the four priests were planning a holiday, he immediately put his villa at their disposal. According to Fr. Jim McGonagle, they had the holiday of a lifetime thanks to their host's generosity.

Divine inspiration

When it came to the end of the holiday they pondered long and hard as to what they should get their host as an appropriate gift. It was at that moment that divine inspiration took over.

A few weeks later we were out for our usual Friday lunch. P.C. tells us he had invited four 'druids' out to the villa in South Africa and, with tears running down his face, he tried to tell us what they had left as a thank you gift. "What would you think CA, maybe a Scotty Cameron putter, maybe a Premier Cru Latour?"

Eventually he managed to blurt it out – it was 'The New Catechism of the Catholic Church', signed by all four with an appropriate little comment.

A miracle?

Long bawls of spontaneous laughter filled that restaurant for at least five minutes. "I couldn't have thought of a more appropriate book to buy me. And you know, C.A., stranger things have happened – maybe there will be a miracle and Old P.C. might find religion. But I sincerely hope not".

Geoffrey Boycott

PS. The legendary Geoffrey Boycott owned a villa right next to Colm and during their stay he invited his temporary next door neighbours over for dinner – a lovely gesture by someone who turned out to be a most gracious host. After dinner he said he was asked to name the eleven best cricketers he had ever played with, so for posterity he commissioned an artist to paint a canvas.

"Would you like to see it"? In expectation they adjourned to the lounge, very curious as to who Geoffrey's choice would be. On the wall was a splendid canvas, showing eleven different poses from just one man – Geoffrey Boycott. Pure class.

Michael's times

Michael's eldest son, Jim

When North-West member Mary McGeough was researching for a special book celebrating 125 years of the North-West she asked Michael's son, Jim if he could provide some background information on his dad's time at North-West. Jim sat down with Michael and jotted down some of his recollections. They make great reading.

In his early days Michael's pastimes and interests were billiards, cinema, tennis, winter sleighing and music. Around the age of twelve or so his father James took on the running of the town council's tennis courts and putting green at the shorefront, as well as continuing to work shifts in McCarter's factory next door. Michael became his helper after school and during holidays.

Around that time Arnold Gilliland and Norman Drew came to work at North West Golf Club, with Norman being assistant to Arnold's professional role. Norman was one of the top Irish golfers of the time, had been a Walker Cup amateur and would be a future Ryder Cup player. Arnold was a renowned club maker. They resided in Bradley's guest house at the shorefront and Norman in particular paid many evening visits to the putting green, resulting in regular matches betweeen him and Michael for a shilling a time.

Shocked to be invited

Michael had also started playing golf proper at Buncrana Municipal Golf Club. Although only fourteen and still at school at the old 'Tech' in 1953, Michael was shocked to be invited to work at North-West Golf Club with Arnold and Norman. He started at the initial pay of ten shillings a week, in the weeks that his employers could afford to actually pay him! Transport to work involved the three of them squeezing into Arnold's old MG sports car, when it wasn't in the garage for repairs, which was often!

His earliest roles including cleaning members' clubs on Mondays after the weekend's play. In those days part of the service was the storing of members' clubs on racks in the Pro Shop. He then moved on to learning club repairs, such as replacing the old twine bindings on wooden clubs, a craft no longer needed of course. Under Arnold's guidance he progressed to the making of wooden clubs out of wooden blocks; sanding, making face pieces, installing sole plates and many repeats of varnishing and buffing.

A new set of clubs

Michael wan't allowed to actually play on the course for the first six months, restricted to early morning hitting of shots on the 11th and 9th fairways with old clubs given to him by his father. That was until the time Michael remembers Norman giving him a John Letters 'Dai Rees' brassie (2 wood) and Norman came out to watch him hit shots with it. Norman got a great surprise at what he saw and Michael remembers him going inside again and bringing Arnold out to watch, saying "look at this boy hitting the ball, I didn't realise he could play so well!" Norman then organised for the John Letters company, with which he was associated, to provide Michael with a new set of clubs and he began playing on the course. Norman moved on to Strabane Golf Club a year or so later.

Offered North-West position

In 1956, when seventeen years old, a relative in America arranged for an Assistant Professional position in California, which Michael was preparing to move to. However, Arnold Gilliland then left North West, and the club council offered Michael the full Professional position, which he accepted. He took on the stocking of the shop, providing a repair service, giving lessons, and, still part of the Pro's role in those days, organised the caddies. There could be around twenty caddies active at weekends. They got two shillings for a round, but extra in bad weather from more generous members, and Michael got sixpence for the organisation. There was a caddy shack behind the shop at the old clubhouse. Nearby was the kitchen door, where the caddies paid a penny for bread and 'caddy jam', as it was known.

In those days a Professional had to be registered with the PGA for five years before playing in tournaments. Early years playing was therefore concentrated on the course at Lisfannon.

at North-West

Michael remembers many games played with James Longwill (Butcher), Danny O'Donnell, Jacom Centra, Bill McNutt (shoemaker) and Sonny Doherty, when he worked with Bill McNutt before going on to become Professional at Buncrana Municipal. These were mainly Wednesday afternoon games, on the weekly Buncrana business 'half-day'. There were also many outings with Jackie 'The X' McLaughlin after his Lynch's Bakery shift, and with Frankie Friel and others.

Beat the pro

Michael remembers that around the early 1960's there was an ongoing competition called 'Beat the Pro', where members could challenge their club Professional to a match, the member playing off their normal handicap and the Pro off scratch. He recalls having a hole-in-one at the then 200 yard or so par 3 third against Plunkett Duffy. John Grant challenged him to a match one morning to be beaten by Michael's 66, when the par was around 73/74, in the 'jungle' hole days, before erosion reduced the course. John insisted on a repeat in the afternoon, when Michael managed a 67! In Michael's memory, he only ever suffered about three or four defeats! This active playing at the time was allowed by his father James having finished at McCarter's and helping him out at the shop.

A few months before his PGA registration was complete, Michael played with Christy O'Connor Senior for the first time, who was a big star then. This was part of an exhibition match day at North West and Christy, having witnessed Michael's play first-hand, advised him to go and play in professional tournaments in Britain. But, this was pre-organised European Tour days and Michael already had his commitments at North West.

Tournament play

When his registration came through he remembers his first big event as the Hennessy Tournament at Royal Dublin, playing with and managing to outscore the great Harry Bradshaw in the first two rounds and was then paired with the famous Fred Daly over the final two rounds. Michael then played events such as the Irish PGA Championship at Lahinch with Christy Senior, the Dunlop Tournament and the Carroll's International, predecessor of the Irish Open, where the likes of Tony Jacklin, Eric Brown and Brian Hugget came to play. He remembers completing his final round at the Carroll's at Royal Dublin and going back out to watch Christy O'Connor playing his last few holes. Eric Brown was in the clubhouse with a two shot lead and Christy finished eagle, birdie, eagle to win. Michael went back to the locker room to see Eric Brown shaking his head in disbelief.

Wedding goes ahead despite the fire!

Michael's wedding date with Veronica was organised for April 1964, but in February came a devastating fire which destroyed the clubhouse, Pro shop included. The temporary measures quickly organised involved a combination of using upstairs in the Trocadero restaurant in town, space in Ferguson's house across the road from the golf club and then two buses parked behind the 10th tee, one for the shop and one for members' changing. The wedding went ahead as planned!

With marriage, children following and club commitments, most of Michael's golf continued to be played at Lisfannon. He can recall that, on the current course layout, he had a hole in one on every par three and an eagle on every other hole except, he thinks, the 6th, 10th and 12th. He remembers his eagle two on the 17th happening one evening in the company of Mickey McCarron.

A round that stands out

One of the rounds that stands out in his memory was the Captain's Prize competition in the first year of the North West Alliance. Many Irish international players came to play from Belfast, Portrush and other places, such as the Hoey brothers and top local players took part, like the McCarrolls and Michael Fitzpatrick. He played that day with his brother-in-law, Fr. Denis McConologue and Frank Friel. It was a cold, windy March day with hail showers. It took two drivers to reach the first and twelfth. Two birdies in the last five holes helped him to a winning score of 68.

Giving lessons was an important part of the service to members, as well as the occasional visiting 'celebrity'. Michael remembers early lessons given to Johnny Giles and Val Doonican at Lisfannon, for example.

On the move to Derry in '72

Michael moved on to City of Derry Golf Club in 1972. North-West was suffering badly from erosion, the club council had decided against purchasing land available across the road and he had a growing family to look after, so the offer of the new position was taken up, despite it being a huge wrench to leave North West.

North West Golf Club provided the grounding for a very successful 36 years at City of Derry, during which he served on the British and Irish PGA executive committee for several years, was Irish region PGA captain, was PGA representative at the U.S. Open and he officiated at the Ryder Cup. He was voted Irish Club Professional of the Century by his peers at the PGA centenary dinner in 2004, where Seve Ballesteros joined him on stage in Dublin to collect his international player award.

Michael retired in 2008. He looks back very fondly on his time at Lisfannon and the people he met and had fun playing golf with and he still thinks of it as his golfing 'home', despite the many years that have passed since.

Jim Doherty 21st July 2011

TRAVELLERS ON MICHAEL'S TOURS

Abel Wilf
Aiken Fred
Allen Maurice
Armstrong Vincent
Bakewell Raymond
Balmer Jock
Barrett Kevin
Barrett Sean
Barrett Willie
Brady Walter
Bell Bobby
Black David
Bland Dan
Blaney Paul
Bonner Michael
Boyce Con
Boyce Francis
Bradley John (Accountant)
Bradley John
Bratton Davy
Bratton Bill
Brennan Maurice
Brennan Paul
Brown Harry
Bruce Norman
Budd Brian
Burnside Walter
Brolly Clive
Byrd Captain
Campbell Alex
Campbell Dan
Campbell Oliver
Campbell Frankie
Canning Dermot
Canning Bill
Canning Stuart
Carey Pius
Carlisle Paul
Carroll Mike
Casey Hugh
Cassidy Tom
Cassidy Kevin
Chambers John
Cleary Paul
Collins Charlie
Condit Sam
Connelly M
Connor Roger
Cooley Danny
Cooley Hugh
Copas J
Coyle Brendan
Coyle Dermot

Coull Bob
Curruthers Les
Cunningham D.
Cunningham Michael
Cunningham Paddy
Daly Tommy
Deehan Tom
Dalton Tim
Deeney Laurence
Del Pinto Gino
Doherty Karl
Doherty Denis
Doherty Michael
Doherty Jack
Doherty Ian
Doherty Patrick
Doherty Joe
Doherty Sean
Doherty Brian
Doherty Jim
Doherty Kevin
Doherty C
Doherty Paul
Doherty Peter
Doherty Thomas
Dougherty Gilbert
Dolan Gabriel
Dolan James
Douglas D
Doyle Sean
Draper Mark
Duddy Brian
Duffy Arthur
Duffy Brian
Duffy PC
Dunbar Eugene
Duncan Neil
Dunlop Willie
Ellis Pat
Elliott Billy
Fagan Patsy
Finlay Trevor
Finn Lenoard
Fitzpatrick Cahir
Foley Joe
Friel Frank
Furnival Jess
Gallagher Mick
Gallagher J.
Gallagher Danny
Gallagher Liam
Gallagher Paul
Gallagher Dermot

Gallagher Eddie
Gault Michael
Gilmore Mervyn
Glenn Trevor
Gormley John sen
Gormley John Jr
Grant Eamon
Grey Archie
Grant Eugene
Graham Ted
Guckian Frank
Gallagher John
Haddock John
Hamill Barry
Hanna Bill
Hannigan Seamus
Hannigan John
Harkin Peter
Harkin Eamon
Harper Pascal
Hassay John
Hasson Declan
Hasson John
Hasson Larry
Hegarty Denis
Hegarty Ted
Hester Sam
Heywood Ernie
Hickey Leo
Hill Ron
Hume Colm
Hutton Dermott
Hutton Jim
Hynes Noel
Irwin Bobby
Irwin Dougie
Jackson George
Jackson Jim
Jarvis Sonny
Jones Davy
Kealy Sean
Keating Pat
Kane Raymond
Kelly Des
Kelly James
Kelly Pat
Kelly Shane
Kernan Seamus
Killeen Gavin
Kirby Eugene
Kyle Jim
Langan Cathal
Lawrence Peter

OVER THE 41 YEARS (NOT A COMPLETE LIST)

Leckey Jim
Leckey Gary
Lees Trevor
Leonard Eddie
Logue Jack
Logue Oliver
Long Brian
Longwill James
Louden John
Loughrey Pat
Love John
Mackey Pat
McLochlainn Donal
Maine J
Maloney Donal
Moran John
MacManus Eamon
McAteer John
McBrearty Seamus
McBride Ken
McBride Eneas
McBride Tommy
McCann Michael
McCarroll Frank Snr
McCarroll Brendan
McCarroll Colm
McCarroll Frank Jr
McCarroll Brian
McCaul Liam
McCauley Eddie
McKeegan Stephen
McCloskey Danny
McCloskey Jimmy
McCloskey Malachy
McClure Brian
McConomy Tony
McCullough Terry
McCullough Michael
McCourt Eamon
McGowan Kingsley
McCready Peter
McDaid Barney
McDaid Peter
McDaid Paul
McDermott Niall
McDermott James
McDermott John
McDermott Paul
McDermott Sean
McDevitt Seamus
McElhone Maurice
McElhinney Billy

McElroy Eamon
McElroy Joe
McGeady James
McGeady Cahir
McGee Michael
McGee Jimmy
McGilloway Declan
McGlinchey Jimmy
McGorrian Seamus
McGonagle Pat
McGrane Sean
McGuire Frank
McHale Dominic
McKane Sean
McKee Brian
McKeegan Cecil
McKeegan Stephen
McKerr Donald
McLaughlin Brendan
McLaughlin Gilbert
McLaughlin C
McLaughlin E
McLaughlin Derek
McLaughlin Phil
McMorran Norman
McMenamin Joe
McMenamin Enda
McNally Danny
McNulty Harry
McNutt Raymond
McWilliams Christie
McWilliams Jim
Meek Chris
Meenagh Andy
Molloy E
Monaghan John
Morrison Paddy
Mulgrew Brian
Mullan Ronnie
Murphy R
Murphy Colm
Murray Tommy
Nagra Bobby
Nagra Sukie
Nash Raymond
Neff Chris
Nicholl Denis
Nolan Sean
O'Brien John
O'Carroll Jamsie
O'Connor B
O'Doherty Eamon
O'Doherty Eugene

O' Doherty Don
O'Doherty Paul
O'Doherty Mark
O'Dwyer Sean
O' Hare Rory
O'Hare James
O'Kane Fonsie
O'Kane Martin
O'Kane Hugh
O'Neill Phelim
O'Neill Ciaran
O'Neill Tommy
O'Sullivan Eoin
Patton Charlie
Pearson George
Phillips Terry
Pollock Davy
Quigg Maurice
Quigley Peter
Renshaw Les
Ramsey Joe
Rodden Billy
Wray Stephen
Rooney Dermod
Ryan Jimmy
Sharma Deep
Shaw Mercer
Sharp Ken
Simms George
Simpson Hector
Stafford Charlie
Smyth Bob
Smyth Hugh
Smith Jackie
Souden W
Stewart Jim
Stewart Teddy
Swain Pat
Sweeney George
Taylor George
Toland Tony
Tourish Liam
Trickett Dave
Villa Peter
Wallace Gordon
Ward Andrew
Ward Cyril
Ward Dixon
Whoriskey Bert
Wilkins Raybon
Wright Billy
Young Noel

Bright future

It is difficult to fathom how golf has advanced in the North-West over the past thirty years. Thanks to the remarkable efforts of a lot of dedicated people, many golf clubs are beyond recognition. And with the addition of the splendid new 27 holes complex at Foyle Golf Centre and the new Faughan Valley Golf Club, the future looks very bright.

That runs against the trend in general as golf has been going through a quiet period since 2008 when, for many people, golf became a very expensive hobby. That aside, more and more new faces are now appearing on the scene and it is great to see them. New faces are the life-blood of golf and where the future lies.

No age boundaries

In what other sport can you see octogenarians out battling in all weathers in the all-important quest to win a few shillings. Bragging rights have no age boundaries – I have listened in to the likes of Pat O'Carolan and Brendan Burke as they ruthlessly dissect their opposition's performance. Life is not a bed of roses if you have just been beaten.

If our golfing forefathers came back now, what would they think – a superb 18 holes layout at Greencastle, a picturesque nine holes course at Redcastle, an upgraded Buncrana Golf Club boasting the longest par 5 on the Wild Atlantic Way – four yards short of 600 and a North-West links which would rival the best in Ireland.

First 'ace'

And my old home course, City of Derry, for which I will always have the greatest of affection. I had my first-ever 'hole-in-one' at the old 15th, the Quarry on 12th April, 1959 using a black shafted 5 iron I got for Christmas. Incidentally I had fifteen more since!

And what would they think of Ballyliffin – they would be mesmerised. From its birth in 1947, it has developed into one of the top golfing venues in Europe. With several GUI and R & A events already under their belt, they will receive the ultimate accolade in 2019 when they host the 'Irish Open'.

A great foursome about to set off. From left, P.C. Duffy, Danny McNally, Billy McElhinney and Danny Cooley.

MICHAEL DOHERTY TOUR TEAM WINNERS

1976	F.E. McCarroll, J. Balmer, H. Quigley, F. Aicken	343 pts
1977	D. McNally, J. Logue, J. Stewart, P. Loughrey	242 pts
1978	No team results available	
1979	F.E. McCarroll jun, B. Duddy, W. Elhinney, P. Doherty	174 pts
1980	P. McCready, N. McMorran, B. Duffy, P. Ellis	175 pts
1981	J. Hannigan, D. Quinn, L. Carruthers, B. Bratton	171 pts
1982	L. McCaul, C. Fitzpatrick, B. Long, W. Burnside	176 pts
1983	B. Doherty, H. McNulty, C. McWilliams, B. McLaughlin	187 pts
1984	E. Gallagher, D.J. O'Doherty, L. Finn, E. O'Doherty	181 pts
1985	D. McGale, J. Foley, L. Carruthers, P. Morrison	178 pts
1986	F.E. McCarroll jun, E. Gallagher, C. Stafford, E. Dunbar	178 pts
1987	C. Boyce, J. Ramsey, D. Irwin, J. Gormley	177 pts
1988	P.C. Duffy, D. McLaughlin, W. Burnside, B. Bratton	183 pts
1989	C. Boyce, B. Rodden, K. Doherty, M. Brennan	191 pts
1990	N. Hynes, M. Quigg, J. Gormley, S. Cassidy	189 pts
1991	C. McGeady, J. Ramsey, W. Burnside, S. Jarvis	191 pts
1992	P.C. Duffy, P. Brennan, M. Quigg, E. Dunbar	183 pts
1993	C. McGeady, C. McWilliams,D. Douglas, J. Moran	191 pts
1994	E. McCourt, K. Doherty, J. McGee, E. Dunbar	192 pts
1995	C. McWilliams, P.C. Duffy, R. Wilkins, T. Daly	191 pts
1996	P.C.Duffy, K. Barrett, K. Doherty, P. Harper	187 pts
1997	B.H. McCarroll, B. Doherty, E. McCauley, E. Dunbar	348 pts
1998	E. Gallagher, T. Toland, P. Mackey, P. Harpur	333 pts
1999	F.E. McCarroll, P. Villa, K. McConomy, E. Dunbar	332 pts
2000	B. Long, F. Campbell, J. McGee, E. Dunbar	323 pts
2001	T. McBride, P.C. Duffy, P. McDaid, B. McElhinney	310 pts
2002	B. Long, T. McBride, Patrick Doherty, W. Barrett	323 pts
2003	M. Brennan, P. Brennan, P. Gallagher, E. Dunbar	332 pts
2004	C. McGeady, M. McGee, D. Bratton, J. Furnival	246 pts
2005	C. O'Neill, P. Villa, F. Campbell, K. Doherty	337 pts
2006	C. Boyce, P. Villa, P. O'Neill, S. Canning	330 pts
2007	S. Wray, B. McDaid, J. Hassay, L. Hickey	349 pts
2008	T. McBride, S. Wray, B. Doherty, D. Jones	336 pts
2009	T. McBride, J. O'Brien, P. Swain, Karl Doherty	329 pts
2010	J. O'Brien, A. Meenagh, P. Swain, L. Hickey	334 pts
2011	M. O'Doherty, P. Mackey, K. Doherty, M. Quigg	331 pts
2012	B. McClure, P. Villa, P. Swain, D. Jones	352 pts
2013	F.E. McCarroll jun, E. McCourt, D. Jones, K. Barrett	337 pts
2014	P. Harkin, E. Dunbar, S. McKane, G. Pearson	345 pts
2015	B. McClure, K. Doherty, M. Quigg, D. McCloskey	344 pts
2016	B. McClure, S. Wray, S. Kelly, S. McKane	334 pts

Andy Robertson – what an interesting man!

The genius behind Ballyliffin's world-beating greens.

What an interesting character Andy Robertson is. Ballyliffin's Links Superintendent, rightly acknowledged as one of the top links specialists in Europe, has quite a story to tell. And you'll get some laughs when you sit down to talk to him.

Not that we had time to sit. Andy was taking a short break from his very busy schedule at Ballyliffin and I was sitting at a computer on the other end of a mobile phone.

How did a man from the very north of Scotland, Reay in Caithness, end up in beautiful Inishowen? From the age of 15 he was a sand-blaster before getting his introduction to golf at the age of 18 as an assistant greenkeeper at Thurso Golf Club.

After six months there he joined a Greens Training Course at Elmwood College in Cupar, Fife where he was to meet a man who would ultimately change his life – Anthony Bonnett, a fellow trainee at Elmwood College and assistant at Sunningdale.

He didn't like flying

Through Anthony, whom he impressed greatly, he was to get a week's work experience at Sunningdale. It meant a flight for the first time in his life for the Reay man and he didn't like it one little bit – he put it in much stronger terms, but we won't go into that.

That experience was amazing – he just loved the course but typical of Andy's honesty, he felt that Sunningdale was in need of essential "house work".

His mentor that week in Sunningdale was Lawson Bingham, originally the course manager at Prestwick and the man who was going to finally chart his career.

Bingham told him that he would contact him as soon as he finished college and was good to his word.

He invited Andy to start work in London in 1990 to prepare Sunningdale for the European Open and it was there that he became an expert in bunker revetting, a skill reserved for the select few.

Bingham moved on to the exclusive Swinley Forest Golf Club but always kept in touch with Andy. One day out of the blue, he contacted Andy to advise him that there was a vacancy at a club in Donegal.

He had a few gallons of stout

He sent in his CV to Ballyliffin on a Tuesday and got a call on Thursday asking him if he could come to an interview on Saturday. It was then that he met club captain, Oliver Gilmore, Patsy Doherty, Karl O'Doherty and Barry Kearney for the first time.

His story is hilarious about how he ended up in the 'Rusty Nail' afterwards and had a few gallons of stout with an old friend. The whole story would take a week to tell but, to make it short and sweet, when he arrived back at his hotel, the receptionist informed him that Ballyliffin's captain, Oliver Gilmore, had been looking for him. That was on 18th May, 1998 and the beginning of the best years of an already eventful life.

And it was a local girl, in typical fashion, who won his heart. Ballyliffin's committee had forgotten to give him one vital piece of advice - when an Inishowen woman gets her hooks into you, you're dead meat. He's been very happily married to Majella Strain from Burnfoot for the past 14 years, with an 8 years old son Fintan, their pride and joy.

There is only one Augusta

The most extraordinary person I have ever had the pleasure of working with in administrative golf is Augusta Neff, captain of North-West ladies branch in 1996 and immediate past president. Generosity of spirit sums her up – nothing is too much for her, no task beyond her huge capabilities. She has been on Council for the past twelve years and is, as everyone would agree, indispensible.

I first came into contact with her in the early 1980's when North-West was in dire straits because of the ravages of coastal erosion which was ripping the beautiful little jewel to shreds.

We had to come up with something urgent so a committee consisting of Cathal Harvey, Kevin McGeough, John O'Brien, Augusta and myself were drafted in to see if we could come up with any ideas how to generate money.

Without remembering too much about it as it was so long ago, we dipped our toes in the water with an initial draw which generated about £20,000 at the time – nice money but not nearly enough.

He proposed a bruiser

Kevin McGeough is a forward thinker and ambitious too – flushed with the success of the first draw, he proposed a bruiser"– 2,000 tickets at £100 each realising a nett profit of £120,000. In 1985 it all sounded a bit mad.

Again the same team was assembled – Harvey, McGeough, O'Brien, Neff and myself. It was at this stage that Augusta

The 6th fairway under several feet of water

came into her own – she was like the Terminator – no one was safe. In a master class of determination she had every tight-arse running round corners when she appeared on the scene.

As a result of the selling power and stamina of all of the five organisers, all 2,000 tickets were sold and the club banked £120,000. It was a truly great effort by five very determined people.

Past captain Stella O'Carolan summed up Augusta so well – "She has endless energy, is generous and caring and as long as North-West needs her, she will always be there."

I couldn't agree more with that observation.

I've just heard recently that she has been made a trustee of the Inishowen club. It's not for me to be making any recommendations to North-West's council but if it was anything to do with me Augusta Neff would unquestionably be an honorary member of a great little club.

Thirty-two years after she helped run the biggest draw in North-West history, Augusta Neff is still at the forefront of golf at Lisfannon as the past President of the ladies branch. I wanted a bit of class so I borrowed this. The occasion – the ladies annual presentation of prizes. From left are Augusta, Kathleen Griffin, Deirdre Britton and Joanne Harkin. Back from left, Lorraine McGettigan, Anne McCloskey, Roisin Timoney, Margaret O'Hea, Aileen McGlynn and Marie McLaughlin.

I could write a book about Larry

I could write a book about Larry Hasson, no question about it. Apart from being a very successful businessman, he was a raconteur, a singer of classical standard, a very kind-hearted man and a very humorous one. One day he was playing at North-West with my brother Frank. At the 7th hole, stroke index 1, Frank struck a shot most unusual for him – a quick hook into the rubbish on the left, about 120 yards from the tee.

250 yards

Up stands Mr. Hasson. For Larry, the carry over the drain from the back sticks was quite a challenge but on this particular day he had a stroke of good fortune – his tee shot hit the bridge, came off a steel hinge and flew a mile up the fairway, so far that it went over the height on the middle of the 7th fairway and finished no less than 250 yards from the tee – for all intents and purposes he was 130 yards outside Frank.

Outhit big Frank

Fast forward to the clubhouse after the round. Both Frank and Larry were in the locker room changing but Larry was unaware that Frank was there. Brendan Burke arrived in and after a few pleasantries asked Larry how he had played. "Great", said Larry, "and I was hitting them so long I outhit big Frank McCarroll at the 7th." As sure as I am sitting here, that is a true story.

Where's my cigar

In his role as president of North-West Golf Club, one of the privileges Larry Hasson had was to play with 'himself', the legendary Christy O'Connor. Miles ahead of Larry after his opening tee shot, Christy looked back, only to see the president looking for his ball. He headed straight back to join the search. In due course the ball was found.

Christy heads back to his ball, waiting for the green to clear. He glances back, only to see Larry searching again. So he heads back again to offer assistance. "What's the problem, Mr. President, was that not your ball?" "Yes, Yes" said the president, "I've got my ball, but now I am looking for my cigar".

Have you got 4?

Cahir McGeady, Danny McNally and myself were waiting our turn to go to the 1st tee at North-West one Sunday afternoon. Round the corner came a vehicle that looked like a hearse (sorry Paul). It was a huge big Volvo estate, driven by Mary Hasson, 98 years old Larry's Hasson's daughter-in-law. The 'hearse' stops, the window spins down and a voice, so strong for someone about to become a centenarian, says "Boys, have you got four?" There was only one Larry Hasson.

Viva el Presidente

The highlight of each year during Larry's spell of presidency at North-West happened at the annual general meetings. Larry had been asked by my father to follow him as president, a role he held for five years. To call the meeting to order at exactly 8pm, he would stand up, shout "Viva el Presidente" at the top of his powerful voice and then break into wonderful song, usually of Italian operatic origin. It was unmissable and without a shadow of doubt, the main reason why most of us turned up.

Pictured on the 1st tee at Poniente are John Hasson, Barry Hamill, a very welcome guest professional, John Chambers and Peter Villa.

Accidents in buggies are commonplace. Peter Villa was lucky to escape with no injuries and his life when his buggy careered into a ravine at the 18th in Son Termens in 2009. Eugene Dunbar was also on the receiving end a few years ago in Poniente and received a serious injury. Take great care!

Navigation specialists

Back in 1999 I went on holiday with Sheila to Florida, with permission granted to bring the clubs. The round that stands out in my memory of some great golfing experiences was the day I played at Falcon's Fire Golf Club. On my own with Sheila driving the buggy, I was introduced to my playing partners, two navigation specialists from Cape Canaveral. I was honoured.

Obviously they didn't see me as a security risk as they delighted in telling me that they had just finished the part they had played in the forthcoming launch of a military satellite called 'Milstar'. I was 'all ears' as they say in Derry. (editor's note:- you're all ears anyway. No wonder your family

called you "Lugser" when you were young).

Bud was everywhere

It became obvious that they were not in the premier league as far as golf was concerned. One in particular, who introduced himself as 'Bud', would have made John Bradley look like a straight hitter. Bud was everywhere – there wasn't a tree plantation, a lake, a 'boondocks' he didn't visit. I had counted that he had parted company with thirteen balls by the time we reached the 12th.

Just as a little aside which I thought would lighten his black mood, I said to him: "Bud, are you sure you are a navigation specialist?" He was outraged. Sheila can confirm this,

he didn't break breath to me over the next four holes. But in the end we parted friends, strangers in the night, exchanging glances and all that sort of stuff.

Gone walkabout

Curiosity killed the cat. During the download of information they freely provided, they told me when it was going to be launched - it was part of a payload from a Titan rocket. I got my hands on the 'Orlando Sentinel' and there it was for all to see. I read it and turned to my beloved – "Sheila, you're not going to believe this – the 'Milstar' project had to be abandoned. As soon as it got into orbit it developed a navigation fault and has gone walkabout". Bud – you are one of my many heroes.

Persistence pays off

Second in 1996, 4th in '97, 3rd in '98 and on the winning team in 1999, Peter Villa's persistence finally paid off in 2000 when he won the Travellers Trophy with a four round total of 133 pts. A huge hitter of the ball, he could find places on Majorcan courses that no-one else knew existed. But in the Millenium year, he sacrificed power for accuracy to deadly effect.

Overall results

1, Peter Villa (12) 133 pts (32,36,33,32); 2, Colm McCarroll (5) 130 pts (34,29,35,32); 3, Brian Long (5) 130 pts (31,35,31,33); 4, Colm Duffy (9) 130 pts (35,34,29,32); 5, Sean Barrett (15) 129 pts (38,27,38,26); 6, Eugene Dunbar (19) 126 pts (32,31,31,30); 7, Maurice Brennan (5) 125 pts (31,27,34,31); 8, Brendan Coyle (9) 125 pts (27,34,32,31); 9, Frank McCarroll (2) 124 pts (33,32,29,30); 10, Frank Campbell (12) 124 pts (9) 30,35,33,26.

Team results

1, Brian Long (5), Frank Campbell (12), Jimmy McGee (12), Eugene Dunbar (19) 323 pts; 2, Frank McCarroll (2), Sean Kealey (12), Jess Furnival (16), Willie Barrett (20) 317 pts; 3, Michael McGee (7), Stephen Wray (11), Andy Meenagh (14), Peter McDaid (16) 316 pts.

Daily results

Poniente – 1, Sean Barrett (16) 38 pts; 2, Paul Brennan (10) 36 pts; 3, P.C. Duffy (9) 36 pts. Santa Ponsa - 1, Peter Villa (12) 36 pts; 2, Brian Long (5) 35 pts; 3, Frank Campbell (12) 35 pts. Poniente – 1, Sean Barrett (16) 38 pts; 2, Patrick Doherty (15) 35 pts; 3, Colm McCarroll (5) 35 pts. Santa Ponsa – 1, Willie Barrett (20) 34 pts; 2, Maurice Brennan (5) 33 pts; 3, Brian Long (5) 33 pts.

John Hasson, Sean McKane, Michael McCullough , Paul Gallagher and Bobby Irwin.

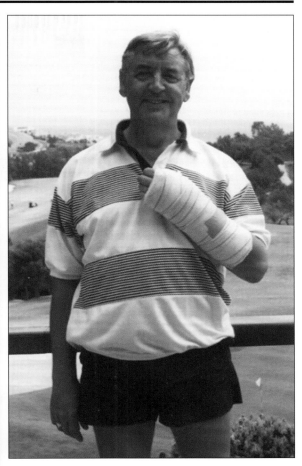

Paul O'Doherty and Tommy McBride before the 'off' in 2002. Paul won at the 73rd hole.

All John McDermott ever needed when he went on Michael's Tour was one arm so he was as happy as the day was long in this picture at Torrequebrada.

Leo Hickey, Steven Wray and Gary Leckey.

Frankie wins in play-off

Renowned for his ability on the soccer pitch with Derry City, eleven handicapper Frankie Campbell joined an elite group in 2001 when he claimed the sought after "Travellers Trophy" after a two holes play-off with Maurice Brennan. In a field of 63 starters the pair finished ahead on 130 pts on Poniente and Santa Ponsa, three ahead of third placed Colm Duffy.

After the first was halved in 5's, a text book par at the dogleg par 5 second was enough to give Frank a very popular victory.

Overall results

1, Frank Campbell 130 pts; 2, Maurice Brennan 130 pts; 3, Colm Duffy 127 pts; 4, Stephen McKeegan 125 pts; 5, Brendan Coyle 124 pts; 6, Brian McClure 123 pts; 7, Brendan McCarroll 123 pts; 8, Eugene Dunbar 123 pts; 9, Eddie Gallagher 122 pts; 10, Brian Long 120 pts.

Team results

1, Tommy McBride, Colm Duffy, Peter McDaid, Billy McElhinney 310 pts; 2, Brian McClure, Eoin O'Sullivan, Paddy Doherty, Eugene Dunbar 309 pts; 3, Frank McCarroll, Brendan Coyle, Joe Ramsey, Cyril Ward 309 pts.

Daily results

1st day (Poniente) – 1, Peter Lawrence (11) 40 pts; 2, Mark O'Doherty (5) 36 pts; 3, Colm Duffy (9) 36 pts. 2nd day (Santa Ponsa) – 1 Paul McDermott (14) 37 pts; 2, Eugene Dunbar (20) 36 pts; 3, Frank Campbell (11) 35 pts. 3rd day (Poniente) – 1, Brendan McCarroll (4) 37 pts; 2, Frank Campbell (11) 35 pts; 3, Paul O'Doherty (9) 35 pts. 4th day (Santa Ponsa) – 1, Eamon MacManus (9) 33 pts; 2, Kevin Barrett (10) 32 pts; 3, Colm Duffy (9) 31 pts.

By virtue of his victory on the final day, Eamon MacManus claimed the Bill Canning Trophy, while the Norman Bruce Trophy for the best 16+ handicapper went to City of Derry´s William McElhinney.

The only reason George Pearson appears in so many photos in this book is because I think he is quite handsome. Pictured before they tee off at Poniente are Pat Mackey, Leo Hickey, Eamon McCourt, Willie Barrett (starter) and George Pearson.

Last year's winner Brian McClure with Mark O'Doherty, John Chambers and Brendan Coyle.

Pictured against a delightful background are Karl Doherty, John Hasson, his dog 'Satan', Brian McClure and Kevin Barrett.

'Whingeing Bishop' tour

I'll bet you any money you haven't heard of the 'Whingeing Bishop' Tour. But it does exist. Named after its organiser who does, for all the world looks like a whingeing bishop, it travels off to top class locations at the end of November each year, playing the likes of San Lorenzo, Penina and La Manga and staying in five star accommodation.

Whatever else the bishop might be, he is a master negotiator, because he somehow comes up with the most extraordinary of deals. He is big deal figure in Invest N.I. and revels in the fact that he loves turning people away. No wonder he is a big deal figure in Invest N.I. Exclusivity is his watchword.

Brutal plan

I have been on several and they are all really special. But 2012 stands out where we were based at La Manga, a fabulous location for golf. The bishop had planned a brutal five round tournament, specifically designed to banjax the pensioners on tour, but we did have a day's rest. Off we went to the picturesque little town, Cartagena, for an afternoon's relaxation.

The first thing we spotted was a catamaran which was available to rent for the day. Come hell or high water we were taking to the high seas. To tell you the truth, we didn't get out of the confines of the harbour, but once you paid your money, the booze was free – fill your boots.

Frankie's 'air guitar'

And to tell you even more truth it was a double banjax. The organiser whittled away our energy reserves on the first two days and we expended the rest on that bloody catamaran. From what I can remember, and that isn't very much, I saw Frankie Friel playing an 'air guitar', big Cahir McGeady doing an Irish jig and myself wrapped round a pole doing a 'pole dance' in the middle of the boat. Jesus, Mary and Joseph, the combined age at the time was approximately 220. The moral of the story is – you're only as old as your last pint.

I know I will have a terrible price to pay for this disclosure – a lengthy ban, followed by expulsion. But I don't care, I just enjoyed having a 'whack' at him.

Before teeing off in the Whingeing Bishop Tour in Sotogrande were Cathal McLaughlin, Tommy (of the hooded three iron), Colm McCarroll jun, Phil Doherty, Colm McCarroll sen, Tony McGovern, Niall Casey and Stuart Brand.

A typical scene on the final day of a Michael Doherty Tour.

Lack of respect

I have witnessed lack of respect for your elders on these trips but none will match my experience on the magnificent San Lorenzo course in Quinta Do Lago in Portugal during a "Whingeing Bishop" tour. I had been showing a bunch of young "whippersnappers" how the game should be played and was in good shape to lead the tournament with three holes to go.

I took the tiger line at the par three 16th and nearly played a perfect shot. Nearly – it was no more than three feet from perfection but now I was stuck in the face of massive bunker. I steadied myself, closed the face to stab it out, but just before impact I lost my balance and fell into the bunker rolling down the side of it till I reached the bottom.

Disgrace

I can't remember who the fourball on the 16th tee were but I thought they were a disgrace to the human race, lying on the ground, bawling their brains out - "When you're down and troubled and you need a helping hand". I was in the presence of the dregs of society.

It took me more than five minutes to extricate myself from that bunker. Which begs a question – can you be declared lost in a bunker if you can't get yourself out within five minutes? I can put my hand to my heart and say that I would never have stooped to the level that those four cretins stooped to that day in Portugal.

Don O'Doherty receiving the Terence Bell Salver which he won at City of Derry in 1979 from May Bell. Also in the picture is Dixon Ward, club captain in 1979 and Bobby Bell.

Now here's a man who knows how to enjoy himself. Frank McCarroll conducting the choir in the La Mancha restaurant, Fuengirola in 1980. I know what he was singing - "The Auld Lammas Fair".

Where's my passenger

I remember my father telling me that North-West's honorary secretary, Bill Sharkey, had asked him for a lift home from Lisfannon one Sunday night – he was the only one left going to Derry with a car and he readily agreed. When they were crossing the railway line, his car stalled and he asked Bill to get out and give it a push which he duly did.

When my father went to work each morning he invariably walked down Westland Street, up Fahan Street, across Butcher Street and on to Shipquay Street.

Half-way down Westland Street the following morning, he looked across Westland Ave and saw this huge man running towards him shouting "McCarroll, McCarroll". It was then and not one second before that he realised that once he got the car up and running the previous night, he drove on to Derry minus a passenger he had totally forgotten about. Work is the curse of the drinking classes.

Ballybofey´s Eddie Gallagher (6) holed this putt at Santa Ponsa in 1986 but he didn't need it. He finished nine points ahead of former Irish International Hugh Smyth (2).

In walks Captain Quint

WE WERE SITTING in the bar in Westport Golf Club during the Irish Close Championship in 1977 when who walks in but Robert Shaw star, of 'Jaws' and the bad guy in James Bond's 'From Russia With Love'. Wearing a yellow sou'wester, he sat at the bar quietly sipping a pint of Guinness and enjoying the craic. I have to say, he was a very imposing looking man. I'll never forget him as Captain Quint in 'Jaws', scraping his nails across a blackboard to get the undivided attention of the townsfolk.

It was not yet the day of the mobile phone, otherwise I would have asked for a 'selfie'. The same goes with Sean Connery at Las Brisas Golf Club in 1988.

Bond, James Bond

PLAYING RIGHT BEHIND the last fourball in the final round of the 1988 Tour at Las Brisas was the one and only Sean Connery. And despite being held up on every shot, he could not have been more gracious. I had the pleasure of having a chat with him a number of times while we waited to play. He packed it in after nine holes but, from what I was told, he happily posed for pictures with all and sundry.

Thrilling finale

The final fourball of the Michael Doherty Spanish Tour is not for the faint hearted. Both Paul O´Doherty (City of Derry) and Tommy McBride (City of Derry) can verify that as they brought the 27th annual tournament to an enthralling finish at Santa Ponsa.

Three ahead of McBride after 70 holes, O´Doherty saw his lead vanish when he faltered over the final two holes. It was nerve-wracking stuff.

Deadlocked on 134 pts, it was to be decided by "sudden-death" – advantage McBride who finished the stronger of the two.

As it so happened, it was O´Doherty who shone in the play-off – a 280 yard drive followed by a six iron to 25 feet and a putt which hung on the lip for a birdie 3. It was a magnificent performance under extreme pressure.

Commiserations to the runner-up who could do little to match his opponent´s classy 4 at the 19th.

The organiser could not have picked a better winner. A stalwart on the tour over the past eleven years, Paul had been a potential winner on a number of occasions but never quite made the breakthrough – his timing was perfect at as this was a unique year.

He got off to the ideal start with a winning 37 pts at Poniente. That was followed with a 33 pts at Santa Ponsa and a further 35 at Poniente which gave him a one point lead over McBride going into the last round.

It was so near yet so far for Tommy. A tidy player who hits the ball a long way, he is also the honorary bookie on the tour. He would have been very short

odds to win the play-off but could do little to counter the winner´s extra-time performance.

Consolation for Tommy came with victory in the team event. Along with his team captain, Brian Long, Patrick Doherty and Willie Barrett, a winning total of 323 pts was recorded.

The prizes were superb. Eugene Dunbar was as generous as ever in the team event while Pat Mackey´s Mercury Marine spared nothing in their sponsorship of the third day. And the tournament was greatly enhanced by the presence of B.T. who were overall sponsors.

Paul O'Doherty, winner in 2002.

Overall results

1, Paul O´Doherty (10), City of Derry, 134 pts; 2, Tommy McBride (10), City of Derry, 134 pt; 3, John O´Brien (9), North-West, 129 pts; 4, Brian Long (6), City of Derry, 126 pts; 5, Stephen McKeegan (3), City of Derry, 125 pts; 6, Maurice Brennan (6), City of Derry, 125pts; 7, Stephen Wray (10), Portadown, 123 pts; 8, Brendan Coyle (10), North-West, 122 pts; 9, Peter Villa (11), Ballyliffin 121 pts; 10, Eugene Dunbar (18), Highgate, 121 pts.

Team event

1, Brian Long, Tommy McBride, Patrick Doherty and Willie Barrett 323 pts; 2, Brendan Coyle, Peter Villa, Sean Barrett and Eugene Dunbar 316 pts; 3, John O´Brien, Stephen Wray, John Hasson and Pascal Harpur 306 pts.

Daily results

Monday (Poniente) - 1, Paul O´Doherty (10) (City of Derry) 37 pts; 2, Clive Brolly (15) (City of Derry) 36 pts; 3, Eamonn Molloy (13) (Lurgan) 35 pts.

Tuesday (Santa Ponsa) - 1, Tommy McBride (10) (City of Derry) 36 pts; 2, Jimmy McGee (13) (North-West) 36 pts; 3, Peter Villa (11) (City of Derry) 36 pts.

Wednesday (Poniente) - 1, Tommy McBride (10) (City of Derry) 36 pts; 2, Frank Friel (North-West) (6) 36 pts; 3, Peter Villa (11) (City of Derry) 36 pts.

Winner of the final day´s play at Santa Ponsa was Portadown´s Brian McClure (7) who had 34 pts. Other results:- 2, Brian Long (6) 32 pts; 3, Billy McElhinney (18) 31 pts.

Winner of the Bill Canning-Seamus McDevitt Memorial Trophy was Brian McClure. The Norman Bruce Trophy was won by Phonsie O´Kane (20) with 117 pts.

Easiest card to mark

ON THE MANY trips I made on Michael's Tour, I have had the pleasure of playing with many great characters. And I can honestly say, I never came across a single disagreeable person. The favourite card that I marked belonged to David Liston with whom I played at Poniente. He had 2 points at the 5th and none at the other 17 holes. Happy days as Don O'Doherty would say.

The team event in 2002 was won by Tommy McBride, Brian Long, Patrick Doherty and Willie Barrett, pictured with team event sponsor, Eugene Dunbar.

Overlooking the scenic La Course are Jackie Smith, Dermott Hutton, Stanley McDermott reading his last will and testament, Cecil McKeegan, Andy Meenagh and Pat Mackey.

Superb "up and down"

Stephen Wray from Portadown was the new champion in 2003. Carrying a shot in the first play-off hole against Ernie Heywood (City of Derry), the popular nine handicapper had a superb "up and down" 4 at the difficult 19th at Santa Ponsa. Both men had tied on 135 pts on a dramatic final day in Majorca.

If you want to win on the continent you need to bring your short game with you and it was around the greens that the Portadown man excelled – he demonstrated that to deadly effect at both the 72nd and 73rd holes.

Fifteen points in arrears going into the last day, City of Derry´s Ernie Heywood played brilliantly to make up the deficit on a course where both tees and pins were cruelly positioned in typical fashion for the Michael Doherty tour fourth round. His round of 38 pts off 3 on Friday was golf of the highest calibre and the highlight of the event.

Leader after three rounds, Paul Brennan (City of Derry) slipped back on the final day. Renowned for his striking ability, Paul couldn´t

manage Santa Ponsa´s tiny greens and that was his Achilles heel. Leading by 10, he fought bravely but had to concede to the deft short game skills of Wray and Heywood.

The trophy this year was renamed in memory of the late Joe Ramsey who had two priorities in his life – his family and the Spanish Tour. His huge contribution to the Tour will not be forgotten.

Overall results

1, Stephen Wray (9), Portadown, 135 pts (36, 32, 34, 33); 2, Ernie Heywood (3), City of Derry 135 pts (32, 31, 34, 38); 3, Paul Brennan (13), City of Derry, 134 pts (42, 30, 40, 22); 4, Brian Long (5), City of Derry 130 pts (29, 28, 36, 37); 5, Con Boyce (3) Rosapenna, 130 pts (36, 33, 30, 31); 6, Michael McGee (8) City of Derry, 129 pts (34, 30, 32, 33); 7, Paul O´Doherty (9) City of Derry, 128 pts (33, 30, 33, 32); 8, Maurice Brennan (7), City of Derry, 127 pts (34, 34, 32, 27); 9, John O´Brien (9), North-West, 126 pts (32, 30, 26, 38); 10, Peter Villa (12), City of Derry, 126 pts (38, 26, 31, 31).

Team event

1, Maurice Brennan, Paul Brennan, Paul Gallagher, Eugene Dunbar 332 pts; 2, Con Boyce, Frank Campbell,

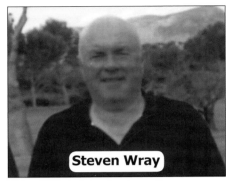
Steven Wray

Brian Doherty, Karl Doherty 329 pts; 3, Brian Long, Stephen Wray, Cyril Ward, Jason Maine 324 pts; 4, Brian McClure, Phelim O´Neill, Davy Jones, Maurice Quigg 320 pts.

Daily results

First day (Poniente) - 1, P. Brennan (13) 42 pts; 2, P. Villa (12) 38 pts; 3, T. McBride (8) 38 pts.

Second day (Santa Ponsa) - 1, F. Campbell (12) 39 pts; 2, W. Barrett (21) 38 pts; 3, M. Brennan (7) 34 pts.

Third day (Poniente) - 1, P. Brennan (13) 40 pts; 2, E. Dunbar (18) 37 pts; 3, B. Long (5) 36 pts.

Results from the fourth day at Santa Ponsa:- 1, John O´Brien (9), North-West, 38 pts; 2, Ernie Heywood (3), City of Derry 38 pts; 3, Brian Long (5), City of Derry, 37 pts.

Horror of horrors

As was often the case, there was a prize for the 'nearest to the hole' at the 15th at Poniente. It was handy for Michael, because he could occasionally go out to observe. He was standing there when I arrived and I was keen to impress. I hit a beauty to four feet behind the hole and the 'old pro' surmised that it would not be beaten.

We dandered up to the green and, as the ball came into view, I became aware that I faced the

horror of horrors, directly under the eyes of my mentor. My best putting days were long over so this was a challenge I hadn't travelled the whole way to Majorca to experience. Just as my putter reached the top of its backswing my body exploded. To put it crudely, it was as if someone had stuck a five thousand live electric cable up my rectum. I had been electrocuted. The ball shot past the hole, headed off the green at gathering speed, down a steep slope and ended in heavy rough.

We broke down

I looked at the pro and he looked at me. After a lifetime's silence – it was probably no more than two seconds, the two of us broke down in roars and tears of laughter.

And I will never forget his observation on what he witnessed. "CA, I'm in a real dilemma. How can I give the prize for 'nearest the hole' in one when you ended up 75 yards away in two. I will have to consult my Special Rule Book, written by myself to cover such unusual predicaments".

As far as I am concerned, and I should know, this is one of the most perfect set-ups I have seen. Beautifully balanced, head behind the ball, it's no wonder Davy Jones hits the ball so straight. Two observations — both the left-hand and right-hand grips could be strengthened. Also some brighter contrasting colours would be a great help as would the dumping of the old fashioned boots into the nearest tide.

Andy Meenagh, Oliver Logue, Joseph Doherty who plays out of Cruit Island, wherever the hell that is and P.C. Duffy.

I don't speak Swahili

It was **Monday 10th May 2004 at 11.25 am precisely on the 1st tee at Poniente. Brendan Coyle, Gavin Killeen and myself waited anxiously on what we had been told the previous night was – "the ace in the pack". Our team were favourites and our fourth man was running a bit late.**

What I witnessed when he appeared out from behind a tree was a decomposed corpse which was still walking. I don't speak Swahili but I could pick up that he said that he was "...so sorry but somebody had been spiking his drink all night".

"Don't worry about it wee John", says I, "you're on your holidays and you are perfectly entitled to a bit of a blow-out". I got him into the buggy beside me and told him just to go along for the ride and maybe he would feel better after nine holes. By the time I got to my drive at the 1st he was snoring like a pig – but I was content – for every snore I heard he was very slowly but surely in recovery mode.

The 3rd is a superb 400 yard par 4, a real challenge. I had gone ahead to my ball and inadvertently forgot about the boys behind. When I realised I turned the buggy at a 45 degree angle to get well out of way.

As a caring partner I looked over every so often to see how John was doing but now he was nowhere to be seen. I immediately looked back up the fairway and there he was, lying flat out on the middle of the fairway.

John Bradley

I dragged him into the buggy, why I'll never know, and chauffeured him round the rest of the course. By the time we got to the 16th, he felt well enough to hit a shot – but that was a bad choice of hole to make a big comeback. But there is always a positive side – John is great fun to be with and by the time he started speaking English again at the 11th, he was the best of "craic".

Up at La Cala in 1999 were from left, Dave Trickett, Paul Gallagher, Danny McNally, Danny Cooley, Con Boyce and Patrick Doherty.

Brendan Coyle pictured immediately after scoring 41 pts round Poniente last year. What a smile! We also have a picture of him after he scored 31 pts on Santa Ponsa the next day – and in that one he looked like he has been told that his pet parakeet had just committed suicide.

Not possible

NO ONE COULD understand how John Hasson managed to have 38 pts on Poniente last year. It just wasn't possible. It was quite late that very same night when we came up with the answer – because of the new layout, John played the last four twice. Quite simple when you think about it.

Too fast

Cahir McGeady was the driver, Larry Hasson the passenger. It was going O.K for the first few holes at Santa Ponsa but eventually it got just too much for Larry. "Cahir", said the wee man, "slow down for God's sake, you are getting to my ball far too fast".

Paul O'Doherty asks "Who gave you permission to take my photo"? Peter Lawrence is getting ready to make another smart-arse remark and Peter Doherty is 'chatting up' Francesco.

A witty person

Don O'Doherty said to me recently that he was going to tell me something about my father that he didn't think I knew. He said "Your father was a very funny person. I bet you don't believe me". Oh I knew it all right– I had heard so many of his great stories

Don said to me, "I'll give you one example of his wit. We were staying in the Waverley Hotel in Princes Street, Edinburgh during the 1977 Tour. He walked into the bar where the group had assembled and solemnly announced that he had just come off the phone to his son Colm and had heard some very disquieting news – the international singing star Josef Locke had been arrested, charged and convicted at the Bishop Street court that day

(buying a drink wasn't one of Joe's strong points).

He had been found guilty of breaking into a £5 note. But, he said, there was good news – the judge let him off because it was a first offence".

Don continued that he heard another story in the Waverley Hotel that night about a Resident Magistrate. The R.M arrived home about 2 in the morning to find himself confronted by his wife Mabel – "where the hell were you to this time of the morning and why is your shirt all covered in boke". He replied "Mabel, my dear, a defendant boked all over my shirt today, so I gave him six months". Mabel replied – "you should have given him a year, because he shit your pants as well".

Both can't be right

IN THE HISTORY section on their club website, Buncrana Golf Club claims that they were founded in 1890. Either they are right or the 'Derry Journal' of Friday, 3rd July 1891 is right. Regarding the official opening of North-West Golf, which took place on Monday, 5th August 1891, the 'Derry Journal' of 3rd July 1891 reports:- 'the ladies have not been forgotten in the arrangements in connection with the club, as immediately adjacent to the railway station at Buncrana an exceedingly good nine hole course has been laid out and is rapidly being got into order.

My favourite picture. Sitting out at the back of my home with the 'old man', enjoying a pre-prandial before we are called to dinner.

LIGHTHOUSE ON THE STRAND

This wonderful old poem was written by Derry's great genius 'Hawker' Lynch. It was one of my father's favourite recitations and many's a time it was specially requested on Michael's trips. My father considered 'Hawker' as a typical disadvantaged Derry man, deprived through circumstances of a proper education, with brains to burn. When you read it, you will see why.

The Black Man stands on Shipquay
Street
While Walker´s on the Wall;
They've placed a big bronze tablet
Before our City Hall
And any day a Derry guide
Will take you by the hand
To see our latest monument
The Lighthouse on the Strand

Its lamp lights up our Ulster Bank
And helps out Meenan´s plan
Although Sir John McFarland talks
Of its expanses grand
But Banaghers new water scheme
Won't wash its golden sands
You will admit when in it you sit
It's a lighthouse on the Strand.

There's a chemist at the corner
Who when your belt feels tight
Will hand you out a number nine
To get relief at night
But if you do be taken short
You can get relief my man
You can go and drop your anchor
At the lighthouse in the Strand

Golf, bridge, snooker and billiards were the big passions in my father's sporting life. He was also a devoted cricket fan, taking me to Beechgrove on manys a Saturday afternoon. This photo was taken at the 1989 North-West Premier Snooker K.O. Cup final between local clubs Duffy's Social Club and George's Bar. Tied at three matches apiece, Duffy's romped home when the aggregate points were accumulated. Front, from left are Terry Murphy (captain of Duffy's), Frank McCarroll (president of N.W.I.A.B.A) and Donal McVeigh (captain of George's). Standing from left are Seamus Gallagher and Paul McWilliams (Duffy's) and Colm McConomy and Seamus McClarey (George's).

All-rounder wins in 2004

Former North-West senior cricketer Cyril Ward stormed to victory in 2004 on Poniente and Santa Ponsa thanks to impressive scores of 38 and 37 points respectively over the final 36 holes.

The weather was the winner in round two when play had to be abandoned after Santa Ponsa officials decided that the course was unplayable.

Overall results

1, Cyril Ward (15) 109 pts (34,38,37); 2, Mark O'Doherty (6) 106 pts (38,35,33); 3, Ernie Heywood (1) 103 pts (33,37,33); 4, Brian McClure (8) 102 pts (31,35,36); 5, Eugene Dunbar (15) 102 pts (32,37,33); 6, Michael McGee (9) 102 pts (38,37,27); 7, Brendan Coyle (9) 100 pts (35,34,31); 8, Paul McDaid (14) 99 pts (35,29,35); 9, Kevin Barrett (10) 98 pts (37,35,26); 10, Adrian Leckey (5) 97 pts (28,34,35).

Team event

Winners of the team event with a total of 246 points (82, 79, 85) were Cahir McGeady, Michael McGee, Davey Bratton and J.C. Furnival on break of tie with Colm Duffy, Pat Swain, Brian Doherty and Eugene Dunbar also on 246 and in third place were Frank McCarroll, Kevin Barrett, Sean Barrett and Bill Braton.

Daily results

Poniente – 1, Michael McGee (9) 38 pts; 2, Mark O'Doherty (6) 38 pts; 3, Jimmy McGee (14) 38 pts. Poniente – 1, Cyril Ward (15) 38 pts; 2, Ernie Heywood (1) 37 pts; 3, Michael McGee (9) 37 pts. Santa Ponsa – 1, Cyril Ward (15) 37 pts; 2, Kevin Doherty (17) 36 pts; 3, Brian McClure (8) 36 pts.

Winners of the team event in 2004 were Michael McGee, Davey Bratton, Cahir McGeady and Jess Furnival. They are pictured with the sponsor, Eugene Dunbar.

Any team with Bob Smyth on it must have a chance of winning. Bob, on the right, is pictured with tour organiser, Andy Meenagh, Tommy McBride and Trevor Finlay.

Sean Ewing

Of the many interesting characters I have come across, I don't think there was anybody more interesting than Sean Ewing. Cahir McGeady and myself were on the practice ground at Poniente when another golfer who had been on the range approached – "Hello Colm, it is a long time since we played together".

It was none other than Sean Ewing with whom I had played in numerous scratch cups and against him in the Donegal Senior Championship. He represented Ballybofey and Stranorlar. Back at home I remembered him as someone involved in the insurance world or something of that nature.

Heard of Son Gual?

During the course of a very interesting conversation, he told me that he had retired to Majorca – he couldn't have been any more than 40 years old and asked us had we ever heard of a course on the other side of Palma airport, Son Gual, which we hadn't. As it turned out, he was one of 119 members there and phoned Son Gual to arrange a suitable time for us. What a fabulous experience that turned out to be.

And for good measure he recommended a classy restaurant in Cala Major and booked a table for us. At a specially chosen table in a most romantic setting, overlooking the Mediterranean, Cahir and I looked into each others' eyes and said that we both wished it was someone else we were looking at. To round off a perfect evening, Sean had picked up the tab for the wine – a gesture so much appreciated.

Rich list

It was some months later when I was reading the 'Sunday Independent' – it happened to have Ireland's 'Rich List' in its columns. Lo and behold, there was Sean Ewing, described as an Irish entrepreneur involved in the world of fund management. He had well over a 100 million in the bank. And when I read that, I thought of my old pal from Meenbanad, Burtonport, Joe Doherty.

Best ever performance

The best ever performance in the history of the Michael Doherty Tour came in 2005 at Poniente and Santa Ponsa when Ernie Heywood won with a four round total of 138 pts off 1. It was great golf by any standards on two magnificent tests of golf. The highlight came in the third round at Poniente where Ernie went round in 70 gross, two under par.

Ernie Heywood (City of Derry) was in a class of his own in 2005. Playing off 1, the left-hander gave an exhibition of shotmaking to win the 30th "Travellers' Trophy" at Santa Ponsa and Poniente with a four round total of 138 pts.

Hitting the ball with great precision he made the running over the opening fifty-four holes with rounds of 32, 35 and 39 pts to share the lead with fellow City of Derry member John Chambers (17).

But it was in the heat of battle that his class shone through. Neck and neck with both John Chambers and Ciaran O´Neill (Greencastle), he played the final four holes as if it was a Sunday afternoon stroll to keep two very competent competitors at bay.

While the gallery was watching the drama in the final fourball, up ahead was a past winner making a run, City of Derry´s Peter Villa had started quietly over the opening 36 holes but nearly pulled off a surprise when he went 35 and 37 points for the final two days to finish on 137 pts, just one behind.

Other performances of note included a fifth place finish for Phelim O´Neill (North-West) on 133 pts and a spirited fight-back by City of Derry´s Mark O´Doherty (6) who fought his way into the top ten after a poor start at Poniente.

All four members of the winning M and E Jewellers team event also finished in the top ten individual competition – a first in the history of the tour.

Overall results

Ernie Heywood (1) 138 pts (32,35,39,32); 2, Peter Villa (12) 137 pts (34,31,35,37); 3, Ciaran O'Neill (7) 136 pts (34,33,34,35); 4, John Chambers (17) 136 pts (35,33,38,30); 5, Phelim O'Neill (14) 136 pts (28,34,33,38); 6, Frank Campbell (14) 133 pts (36,30,30,37); 7, Tommy McBride (7) 133 pts (36,32,28,37); 8, Maurice Brennan (5) 132 pts (35,32,30,35); 9, Mark O'Doherty (6) 131 pts (27,31,35,38); 10, Karl Doherty (17) 131 pts (30,31,37,33).

Team event

1, Ciaran O'Neill (7), Peter Villa (12), Frank Campbell (14), Karl Doherty (17) 337 pts; 2, Brian McClure (7), Sean Barrett (12), Maurice Quigg (16), John Chambers (17) 334 pts; 3, Francis Boyce (6), Eugene Dunbar (13), Cyril Ward (14), Jess Furnival (19) 329 pts.

Daily results

The first day results at Poniente were:- 1, Tommie McBride (5) 36 pts; 2, Frank Campbell (14) 36 pts; 3, Maurice Brennan (5) 35 pts.

The second day results at Santa Ponsa were:- 1, Brian Mulgrew (16) 37 pts; 2, Paul McDaid (14) 35 pts; 3, Ernie Heywood (1) 35 pts.

The third day results at San Termens were:- 1, Ernie Heywood (1) 39 pts; 2, John Chambers (12) 38 pts.

He played his part in Greencastle

GREENCASTLE GOLF CLUB had a very friendly and beneficial relationship with Michael over many years writes Joe McCafferty, past captain of Greencastle. When new land was acquired in the late 1990s Michael's advice was sought and generously given. He played a key role in the development of the land, giving generously of his knowledge and expertise.

But sometimes wannabe amateur golf designers take things into their own hands and Michael's principles of quality and safety were disregarded in the pursuit of length and increasing the par, with almost disastrous consequences.

When Michael's good friend and fellow course designer, David Jones, was contracted to oversee changes, many of Michael's original ideas were restored to prominence and the golf course and club has reaped the rewards.

Greencastle has long been regarded as one of the most scenic of golf courses in Ireland with its views of Rathlin and the Scottish isles and the design of the tees on the new land has certainly made the most of the natural landscape. Michael and David's contribution to a splendid course on the shores of the Foyle was very much appreciated.

On the first tee at Poniente are Brian Doherty, Maurice Brennan, Paul Gallagher, Peter Lawrence and Bobby Irwin.

Peter Doherty, Karl Doherty, Gary Leckey and Paul O'Doherty.

An urgent mission

PC Duffy had read in some obscure magazine of a guaranteed cure for the 'yips' – hypnotism. Eugene Dunbar and himself had been on a trip and when they arrived back at Belfast International Airport he asked Eugene to divert to Belfast for an hour as he had an urgent mission. Dunbar had no idea of what he was up to.

On PC's instructions, Eugene pulled up outside a house on the Ravenhill Road and was told to wait for thirty minutes. Curiosity got the better of the chauffeur so he got out to see who was on the nameplate beside the front door. It was Edwin Heath, the renowned hypnotist and star of stage and television.

Beside himself with glee

Dunbar was beside himself with glee – he had just chanced upon the story of the century. In due course, PC comes out and the car heads towards Derry. There was no explanation offered so Dunbar went into interrogation mode – "I know why you were there, Duffy, spill the beans or I'll tell the whole town about it when I get back".

"If you promise Eugene, I will tell you but this has to be our secret". On that basis he blurted out the gory details. He had read that hypnotism could cure anything and 'yips' were no exception – hence the appointment with the most celebrated hypnotist in the land.

The best laid schemes

After about twenty minutes of intense induction, Heath was ready for the mental implant. He whispered in his ear – "you are the greatest putter in the world Colm, you are the greatest putter in the world". But there is one thing that Edwin hadn't reckoned with – PC's intellect. In the softest of voices Duffy said to the hypnotist – "I am the greatest putter in the world Edwin, and you are the biggest liar in the world". The best laid schemes o' mice an' men gang aft a-gley.

Third party

It was in the days before mobile phones and Dunbar claimed he had "taken short" coming into Dungiven and had stopped for a few minutes. But during that stop he made a phone call and by the time they had got to the Killunaght Road, the word was out. And by the time the poor man got to Derry, the rules experts had deemed that he had called in a "third party" and would be ineligible to take part in the forthcoming Tour. It was yet another magical story from the amazing world of Patrick Columba Duffy.

Tour organiser Andy Meenagh came up with a novel idea when he brought a replica blow-up dummy of Willie Barrett to save him from the pose physically in every photo. If I had my way, I wouldn't be long getting the air out of the dummy. With Willie on this occasion are Steven Wray, Barry Hamill, Brian Long and Karl Doherty.

Feast your eyes. OK, so I'm good looking, fit as a fiddle and I like to pose — if you don't like it, hand the book back and see if they will give you a refund.

A massive hitter of the ball, 2000 winner Peter Villa has developed sat nav problems in recent years. They believe it's to do with stray beams from alien satellites. Sometimes his tee-shots lock into alien beams with quite disastrous results. They could go anywhere — the last time I played with him I saw places in Ballyliffin I never thought existed.

Tommy O'Neill is downloading details of his round at Santa Ponsa last year to Pat Swain who looks profoundly interested. As does Michael Gault who is one of those people who loves to hear of every errant shot a partner plays. It is all part of the comradeship which runs part and parcel with the Michael Doherty Tour.

A model of consistency

Runner-up in 2005, Ciaran O'Neill produced a storming final round at Santa Ponsa of 39 pts to post a total of 145 pts and record a superb win by a margin of eight points. He was a model of consistency returning rounds of 38, 32, 36 and 39 pts. The field of 56 enjoyed a great week's weather with a temperature of 35 degrees on the final day.

The results were

1, Ciaran O'Neill (9) 145 pts; 2, Maurice Brennan (6) 137 pts; 3, Peter Villa (11) 137 pts; 4, Ernie Heywood (2) 134 pts; 5, Eamon McCourt (10) 131 pts; 6, Mark O'Doherty (4) 130 pts; 7, Sean Barrett (14) 130 pts; 8, Colm Duffy (12) 130; 9, Jess Furnival (15) 130 pts; 10, Con Boyce (4) 128 pts.

Team event

1, Con Boyce (4), Peter Villa (11), Phelim O'Neill (13), Sidney Canning (19) 330 pts; 2, Peter Harkin (7), Sean Barrett (14), Pat Mackey (13), Willie Barrett (19) 326 pts; 3, Maurice Brennan (6), Stephen Wray (10), John Hasson (16), Michael McCullough (16) 321 pts.

Daily winners

Poniente – 1, Jess Furnival (15) 39 pts; 2, Ciaran O'Neill (9) 38 pts; 3, Maurice Brennan (6) 35 pts. Santa Ponsa – 1, Peter Villa (11) 39 pts; 2, Jimmy McGee (14)

Ciaran O'Neill, winner in 2005.

35 pts; 3, Mark O'Doherty (4) 34 pts. Poniente – 1, Peter Villa (10) 40 pts; 2, Ernie Heywood (2) 38 pts; 3, Maurice Brennan (6) 37 pts. Santa Ponsa – 1, Sean Barrett (14) 39 pts; 2, Eamon McCourt (10) 39 pts; 3, Ciaran O'Neill (8) 39 pts.

A very welcome newcomer to the Michael Doherty Tour last year was City of Derry's new honorary secretary, Shane Kelly. He was in illustrious company as his fourball contained the very popular winner, Brian McClure. Pictured from left are Shane Kelly, Sean McKane, Stephen Wray and Brian McClure.

Two normal sized humans and two bruisers. On the first tee at Poniente are, from left, Steven McKeegan, Pat Swain, John Chambers and Brian McClure.

Four old pals relaxing with a suitable relaxant after a long day on the golf course. Seated from left are Bert Whoriskey, John Bradley, Davy Jones and Barney McDaid.

Chambers' career best in Majorca

City of Derry's John Chambers secured one of the most sought after prizes when winning the annual Joe Ramsey Travellers' Trophy in a sun drenched Majorca in 2007, the 15 handicapper posted an excellent 143 points total for the 72 holes event, winning by the slenderest of margins from Rosapenna's Con Boyce (5).

Having taken up the sport just a few years previously, John's highlight round was a superb score of 42 points in the third round on the difficult Poniente and, interestingly, it was this course which produced the best scoring of the week with North-West's Jimmy McGee and City of Derry's Bill Bratton, both carding scores of 41 points on what is normally a very difficult track.

Chambers actually finished fourth in the 2005 event and when posting scores of 34 and 35 points over the opening two rounds, he was well in contention having taken fifth spot but his third round effort saw him burst to the forefront before carrying a two point lead into the final round at Santa Ponsa on Thursday.

A final card totalling 32 points proved just enough to see the winner squeeze ahead of the prominent category one performer, Con Boyce with City of Derry's Mark O'Doherty edging out fellow Prehen man, Bill Bratton, for third place, both players having carded final scores of 141 points.

Meanwhile, in the much sought after team event, the international quartet of Stephen Wray (Portadown) Barney McDaid (City of Derry), John Hassey (El Pariso, Spain) and Leo Hickey (Perth, Australia) reigned supreme having basically secured victory with scores of 83, 90, 92 and a final round total of 84 giving them 349 points, enjoying a surprise eight points cushion on the chasing pack.

John Chambers, winner in 2007.

Full Results

Full results were – Joe Ramsey Travellers' Trophy Tour – 1, John Chambers (15), 143 points; 2, Con Boyce (5), 142; 3, break of tie, Mark O'Doherty (5) 141; 4, Bill Bratton (21), 141; 5, John Hassey (14), 141; 6, break of tie, Karl Doherty (16), 140; Maurice Brennan (7) 140; 8, Cahir McGeady (5), 138; 9, break of tie, Eamon McCourt (9), 137; 10, Frank McCarroll (3), 137.

M. & E. Jewellers (London) team event – 1, Stephen Wray, Barney McDaid, John Hassey and Leo Hickey 349 points; 2, Ciaran O'Neill, John O'Brien, John Chambers and Maurice Quigg, 341; 3, Gary Leckey, Brendan Coyle, Michael MCullagh and Karl Doherty, 340.

Mercury Marine 18 holes team event – 1, Con Boyce, Brian Doherty, Michael McCullagh and Phonsie O'Kane, 90 points.

Norman Bruce Trophy – 1, Davey Jones (16), 129 points.

My old drinking partner, Barney McDaid with Eamon McCourt.

The personification of happiness.

"Where did you get that hat"? Oliver Logue with Trevor Finlay and Michael Gault.

Three former winners, Maurice Quigg, Peter Villa and Brian Long. They were joined by Kevin Barrett who, like his two brothers, has never won anything.

Who am I?

I was born on 3rd March 1948 to Buncrana beauty queen Rosaleen McCrudden and Richard Gallagher, a Derry man. They were on holidays in Tenerife, little expecting that I would arrive early (for the first time in my life). I weighed in at 12 lbs and 9 ounces and the Spanish nurses in the Hospiten just loved me to bits. I was able to speak fluent English and Spanish by the time I was three weeks old, by which time I weighed two and a half stone.

The nurses first realised I was an habitual liar when I pretended

I broke my leg on a clandestine visit to the "Dubliner" where I had heard that a Circus midget was

throwing a shape and I might have a chance of a bit of action.

As I got older it got worse – so bad in fact that I no longer knew if I was lying or telling the truth. I went for three sessions with local Derry consultant, Dr. Quigg D.B.L, who told me that my name was Bob Smyth and I was favourite to win the 2017 Spanish Tour. I just didn't believe him – I began to think he was an even bigger liar than me, and that's saying something. Please help me – tell me who I am. Somewhere in the back of my head I think me mammy christened me Munchhausen Gallagher.

All smiles on the first tee. From left are Pat Mackey, Cahir McGeady, Michael McCullough, Kevin Barrett and Danny McNally.

Prior to teeing off at Poniente in 2005 were John Chambers, Ciaran O'Neill, Peter Lawrence and Cyril Ward. Pound for pound one of the longest hitters on the Tour, Peter Lawrence will give you a guided tour of every tree plantation, of every fairway you shouldn't be playing on, of every boondock on the Poniente and Santa Ponsa estates.

The engine room where all the 'behind the scenes' work goes on. Frank McCarroll junior and Andy Meenagh check cards while Sam Condit applies his computer skills with his usual aplomb.

Ballyliffin to host 'Irish Open'

At this moment in time, as I write this article, it has not been officially confirmed but the marvellous news is out that Ballyliffin will host the 2019 'Irish Open'. What a reward that will be for a dedicated group of people, and their predecessors, going way back to 1947.

The whole of the North-West, stretching right through Derry, Co. Derry, Co. Tyrone and, of course Donegal, can expect a bonanza on a scale not seen before.

I can't help but think of the pioneers who had the vision to start it all. Names such as Dr. Frank Friel, my uncle Jim McCarroll and Michael D. White are but three – I know there are many more but these are the names I can remember because I had the privilege of knowing all three.

Uncle Jim told me a story which fascinated me. As a veterinary surgeon in Inishowen, he worked tirelessly seven days a week but still found time to put a lawnmower into the back of his Landrover and mow the greens on the nine holes links on the Pollan Green. So many people spring to mind as I sit here at my computer – Martin Hopkins, James McLaughlin, Barney Harkin and the great man himself, Joe Masterson. It was Joe who came up with the idea of an Open Week which he started in 1968. Incidentally, that was the year the annual Clonmany Festival Week was launched by someone for whom I have the greatest admiration, Hugo Boyce.

The driving force

There have been so many people who have given so freely of their time to bring Ballyliffin to where it is today. The likes of John "White" Doherty and Packie Farren spring to mind but the person I would have to single out is Patsy Doherty.

As captain in 2011, I had the chance to see for myself what a man he is. The club's greens convenor, he is the driving force behind Ballyliffin's reputation for putting surfaces to rival the best in the world. Nothing is left to chance. If the very latest in greens technology was required, he made sure that Ballyliffin was not left behind. And with the pride of Scotland, Andy Robertson, beside him, the best players in the world are in for some treat.

In his stride

What would Jim Clafferty think if he came back for a fortnight in July 2019? I honestly believe he would take it in his stride, charming the likes of Rory McIlroy, Rickie Fowler and the host of household names who will grace the fairways of "Glashedy". Many's a great night we had in that little clubhouse with Jim regaling us with his unique little stories. I don't want to sound sentimental but I often think back to days gone by – we won't see the likes of it again. But I had my little part to play in a great story and I am very proud of that.

Roll on 2019. Between the 'British Open' at Royal Portrush and the 'Irish Open' at Ballyliffin what amazing sporting spectaculars we can look forward to.

A priceless letter

The legendary Pat Ruddy with Ballyliffin's greens convenor, Patsy Doherty.

In a quite remarkable letter which the legendary Pat Ruddy sent to North-West captain Charlie Nicell on 15th May 2002 he provided two very comprehensive plans for the development of a most precious piece of land. "Plan A", as he described it, was the basic thing while "Plan B" was altogether much more ambitious. Charlie gave me a copy at the time as he knew I would be particularly interested in it. If it is not now in the public domain, I would be delighted to pass it on to North-West head green keeper Damian Doherty or the club's greens convenor.

The final piece of the great man's letter is priceless – "I return herewith your maps and hope that you enjoy the next stage of the exercise and wish happiness and fulfilment to all involved. As the visits to North-West are so enjoyable, the delightful tea and scones which I was given will fully discharge my "fee" for the exertions involved.

Paul O'Doherty receiving the top prize in the 2002 tour from Michael Cunningham, BT, sponsors of the event.

I ask myself an honest question. Is there a decent golfer among them?. From left to right are Danny McCloskey, John Hasson, Joe Doherty, P.C. Duffy and Willie Barrett.

National glory after 110 years

So what does it mean to win a green pennant? Brian McElhinney, who had already won the British Amateur title, is grinning like a cat who got the cream. Michael McGeady, playing his last round as an amateur, is losing the fight to hold back the tears and Garrett Mallon is kissing his caddie on the cheek. So reported Philip Reid of the Irish Times in his excellent reportage of the All-Ireland Final of the Irish Senior Cup at Rosslare in September 2005. It had taken 110 years since the club was founded in 1891 to savour national glory but it had finally been achieved. And very proudly, I was there to witness the nerve tingling finale.

North-West's top two, McElhinney and McGeady, set an early pace. Michael won easily by 5/4 while Brian was a stunning 6 under par when his match ended at the 16th. When Paul Van Dessell and Pauric O'Flaherty both lost, it was all down to the most dogged competitor I have come across, Garrett Mallon.

Seized the initiative

One down with four to play, Garrett won the 15th with a birdie and then seized the initiative with a classy approach from a fairway bunker to make par and go dormie. And when he holed out for a birdie at the 18th, the green pennant was on its way to Donegal. Behind a victory of that magnitude, there has to be an inspirational driving force. And that force was Frankie Friel who had had a life-time's experience in senior golf to impart to his young charges. For many years he had tirelessly championed senior golf at both North-West and in Donegal. On Saturday 17th September 2005 he got his reward.

The heroes of North-West who brought glory to the Inishowen club when they won the Irish Senior Cup at Rosslare in 2005 defeating Hermitage by 3/2 in a great final. Front from left are Vincent Grant jun, Lindsay Shanks, president of the GUI, Frank McHale, captain North-West, Dermott Coyle, president North-West and Frank Friel, non-playing captain. Back from left are Padraig MacLochlainn, Paul Van Dessell, Padraig O'Flaherty, Michael McGeady, Garrett Mallon and Brian McElhinney.

The development of junior golf in Donegal was a priority for a hard-working group which included Seamus McBriarty, Frank Friel and Barry Ramsay. This picture taken some years ago at North-West includes three youthful prospects, Dana Clinton, Julie Bradley and Gemma Hegarty.

A dirty big fry was the ideal way to get the day off to the perfect start. If you can survive it, you can survive anything. Getting stuck in are Mark O'Doherty, Brian Doherty and Martin O'Kane.

Visually enjoyable experience

Faughan Valley Golf Centre lies just outside Derry on the A2 road to Limavady. The brainchild of the Forbes family, it is built on the free draining banks of the river Faughan. The site provides the golfer with a demanding yet visually enjoyable experience.

The river Faughan borders the course for some 2,500 yards and the many other features within the 5,453 yards par 69 course ensure a stern test of golfing ability yet the many teeing options on signature holes afford golfers of lesser ability the chance to enjoy the challenge. The emphasis is on friendliness rather than formality.

Opened in 2001, one of its many features is its versatility, accommodating both green fees and offering full G.U.I. affiliated membership. The centre also provides club hire.

Excellent record

The centre itself caters for all G.U.I. Ulster Branch competitions commencing with the underage Fred Daly Trophy and enjoys an excellent record in several of the Qualifying stages. The club reached the semi-final stages of the Jimmy Bruen Shield on two occasions, 2014 and 2016.

In the few years of its existence the centre has produced many fine young golfers. While too numerous to mention I feel that pride of place should be awarded to Colin Starrett who completed his two year training course at The National Golf Academy, Carton House and is now firmly established as a PGA Assistant Professional at the exclusive Portmarnock Club in Dublin.

Evidence of the Centre's high standing in Irish golf circles is that The Centre can boast its own contracted Teaching Professional, Noel Callan who is available for lessons.

GUI representative

That Faughan Valley has a representative on the G.U.I. Ulster Branch Match and Handicapping Committee is further evidence of the massive strides the Centre has made. Trevor Lewers is the current incumbent and has already used his influence to persuade the Ulster Branch to avail of Faughan Valley as a regional venue in 2014 for the Pierce Purcell Shield. So impressed were they with the presentation that is has been awarded the venue for 2018.

The social end of the Centre is not neglected. A friendly home and away fixture is played annually between the Centre and the centre across the river, Foyle International Golf Centre. With planning for a state of the art driving range and car parking the future looks bright for Faughan Valley Golf Centre.

Don O'Doherty

2010 was yet another big year from one of the most significant contributors to the world of sport in the north-west, Don O'Doherty. He was hosting his president's day at Faughan Valley

Trevor Lewers from Faughan Valley Golf Club is a representative on the G.U.I. Ulster Match and Handicapping Committee. Trevor used his influence to persuade the Ulster Branch to use Faughan Valley as a regional venue for the Pierce Purcell Shield in 2014 and it will be back there in 2018.

Two old friends, Davy Jones and Eamon McCourt, having a break.

With more money than sense, Oliver Logue says good-bye to a tiny fraction of his pension fund. The happy recipient is Kevin Barrett, while a handsome Trevor Finlay looks on.

A golfing ambassador

Freda Craig

ONE OF THE outstanding golfing ambassadors in the North-West was the late Freda Craig. Freda's great love was golf, a game she played from an early age. Her formative years were spent at both North-West and City of Derry. She had an interesting association with the Donegal club – her uncle, David Craig, was one of the founding members of North-West in 1891.

While she was a very competent 6 handicapper in her day, it was in golf administration that she excelled. When she agreed to take the post of honorary secretary of the ladies branch at City of Derry, she would have expected to serve for a few years. More than fifty years later, this remarkable lady was still at the helm

What a performance

THE BEST EVER performance in the history of the Michael Doherty Tour came in 2005 at Poniente and Santa Ponsa when Ernie Heywood won with a four round total of 138 pts off 1. It was great golf by any standards. The highlight came in the third round at Poniente where Ernie went round in 70 gross, two under par.

Palma to Soller – he was thrilled

The year was 2010 and of course we were in Majorca. I was conscious by this time that Colm Duffy's health was deteriorating and, like many other good friends, I was doing my best to keep his spirits up. I came up with a masterstroke which we could enjoy – a train journey on the famous trip from Palma to Soller on a quaint train with wooden carriages. He was thrilled, as I had managed to book the 3.10 to Soller. It was a dream. He immediately phoned his secretary Avril to relay the good news and added a little dimension to it – his favourite film of all time was "3.10 to Yuma" and he was living his dream.

Tunnels out of boundo

It all started so well. Uncomfortable as it was, he was enjoying every moment and looking forward to seeing a new beauty spot in Majorca. But no-one told us there would be any tunnels – nor did anyone tell me that PC was a manic claustrophobic. When we emerged from four kilometres of underground passage way, Duffy was a different animal. "Why didn't you tell me about tunnels, you stupid moron,

why did you not check out these arse breaking seats." The list went on.

Soller was all it was cut out to be – a beautiful cove full of shops, restaurants and, of course, the train which ran right along the beach. It was idyllic.

When it was time to go I jokingly said to PC that I had two return tickets - he jumped out of his seat, straight into a taxi and said "if you don't come now with me, you're on that train".

The crickets weren't singing

We met to go for dinner at 8pm. The mood was still black so I tried to lighten the conversation on the way down into Puerto Portals. "Can you hear the crickets PC, they are singing"..

"They are not singing" came the reply – "they are laughing, They're feckin' well laughing at us".

I knew I was in for a tough one – he complained about the menu, the wine, the service and anything that came into his head. But PC is full of surprises – when it came to giving a tip he forked out a fortune. As we left I swear I heard one waiter say to another – "we could do with a couple of nutters like them every night."

Jackie Johnstone, who made a welcome return to the Tour recently, pictured with big hitting Gary Leckey.

Patsy Dan – the wordsmith

PC DUFFY WAS a great storyteller and would always get your attention. On this occasion, he had landed in Tory on "Olivera" for the week-end with his great friend Pauric McGinty. Needing to get back to the yacht which was moored a 100 yards from the pier, he spotted a little currach which would be ideal for the hour long mission. With due reverence he went along to Patsy Dan, the "King of Tory" to find out if the owner of the currach would mind if he borrowed it for a short period.

Here was the King's response – "well now Colm, if he knew you half as well as I do he wouldn't, but he doesn't, so he would".

Stick that one in your pipe and smoke it.

I'm very fond of this photograph. From left are Colm Duffy, Denis 'Ginger' Doherty, Frank Friel, Peter McCready and Michael Doherty.

Desperation

In my time I have putted right-handed, left-handed, cack-handed, used a 48" long putter, used my driver, three wood and three iron – desperation is a terrible thing. But bad as I have been, I can offer no tale to compare with that of P.C. Duffy. During a practice round in Son Antem in Majorca, myself and P.C. were pitted against the formidable pairing of brother Brendan and Cahir McGeady. What I witnessed on the first green was an image that will be implanted in my brain to my dying day.

Specially made

On the par five in three, P.C.'s putt for a birdie came up four feet short. He marks his ball and heads for his bag. After fidgeting about for a bit, he produces a putter 19" long. Before McGeady could utter a word of protest, P.C. told him that it had been specially made for him by Michael who had assured him it had fulfilled the legal minimum size of 18".

In order to use it, P.C. had to do something he hadn't done for forty years – he had to get down on his knees. In a penitential position,

he potted the ball with supreme confidence. We were cock-a-hoop. We all laughed till we were ill.

So bony

But there was a downside to using such a unique, innovative method. P.C.'s kneecaps were so bony, they left two craters in the green. We tried to repair them but to no avail. Would the opposition allow him to use a towel to kneel on for the rest of the round – "not on your nelly", was the grumpy, abrupt response from the man whom P.C. was to christen "Jumbo Osaki".

Mark's runaway win

City of Derry´s talented six handicapper, Mark O´Doherty, finally achieved one of his ambitions when winning the annual Joe Ramsey Travellers ´Trophy Tour to Majorca 2008. His record breaking score of 149 points for the 72 holes tournament was certainly impressive.

In fact, the local electrical engineer had been "knocking on the door" in this particular competition for quite some time, but it was his liking for the Santa Ponsa I course which saw him cruise to victory having carded two outstanding scores over the final two rounds.

With the tour party of 44 experiencing a difficult start to the event with rain and wind compounding the difficulties associated with the Poniente course during the opening round, Mark still managed to record 37 points, a score which saw him occupy eighth position. While the overcast conditions at the Jack Nicklaus designed Golf Park made life more comfortable for the 31st year of the Michael Doherty led event, Mark´s 31

points saw him drop down the leader board into joint 17th spot, requiring a major effort if he was to figure on the podium.

And it was clear that the visit to Santa Ponsa I was to prove profitable when he carded a magnificent score of 41 points to top the "day prize" leader board and, indeed, share overall leadership with Tommy McBride to occupy a place in what was a high profile final fourball on the same course for the deciding round.

With O´Doherty and McBride joining previous winners Ciaran O´Neill and the vastly experienced Maurice Brennan in the final fourball, it proved a test of both nerve and skill and Mark stood up well to the challenge to post another "day victory" of 40 points to guarantee the top honour.

Interestingly, Mark also matched the achievement of his brother Paul, who reigned supreme in this event back in 2002.

Meanwhile, in the highly competitive and enjoyable team event, the quartet of Tommy McBride, Stephen Wray, Brian Doherty and Davy Jones reigned supreme – McBride gaining some

consolation having finished fourth overall in the individual competition.

Full results were

Joe Ramsey Travellers´ Tour Trophy – 1, Mark O´Doherty 37, 31, 41, 40 – 149 points; 2, break of tie Maurice Brennan 37, 33, 35, 37 – 142; 3, Ciaran O´Neill 36, 32, 38, 36 – 142; 4, Tommy McBride 39, 35, 35, 30 – 139.

Team results

1, Tommy McBride, Stephen Wray, Brian Doherty and Davy Jones; 2, Colm McCarroll, John Chambers, P.C. Duffy and Karl Doherty; 3, Paul O´Doherty, Peter Villa, Bobby Irwin and John Hasson.

Daily winners

Poniente – 1, break of tie, Maurice Quigg, 39 points; 2, Tommy McBride, 39; 3, break of tie, Karl Doherty 38.
Golf Park – 1, Brendan Coyle 37 points; 2, Peter Harkin, 36; 3, break of tie , Tommy McBride, 35.
Santa Ponsa I – Mark O´Doherty 41 points; 2, Ciaran O´Neill, 38; 3. Peter Villa, 37.
Santa Ponsa I – 1, Mark O´Doherty 40 points; 2, John O´Brien 38; 3, break of tie, Maurice Brennan 37.

The 2008 team winners, pictured with Eugene Dunbar, were Brian Doherty, Davy Jones, Steven Wray and Tommy McBride.

In pensive mood are Pat Swain and Danny McCloskey.

649 yard par 5

Opened in 1977, Santa Ponsa I is another of the finest courses in Europe. 6,543 metres from the championship tees, it has one of the longest par 5's in existence, the 10th stretching out to 649 yards from the white sticks.

Designed by Folco Nardi, together with Pepe Gancedo, Golf Santa Ponsa I is renowned for its lakes and great variety of trees (olive, pine, almond etc). Thanks to its generous fairways big hitters like Bob Smyth can let fly. It has hosted many tournaments including the Spanish PGA Championship and the Spanish Amateur Championship which I had the pleasure of taking part in 1982.

Important personalities who have visited the club include several Kings of Spain, H.R.H. Prince Felipe, H.R.H. Juan de Borbón, Prince Andrew of England, Kings of Sweden, Duques of Luxemburg, President Carter, Bruno Kreisky, Michael Douglas, George Pearson, Nigel Mansell, Franz Beckenbauer and Ingemar Johanson.

The four amigos, Tommy McBride, Ciaran O'Neill, Mark O'Doherty and Maurice Brennan.

Ciaran records "double"

Winner of the annual "Travellers' Trophy" in 2006, Ciaran O'Neill, put his name on the trophy again when he won the 31st Spanish Tour at Santa Ponsa with a four round total of 137 points.

It was an excellent performance by the Greencastle eight handicapper whose precision iron play was to make the vital difference over four days of demanding golf.

The results were

1, Ciaran O'Neill (8), Greencastle, 137 pts (31,34,37,35); 2, Karl Doherty (17) 136 pts (33,31,36,36); 3, Paul Gallagher (14) 133 pts (35,31,31,36); 4, Michael McCullough (13) 131 pts (35,29,28,39); 5, Maurice Quigg (18) 129 pts (33,32,32,32); 6, Phelim O'Neill (16) 128 pts; 7, Mark O'Doherty (6) 128 pts; 8, John Chambers (14) 127 pts; 9, Tommy McBride (8) 127 pts; 10, Sam Condit (14) 126 pts.

Daily winners

Son Antem – 1, Michael McCullough (13) 35 pts; 2, Paul Gallagher (14) 35 pts; 3, Eamon McCourt (9) 34 pts. Golf Park – 1, Mark O'Doherty (6) 38 pts; 2, John Chambers (14) 37 pts; 3, Tommy McBride (8) 35 pts. Son Quint – 1, Mark O'Doherty (6) 37 pts; 2, Ciaran O'Neill (8) 37 pts; 3, Karl Doherty (17) 36 pts. Santa Ponsa – 1, Danny McCloskey, (23) North-West, 41 pts; 2, Michael McCullough (13) 39 pts; 3, Sam Condit (14) 37 pts.

Team results

1, Tommy McBride, John O'Brien, Pat Swain and Karl Doherty 329 pts; 2, Eamon McCourt, Michael McCullough, Tommy O'Neill and Maurice Quigg 328 pts; 3, Frank McCarroll, Andy Meenagh, Sam Condit and Paul Gallagher.

Kevin Barrett, Cyril Ward and an elegant looking Mr. Dunbar before the off.

Mr. Dunbar, suave as ever, pictured with Sean McKane, George Pearson and Peter Harkin.

When you are a cuddly big bear you are bound to attract attention. Swarming like bees round Cahir McGeady are Eamon McCourt, Barney McDaid and Phelim O'Neill.

A little indiscretion

Another of my great old friends was Davy Henderson. A member at both City of Derry and North-West, he gravitated towards Lisfannon in later years. Davy and I were very similar in looks and manys a time he claimed that he was the result of a little indiscretion committed by F.E. senior many years before and he was entitled to a cut in the 'Journal' profits.

Mary McCarroll had a little dog, a Jack Russell, her pride and joy. One Saturday she had it down at Lisfannon and dog lover that he was, Davy was giving it his undivided attention. After the usual cooing and petting, he headed for the first tee. From there he was to witness a sight that fired him into immediate action. A little Jack Russell was prancing about on the 9th fairway when this gigantic gypsy appeared over the fence, running towards the dog. Davy dropped everything and went eye-ball to eye-ball with this gorilla. Attack is the best method of defence so Davy threw as hard a left-hook as he could throw. Did the opponent cope over? Not a bit of it. He shook his head and said to Davy, "I'll kill you, you bastard and threw one into Davy's sternum, breaking two ribs in the process.

Disbelief

Looking on in disbelief was Mary McCarroll, holding on to her wee Jack Russell, and quickly coming to the conclusion that there were two identical Jack Russells, one owned by her and one by the Bruiser standing on the 9th fairway.

Unsporting

The sequel was quite interesting. Cahir McGeady and myself were playing my brother Frank and Danny McNally. The match was a 'hum dinger' with no favours asked or given. Then something happened on the 9th tee which I believe to this day went way beyond the bounds of sportsmanship. I had just teed up and had made all of the mental preparations needed to unleash yet another perfect drive when Frank politely interrupted – "Do you see that gorilla parked in the caravan opposite the 9th green; when you get down to the green he's going to think you are Davy coming back for a second round.

Happy ending

I recoiled in horror. The odds of exactly that happening were about 2 to 5 on. After I called Frank what the gypsy had called Davy two hours before, I put on a hat, played down the left wing and kept a wedge constantly on hand to defend myself if necessary. Thankfully it wasn't needed. In fact there was a very happy ending – McGeady and myself won on the 18th green.

I am sitting in my first floor office at home, captioning for the past seven hours. I swear to Christ that if I see these three faces again before I finish I am going to put my boot through this computer. I feel better now.

You can tell it in his eyes. Tommy McBride has 'pushed the boat' out the night before and is asking Willie for a few more shots back, just for one day. In contrast, not a drop of the 'devil's buttermilk' has passed through Danny McCloskey's lips.

This is how it feels when you have just finished your final round as members of the ignoble 'dawn patrol'. Having hit more than 650 shots between the four of them, looked for balls at every hole and scored a combined total of 42 pts you are entitled to look as if you had just been mauled by a pride of lions.

Third win for McCarroll

Thirty years after he first won the Michael Doherty Tour at Mijas in 1980, Colm McCarroll lifted the "Travellers' Trophy" for the third time when he posted a four round total of 143 pts in Majorca in 2010.

It was over the final 36 holes that McCarroll found his touch. In the middle of the field at the half-way stage, he made his move with a superb 40 pts at Son Quint on the third day to take the overall lead and followed that with a solid 37 pts at Santa Ponsa to win by a four point margin.

Two birdies on the back nine at Santa Ponsa proved crucial – one at the notorious 220 yards 12th and the other at the dog-leg par four 17th which effectively won the tournament.

McCarroll's nearest challenger was City of Derry past captain Brian Long, who gave an exhibition of "striking" over the 72 holes which would have done justice to any top player. Like the winner, Brian was well in arrears after 36 holes but consecutive rounds of 38 pts saw him climb into second place on 139 pts.

The results were

1, Colm McCarroll (8) 143 pts (33,33,40,37); 2, Brian Long (6) 139 pts (28,35,38,38); 3, Leo Hickey (20), Joondalup, 136 pts (30,39,28,39); 4, Eamon McCourt (9) 134 pts (31,32,40,31); 5, Paul Gallagher (14) 132 pts (33,34,29,36); 6, Karl Doherty (17) 132 pts (34,34,33,31); 7, Andy Meenagh (12) 131 pts (35,32,36,28); 8, Brian McClure (8) 128 pts (35,32,28,32); 9, Stephen Wray (10) 125 pts (33,29,31,32); 10, Brendan Coyle (10) 125 pts (37,29,33,26).

Daily winners

Poniente – 1, Brendan Coyle (10) 37 pts; 2, Frank McCarroll (5) 36 pts; 3, Cahir McGeady (9) 36 pts. Son Vida – 1, Leo Hickey (20) 39 pts; 2, Cahir McGeady (9) 37 pts; 3, Maurice Quigg (17) 36 pts. Son Quint – 1, Eamon McCourt (9) 40 pts; 2, Colm McCarroll (8) 40 pts; 3, Brian Long (6) 38 pts. Santa Ponsa – 1, Leo Hickey (20) 39 pts; 2, Brian Long (6) 38 pts; 3, Colm McCarroll (8) 37 pts.

Team results

1, John O'Brien, Andy Meenagh, Pat Swain and Leo Hickey 334 pts; 2, Eamon McCourt, Michael McCullough, Sam Condit and Sean McKane 327 pts; 3, Colm McCarroll, John Chambers, Colm Duffy and Karl Doherty 327 pts.

Jackie Johnston enjoying the fun as usual. This a photograph of a 'dawn patrol', a four ball with special qualities. Making up the team of shame are Bob Smyth, Davy Jones, the steward at Santa Ponsa, Colm McCarroll and Willie Barrett.

Munroe's Karaoke star Willie Barrett, on the 1st tee at Santa Ponsa with John Hasson, Sean McKane, Michael McCullough, Paul Gallagher and Bobby Irwin.

Just before a presentation ceremony are, left to right, Chris Neff, Archie Grey, Cahir McGeady, Willie Dunlop and Patrick Doherty.

A deserving winner

City of Derry six handicapper, Brian Long, proved a model of consistency in Majorca in the final round of the 34th Traveller´s Trophy tour, his performance at Santa Ponsa deservingly securing top honours.

Long, played some of the finest golf ever seen on this tour on what was a very difficult Santa Ponsa course.

In the end, Brian recorded a massive total of 145 points for the week and with 38 points on this final day had also won the day prize in addition to lifting the Travellers ´Trophy from its original sponsor and winner in 1978, Mr. P.C. Duffy, for the first time after some 15 years on the tour.

Gary Leckey claimed the runners-up spot with 135 points, while Karl Doherty made

enough ground over the final day to score 132 points, one ahead of fourth-placed finisher, Sean McKane.

Meanwhile the winning quartet in the team competition was the fourball led by Mark O´Doherty, including North-West Vice-Captain, Pat Mackey, Karl Doherty and Maurice Quigg who excelled over the last three days to win with 331 points.

The results were

1, Brian Long (6) 145 pts (37,32,38,38); 2, Gary Leckey (11) 135 pts (41,29,39,26); 3, Karl Doherty (16) 132 pts (29,31,42,30); 4, Sean McKane (20) 131 pts (35,35,40,21); 5, Maurice Brennan (6) 130 pts (33,29,33,35).

Daily winners

Poniente – Gary Leckey (11) 41 pts; Santa Ponsa – Sean McKane (20) 35 pts; Poniente – Karl Doherty (16) 42 pts; Santa

Brian Long

Ponsa – Brian Long (6) 38 pts.

Team results

Mark O´Doherty, Pat Mackey, Karl Doherty and Maurice Quigg 331 points; 2, Brian Long, Cahir McGeady, Michael McCullough and Jack Johnstone 326; 3, Frankie Friel, Hugh Casey, Andy Meenagh and Trevor Finlay 326.

At the 2011 presentation ceremony which took place at Santa Ponsa. From left are Colm Duffy, sponsor of the Travellers Trophy, Brian Long (winner), Gary Leckey (2nd) and Karl Doherty (3rd). Willie Barrett makes up the group.

Not often do you have four winners in the same fourball. Pictured at Poniente are Brian McClure, Steven Wray, Maurice Brennan and Paul O'Doherty.

Karl Doherty, Brian McClure, Maurice Quigg and Danny McCartney.

The Carrycullion Classic

With the assistance of his dear old friend at City of Derry, Seamus McBriarty (North-West) set off on his first-ever tour, the North-West Scottish Tour, in September 1978. It was the beginning of a great annual event, renamed the Carrycullion Classic, which was to run virtually annually until 2013. But sadly, when Seamus died on 15th February 2008, its days were numbered. Like the 'old pro', Seamus was from the old school. He began his career at Fortwilliam in Belfast and after learning the ropes, he emigrated to Canada where he was based at Cedar Brae Golf Club. But the lure of Ireland was too much and at the tender age of 21, he returned to take up a post at North-West.

Duty and humour

He was an immediate hit. A great sense of both duty and humour, he was the life and soul of many a 'shindig' which would start up at the drop of a hat. An accomplished guitarist with a great love for music, he could belt out a succession of classic songs in venues all over the continent.

His teaching skills were so subtle. Feel and touch, very much like Michael, were far more important than blasting a ball 300 yards to the far corners of the earth.

I tried very hard to keep the event going in his memory but sadly it turned out an uphill battle I was never going to win. An abiding memory was a phone call I received from Seamus's wife Briege when I produced a little 16 page tribute to him in 2014 – I will always treasure that call.

The 2005 'Carrycullion Classic'. From left are Maurice Toland, Marcus Roulstone, Sam Condit and Seamus McBriarty. It is evident from the photo that poor Seamus was fighting very bravely against a serious illness.

A very popular winner in 2016 was Ballynahinch single figure golfer, Brian McClure. Brian has been a faithful supporter of Michael's trips for many years.

Pictured at the 2016 presentation dinner are, from left, Neil Duncan, Shane Kelly, honorary secretary of City of Derry Golf Club, Gary Leckey and George Pearson.

Cheers Georgie – it's your round next. Eamon McCourt looks like he has just shot 25 pts, something similar to Gary Leckey, while the suave Eugene Dunbar has obviously something to celebrate about.

Doubles or quits

A BELFAST BUSINESS man, a six handicapper, visited a shop he owned in Derry on a monthly basis and, on completing his work at the shop, he would motor to Lisfannon and force Michael to play him for a large wager over 18 holes. Michael was reluctant to take on the challenge but did so under pressure. On many of the occasions Michael would have won by the 14th or 15th hole but the challenger would then go for double or quits over the last few holes only to be beaten again – a nice little earner for Michael in his early years!

Vincent Grant

Shaft bent

FOR THOSE WHO remember the Manchester United teams of great old days, Derry man Jim Shields was a member of the squad which included the great Johnny Giles in the late 1950's and early 60's. Sadly a serious injury was to curtail a blossoming career. To this day he is a tidy golfer and when the Seamus McBriarty's 'Carrycullion Classic' trips were in full flow, he was a regular.

I will never forget a practice swing he made on the 1st tee of the Laguna course in Vilamoura. Unaware that a Garda Sergeant was standing behind him, he made a swing which crashed into the side of the unfortunate policeman's head. The outcome was extraordinary. While Jim's driver was bent at the top of the shaft, the Garda suffered no apparent damage.

It is hard to believe that this photograph goes back to 1997 when Seamus McBriarty brought his trip to Majorca. No less than 35 travelled that year. The picture was taken behind the 18th at the magnificent Son Vida complex, overlooking Palma Bay. Front, from left, are Paddy O'Carroll, Eugene Falconer, Paddy Doherty, Martin Doherty, Paul Doherty, Jimmy Ryan, Dermott Fullerton, Kevin Green, Vincent Quigley, John Deeney, Paul Gallagher, Frank Friel, Robert Scott, Pat Mullin and Artie Duffy. Standing, from left, are Dermott Coyle, club president Eamon MacManus, Stanley McDermott, John McDermott, Colm McCarroll, James O'Carroll, Jimmy McGee, Michael Furey, Peter Doherty, Paul Slevin, Tommy Deehan, Seamus McBriarty, Seamus Cassidy, Bobby Irwin, Oliver Logue, Eddie McCauley, Gilbert McLaughlin, Patsy McCallion, Eamon Quigley and Kieran Doherty.

One of the many 'Carrycullion Classic' trips organised by Seamus McBriarty. In 1981 he picked Killarney and what a magnificent choice that was. Included in the itinerary were both the Killarney courses and Waterville. Kneeling, left to right, are Willie Dunlop, Mickey McCarron, Hugh Quigley, Seamus McBriarty, Eamon McCallion, Hugh Duffy and Pat McGonagle. Second row, from left, John Louden, Pat Ellis, Joe Roberts, Francis Duffy, Paul Crotty (captain, North-West), Seamus Anderson, Dermott Coyle, Brian McCarroll and Brendan McCarroll. Back, from left, are Michael Furey, Jimmy Kilburn, Sean Doherty, Daithi Murphy, Patsy Fagan, Tom Deehan, Joe Mallon, Liam Jackson, Sean O'Kane, Brian Daly, Plunkett Duffy and Colm McCarroll.

Trip of a lifetime

Having travelled on most of Michael's golfing trips over the past forty years, I can recall many unforgettable moments, beautiful places and wonderful golf courses played including the hallowed grounds of St Andrews, Carnoustie and Muirfield in Scotland and the superb courses on the Costa del Sol and Majorca, but for me the trip to California in 1995 was by far "the trip of a life time".

The trip was organised and led by Michael with his brother Denis, Eddie Gallagher, Patrick Doherty, Wilf Abel, Colm Duffy, Colm McCarroll and myself.

We arrived in Los Angeles, picked up our transport and travelled to the beautiful San Diego complex of Rancho Bernardo where we stayed for two nights and played Rancho Bernardo and the Aviara Country Club.

We then travelled to Palm Springs where we stayed in the magnificent La Qinta complex for four nights and played some of the most famous courses in the area, PGA West and La Quinta. But I think for all of us being in Palm Springs was one of the highlights of our trip. This is the place where the rich and famous come for their holidays or winter breaks but it's also home to the American Indian who settled in the desert long before the white settlers arrived There was an amazing sense of history about the place and we could have spent our entire two weeks there sight-seeing and playing different courses every day. Our next destination was the Monterey Marriott Hotel in Monterey and the famous Monterey Peninsula, a seventeen mile trip which took in Carmel where Clint Eastwood and Doris Day live to this day. It's also home of many world famous golf courses including Spy Glass Hill and of course Pebble Beach to name but a few. Our only disappointment was we did not get to play Pebble Beach although CA and myself managed to get a photo of ourselves on the 1st tee of the iconic course.

Next on the agenda was San Francisco. We stayed in The Weston Hotel in Cleary Street in the centre of town where we had the opportunity to spend a couple of days taking in some of the famous sights. That included a boat trip round Alcatraz where we were informed that salt had corroded the brick work so badly that its days as an impenetrable fortress were gone.

We were booked to play two courses, Half Moon Bay and the world famous Olympic Club one of America's most exclusive clubs. We were warmly welcomed by a delightful man, Dennis Moriarty, the Olympic Club president who had the uncanny knack of giving us a truly "Irish" welcome. I know that he played with Michael that day who, despite the terrible agony he was suffering with Ankylosis Spondylitis, managed to charm his American host with some marvellous anecdotes about one of his golfing heroes, Ben Hogan.

A memorable lunch and some very astute comments about Michael from Mr. Moriarty told us exactly why he had been chosen to be the leading representative of a truly magnificent club. And he came from Ireland which helped enormously as well. Thank you Michael for the memories.

Cahir McGeady

Pictured on the Monterey Beach during Michael's 1995 trip to California are, from left, P.C. Duffy, Denis 'Ginger' Doherty, Eddie Gallagher, Colm McCarroll, Michael Doherty and Patrick Doherty.

Another great memory from Michael's trip to California. The photo was taken on the 1st tee of the equisite Aviara club in Carlsbad, just above San Diego. From left, Colm McCarroll, Cahir McGeady, Denis 'Ginger' Doherty and P.C. A formidable pairing, P.C Duffy and myself gave the two boys an early bath.

Standing on the first tee of the world famous Pebble Beach Golf Club. Sadly it was not on the itinerary.

What grand memories

Dear Colm,

What grand memories you rekindle. It was late 1995 when I had just become President of the Olympic Club and I had the honour of welcoming Michael and his party to our club. Believe it or not, I have often entertained my friends with the memory of that round on the Lake Course when our Irish guest Michael recounted with unerring detail where Ben Hogan was on the fairway for various vital shots in the 1955 Open. His photographic memory of Hogan's achievements was quite remarkable. And there was the music in the club house after the round which still resonates with me. Good luck with the book – you are honouring a very special man.

Dennis Moriarty
Former president of the Olympic Club, San Francisco

Editor's note – what a remarkable impact the Irish made in the USA. Dennis's father emigrated to America from Killarney in or around 1915 while his mother, an O'Connell from Abbeyfeale in Limerick made the same momentous decision at about the same time.

Viva Las Vegas

This picture was taken during one of Michael's great trips, this time to Las Vegas, Arizona. P.C. Duffy, Eddie Gallagher, Peter Villa, Eugene Dunbar and Joe Doherty were the contenders. Sadly for poor Eddie, he was terminally ill at that stage and it was to be his last big golfing adventure.

On one of the days the party went north on Highway 95 to the Paiute Golf Resort, right in the middle of the Paiute Indian Reservation. It was in the wilderness, but the scenery was quite spectacular. On that day they had the pleasure of playing with a member of the Paiute tribute – a delightful character who made the party feel so welcome.

Pictured in Phoenix on the first tee are P.C. Duffy, Denis "Ginger" Doherty and Joe Doherty.

Another example

Another example of Michael's influence came months after his fabulous sixteen day trip to California in 1995. We had been the guests of a man with strong Inishowen connections, Tom O'Kane. A member of the Olympic Club in San Franscisco, Tom had arranged for us to play the 'Lakes' course, which had hosted the U.S. Open five times and the U.S. Amateur three times.

Six months later I was to get a call from San Francisco. It was Tom and he was in a bit of a dilemma - he had been asked by his boss to set up a schedule for a forthcoming European Golf holiday and St. Andrew's was a 'must'. He was having no luck getting a tee-time and was there any way I could help. I told him to leave it with me.

Job done

I immediately called Michael and explained the situation - he told me to leave it with him. Forty-five minutes later I got a call back from Michael – "CA, I have an old club-maker friend who has a shop just opposite the 18th green at St. Andrew's and is a member. I have just been off the phone to him and he has booked a time of 9.12am (I remember it well) at St. Andrew's on the appropriate date for the American visitor. And, as a little bonus if he wishes to avail of it, he is booked to play at Carnoustie the following day.

Tom was flabbergasted when I rang him back but I was very quick to let him know that it had got nothing to do with me – Michael was the fixer, the 'man with the plan', the person with the contacts right throughout the golfing world.

Alex Campbell, Bill Bratton and Sidney Canning in fine form.

After a week of golf and relaxation John McDermott, Bobby Irwin and Brendan Coyle just can't wait to get back home to the lovely wives and back to work on Monday.

Who's that man with the handsome smile. Looking as if he is really enjoying himself is Tommy Daly.

Portstewart in July

IF I AM alive and spared, I look forward to travelling down to Portstewart for the 2017 'Irish Open' which takes place from Thursday 6th to Sunday 9th July. It will be a great occasion on a wonderful golf links. Ireland has a number of truly outstanding golfing gems and Portstewart is one of them. Make sure you get a ticket, which will be at a premium – that's guaranteed.

The last time we had the privilege of hosting the 'Irish Open' in Ulster was in 2012 when Royal Portrush was the venue. Such was the success of that event, the R and A was persuaded to bring the 'British Open' back to Northern Ireland for the first time since 1951. My father was there on all four days and his legion of stories had eager listeners such as myself transfixed.

Multi-lingual

MICHAEL, FRANK, CAHIR and myself were sitting in a little restaurant beside the Piano Bar when Michael complimented the waiter on the fluency of his English. "I can speak five languages fluently", the waiter told us. Just for fun, Michael said to him: "here is one you don't speak" and proceeded to speak in Irish.

"I apologise", said the waiter, "I can speak six languages and proceeded to engage in a conversation with Michael in Irish. A University student who specialised in languages, he had spent a summer in the Gaeltacht. Needless to state, we were dumbfounded.

Anglo Irish Accord

The occasion was the Ulster play-offs for the All-Ireland Johnny Walker Trophy at Castlerock with the reward a trip to Royal Dublin for the All-Ireland finals. Against all the odds, Derry and Donegal respectively hammered Antrim and Down in the morning and were contesting the afternoon's play-off.

The boys from Cherryvalley and surrounding districts were less than pleased. They had travelled from Belfast to see the likes of Garth McGimpsey and co. give a peerless performance.

To make a long story short, Co. Derry made it through to the finals and at a special dinner in Castlerock club house afterwards it was a sombre occasion with the top table looking like someone very close to them had died.

The bomb was dropped

Then came the speechifying. The Ulster Chairman among others spoke and as the evening drew to a close, the bomb was dropped. Alfie Collis, secretary of the GUI Ulster Branch, stood up and said – "members of the top table, members of the Co. Londonderry and Donegal teams, please be upstanding and drink a toast to "Her Majesty the Queen".

It was a masterstroke. Slowly but surely the assembled party, dyed in the wool Fenians, rose to pay their respects. I glanced over at Fr. Anthony Griffith – not a well man I thought.

I sat down and turned to P.C - "Can't let this one go". Without a second thought I stood up, struck my glass with a spoon and said "Could the top table and members of the Donegal and Derry teams be upstanding and drink a toast to "His Holiness the Pope". A classic case of Anglo Irish Accord.

GUI secretary Alfie Collis and Colm McCarroll share a laugh about the 'toasts' which had just taken place.

Amongst the prizewinners in the team event in 1981 were Christie McWilliams, John Gormley, Frank Guckian and John Bradley.

Fit and rarin' to go are Davy Jones, Barney McDaid, Joe Doherty and Pat Swain

Who is the dude in the white hat? When it came to sartorial elegance there was only one Karl Doherty.

Arklow rookie romps it

The 35th Michael Doherty Golf Tour to Majorca was won by Arklow rookie Sean Doyle playing off 15 on the challenging Santa Ponsa course.

With an all-time tour record score of 156 points, Doyle held off all challengers when he posted a stableford score of 34 points. Brian McClure (9) of the Ballynahinch club finished in second place with 151 points, one point ahead of both Tommy McBride (5) and Karl Doherty (16) who amassed 150 points over the four days of the tournament.

The fourth day was won by Tommy McBride with a brilliantly compiled 42 points, two points ahead of another City of Derry player, George Pearson (22).

The results were

1, Sean Doyle (15), Arklow, 156 pts (44,40,38,34); 2, Brian McClure (8), Ballynahinch, 151 pts (38,34,40,39); 3, Tommy McBride (5) 150 pts (39,36,40,29); 4, Karl Doherty (16) 150 pts (44,37,42,30); 5, George Pearson (24) 149 pts (36,36,37,40).

Daily winners

Poniente – Sean Doyle (15) 44 pts; Santa Ponsa – Gary Leckey (11) 41 pts; Poniente – Stephen Wray (10), Portadown, 42 pts; Santa Ponsa – Tommy McBride (5) 42 pts.

Team winners

1, Brian McClure, Peter Villa, Pat Swain and David Jones 352

Sean Doyle

pts; 2 – Tommy McBride, Paul Gallagher, Trevor Finlay and Leo Hickey 346 pts. 3 - Brian Long, Eamon McCourt, John Hasson and Kevin Barrett.

Bob Smyth shows his four ball how to dress properly, using a tea caddy his granny knitted for him way back in the 1960's. With Bob are Leo Hickey, Brian McClure and Michael McCullough.

Arklow rookie Sean Doyle was the winner in Majorca in 2012. The final day group is pictured behind the 18th green at Santa Ponsa. Standing, from left, are Sean McKane, John Hasson, Trevor Finlay, Hugh Casey, Danny McCloskey (?), Maurice Quigg, Gary Leckey, Joe Doherty, Patrick Doherty, Leo Hickey, Paul Gallagher, Sammy Smallwoods, Michael McCullough, Sean Doyle, Andy Meenagh, Pat Mackey, Peter Doherty, Davy Jones, Peter Harkin, Frank McCarroll, Colm McCarroll, Colm Duffy, Maurice Brennan, Willie Barrett, Eamon McCourt, Karl Doherty, John Morrow and John McClafferty. Front, from left, are Brian McClure, Stephen Wray, George Pearson, Barney McDaid, Pat Swain, Cahir McGeady, Eugene Dunbar, Peter Villa and John Chambers.

Maurice holds nerve in play-off

Extra tie-holes decides 36th Travellers' Trophy in sunny Majorca

Maurice Quigg realised a personal ambition in Majorca in 2013, the local florist finally claiming the Traveller's Trophy after a 32 year wait.

And the 18 handicapper had to call on his experience and, indeed, hold his nerve when he finished level on points with two other players when entering a three-way playoff, another first for the long standing annual City of Derry tour.

Having recorded a total of 142 points for the 72 holes tournament, Maurice was joined on the podium by fellow Prehen members Eamon McCourt (11) and Sean McKane (21) who also returned 142 points.

In the opening tie-hole both Quigg and McCourt recorded regulation pars while McKane carded a bogey 5 and therefore, dropped out of contention.

At the second tie hole, a par five, McCourt put his second shot into the trees to the left of the fairway, thus struggling to find the green in three passing a clear-cut advantage to Quigg and Maurice was quick to react.

In fact, he played three perfect safe shots to find the green and facing an easy two putts for his par, he subsequently secured victory, a remarkable feat for one of the Prehen club´s stalwarts who had been playing in the Michael Doherty tour for the past 32 years.

The results were

1, Maurice Quigg (18) 142 pts (36,36,33,37); 2, Eamon McCourt (11) 142 pts (35,33,41,33); 3, Sean McKane (21) 142 pts (39,32,39,32); 4, Brian McClure (9) 135 pts (30,32,40,33); 5, Stephen Wray (12) 135 pts (34,36,33,32).

Daily winners

Poniente – Sean McKane (21) 39 pts; Santa Ponsa – Maurice Quigg (18) 36 pts; Poniente – Eamon McCourt (11) 41 pts; Santa Ponsa – Maurice Quigg (18) 37 pts.

Team winners

1, Frank McCarroll, Eamon McCourt, David Jones and Kevin Barrett 337 pts; 2 – Brian McClure, Michael McCullough, Pat Swain and Danny McCloskey 336 pts.

Maurice Quigg, winner of the 2013 Michael Doherty Tour, pictured with Brendan Coyle, Steven Wray and Brian Doherty.

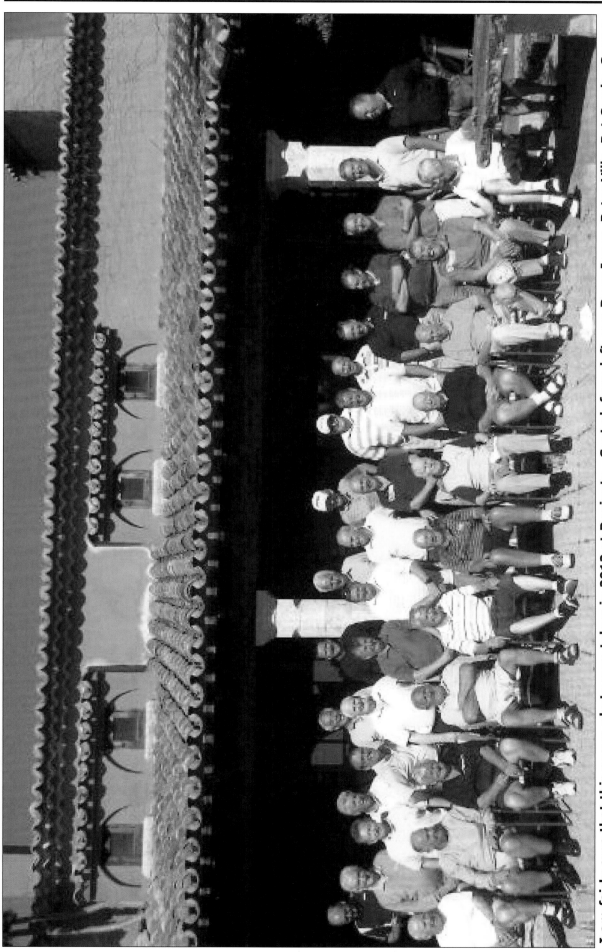

I am fairly sure that this group photo was taken in 2012 at Poniente. Seated, from left, are Davy Jones, Peter Villa, Pat Swain, George Pearson, Joe Doherty, Colm McCarroll, Barney McDaid, Bob Smyth, Danny McCloskey, Pat Mackey and Eugene Dunbar. Second row, from left, Willie Barrett, Brendan Coyle, John Hasson, Karl Doherty, Maurice Quigg, Danny McNally, Eamon McCourt, Trevor Finlay, Oliver Logue, Stephen Wray, Gary Leckey, Brian McClure, Leo Hickey, Michael McCullough, Kevin Barrett and Sean O'Kane. Back, from, left, Andy Meenagh, Brian Long, Colm Duffy, Frank McCarroll, Cahir McGeady and someone that I must know but can't identify.

Little sympathy

If you have problems with your chipping, you will get little sympathy from me. I am about to disclose the most embarrassing moment of my sixty or so years in golf. It was at the 8th at North-West, the 'Piffler" and I had missed the green on the right. I could have taken a putter and 'hoked' it on some sort of way, but I am made of sterner stuff than that.

I took out my 60 degree wedge with only one thought in my mind – swing back slowly, swing through slowly. Three practice swings were needed to get exactly the right speed of swing. I was ready to impress Danny McNally, Frank McCarroll and Cahir McGeady, three people with less confidence than I had that I would pull off this shot which, if I had been diving, would have been a triple twist, seven turn backward flip with a 4.6 degree of difficulty. McGeady was standing behind me, curious to see how I was going to pull it off.

Heard a click

There was no problem with the backswing but as I struck the ball I heard a little 'click' and then as I followed on through I heard another. By this time my body was in spasm. I accelerated the clubhead which held on to the ball and the next thing I knew it went over my head and hit McGeady on the shoulder.

What followed was a deathly silence, not unlike the announcement of a sudden bereavement. Deep, unasked for sympathy then followed and that was followed by a display of gross bad manners – the three of them exploded into roars of laughter as I struggled to come to terms what had just happened.

It was over

How many shots had I just taken? How many 'clicks' were there? Then I started to laugh, harder than any of them. Then there were tears – to this day I do not know if they were the result of the laughter or the realisation that my last moments as a force in golf were over.

The annual 'Autumn Trip to Majorca' for a trophy presented by Colm McCarroll travelled out later in the year. While it didn't have the same numbers it was every bit as much fun as the trip in May. Front from left are Sean McKane, Colm McCarroll, Peter Villa and Gary Leckey. Back from left are Barney McDaid, Michael McCullough, Jimmy McGee, Peter Harkin, Brendan Coyle, Paul Doherty, Maurice Quigg, Andy Meenagh and George Pearson.

Paul Gallagher snuggles up to Gary Leckey before they start play in Poniente.

Manuel 'Ginger' Doherty, makes sure everybody is replete during one of the many parties held on the Michael Doherty Tours.

Mark O'Doherty, Peter Doherty, the cool dude from Perth, Australia and Davy Jones from the Waterside.

Performance of his career

City of Derry´s Eamon McCourt realised a long-standing ambition in Majorca in 2014 when producing the performance of his career to claim the much sought after Travellers' Trophy.

And it was a fitting victory for the affable 11 handicapper who smashed the previous record with his 157 points overall total. Eamon has played in this tour for 22 years and, indeed, has finished in the runners-up position on several occasions.

His victory was built on a platform of consistency and having carded superb daily totals of 39, 39, 39 and 40 points – for a 72 holes total of 157 – and a sensational 10 points cushion on his nearest rival.

"Obviously, I´ve never played better," admitted the Prehen man afterwards.

"I drove the ball really well and even playing in the final round, I never felt nervous. The ball always seemed to go where I had directed it and I took full advantage of scoring when on the greens," he smiled.

"I've had a few close calls over the years but to finally win the Travellers' has always been a personal ambition."

Eamon failed to score at just one hole over the four days – on a short par four during the opening round at Poniente – so it was no surprise that his consistency kept him to the fore after every round.

He also won the final day´s individual prize with that magnificent 40 points finish and his 157 points is now the record tournament score over the 37 years of the event.

The runner-up was Sean McKane (19), City of Derry on 147 with North-West´s Colm McCarroll (9) in third spot on 144.

McKane also played superbly over the 72 holes after he also lost out in last year´s play-off, he failed to make any dent in the six point lead which McCourt held when they teed-off in the final fourball at Santa Ponsa.

The results were

1, Eamon McCourt (11) 157 pts (39,39,39,40); 2, Sean McKane (19) 147 pts (37,37,37,36); 3, Colm McCarroll (9) 144 pts (33,39,35,37); 4, Brian McClure (7) 141 pts (38,34,36,33); 5, Andy Meenagh (15) 141 pts (36,31,43,31).

Daily winners

Poniente – Eamon McCourt (11) 39 pts; Santa Ponsa – Leo Hickey (19) 39 pts; Poniente – Andy Meenagh (15) 43 pts; Santa Ponsa – Eamon McCourt (11) 40 pts.

Team results

1 – Peter Harkin, Eugene Dunbar, Sean McKane and George Pearson 345 pts; 2 – Brian Long, Brian Doherty, Kevin Barrett and Michael Gault 344 pts.

Winners of the team event in 2014 were George Pearson, Peter Harkin, Eugene Dunbar and Sean McKane. Pat Swain presented the prizes.

Winner in 2014 with the best ever total of 157 pts was Eamon McCourt who receives the Travellers Trophy from the tour organiser, Andy Meenagh.

No one was prouder in 2014 of Eamon McCourt than John Hasson.

My son Colm said to me, "Dad, who is the strange little man who keeps appearing in these photos. Do you want me to airbrush him out"? My response was stern "don't even think of it son, that's a very important annual revenue stream for me". From left are George Pearson, Brian Long, Michael McCullough and Kevin Barrett.

Gap of 21 years bridged

Scoring 33 points on the final day of the 38th Michael Doherty Tour at Santa Ponsa, North-West Golf Club member, Eugene Dunbar, held off all his challengers to claim the 38th tour with 143 points.

And by doing so the 15 handicapper bridged a gap of 21 years having claimed the trophy when a member of the Highgate Club in London back in 1994.

Fellow Lisfannon member, Brendan Coyle (11), finished one point behind and almost pipped Dunbar when returning 36 points on what was probably the hottest day of any of the previous 37 tours.

The results were

1, Eugene Dunbar (14) 143 pts (36,34,40,33); 2, Brendan Coyle (11) 142 pts (37,32,37,36); 3, Stephen Wray (11) 140 pts (34,32,34,40); 4, Paul O'Doherty (8) 138 pts (38,34,36,33); 5, George Pearson (21) 138 pts (38,38,31,31).

Team results

1 – Brian McClure, Karl Doherty, Maurice Quigg and Danny McCloskey 344 pts; 2 – Tommy McBride, Eugene Dunbar, Sean McKane and Michael Gault 335 pts.

Daily winners

Poniente – George Pearson (21) City of Derry, 38 pts; 2, break of tie, Paul O´Doherty (8), Greencastle, 37 pts; 3, Gary Lecky (10), City of Derry, 37 pts. Santa Ponsa – Peter Doherty, Joondalup, Australia, 42 pts; Poniente – Eugene Dunbar (14) 40 pts; Santa Ponsa – Stephen Wray (11) 40 pts.

2015 was Dunbar's year. The smooth swinging left-hander from North-West won for the second time with a fine score of 143 pts. His final shot will be long remembered – an 8 iron to six inches at the last. He is pictured here with Steven Wray (3rd), Brendan Coyle (2nd), Maurice Quigg who presented the prizes, Andy Meenagh and Willie Barrett.

Davy 'made hay'

The year was 1976 and the venue Downfield, a magnificent test but tight. The fourball was Cahir McGeady, Don O'Doherty, Sam Hestor and Davy Bredin – a very pleasant foursome which, for most of the round, was a three ball.

Cahir explained what happened. "Long before we had ever heard of sat nav, Davy Bredin's sat nav was 'up the left'. He was hitting the ball to every corner of Scotland, so his card was also 'up the left' after seven holes".

But 'everything's mixed with mercy' as they say - Davy was finding abandoned balls like they were going out of fashion. So without finishing a single hole on the back nine, he 'made hay while the sun shone', filling his bag to the hilt with Warwicks, Dunlop 65's, Slazengers, Penfolds and anything else he could lay his hands on. In total he found 37, not bad for a day's work.

On the first tee in the final round are, from left, Brendan Coyle, Pat Swain, Cahir McGeady and Oliver Logue.

Nothing Ventured, Nothing Gained!

Colm Duffy may not have been the best golfer or Bridge player of his generation in the North-West, but he was indisputably the most competitive. This competitiveness was honed in his youth, when he excelled at long-distance running – at St. Columb's College and at local athletic events. Even then he did it his way – having won the 880 at the College Sports, he was unduly handicapped for the mile – Colm's response was to walk the race – much to the chagrin of authorities. Point made.

Only he knew

He and Michael Doherty had many memorable trips abroad to Europe and the USA. In January 1981 he invited me along with Billy Patterson (of the singing group), and a friend from Ballybofey, to the States. Only he knew where we were headed – we spent some time in Chicago, we touched down in San Fransisco, found ourselves in Phoenix, Arizona (where we each bought a Ping Putter, which I still use), we visited the Hoover Dam, dressed up in Wild-west attire in Tombstone, ran out of money in Las Vegas (in those days we had no credit cards), but PC wired to Ireland and by Western Union help arrived.

To crown it all we ended up in Hawaii, and eventually arrived back home – exhausted, but with memories for a lifetime.

He was gracious

Even though PC did not like to be beaten on the golf course or at the Bridge Table (and he wasn't very patient with his partners) he was always a gracious loser. In the early 80's he won both the Club Championship and the Junior Scratch Cup at City of Derry in one season, and the following year reached the final of both again – only to fall at the final hurdles.

He has played a big part in the promotion of Golf and Bridge in the Derry area – for a number of years the sponsor of the City of Derry Inter-Pro, and the City of Derry Bridge Congress.

His generosity also behind the scenes to the underdog was never flaunted.

He left his mark

Fr. Jim McGonagle

'No holds barred' fourball

When I look back on a lifetime in golf, I can honestly say that there was nothing I enjoyed more than a good 'no holds barred' fourball. You weren't out there to make friends – the object of the exercise was to defeat them first and foremost, and to humiliate them if at all possible. Bragging rights in a clubhouse bar was the ultimate reward you strove for. What's the point otherwise.

My father taught me that one while I was still in nappies. Over the years I have had sleepless nights over missing a crucial four footer to save the day, while sleeping like a baby as I reflected on the twenty footer that caused my opponents apoplexy. "Happy days", as Don O'Doherty would say.

Hospitable welcome

My son-in-law's father, Gabriel, a sergeant in the Garda Siochana, loved coming to Inishowen to visit his son, daughter-in-law and grandchildren. A keen 12 handicapper, he loved nothing more than playing North-West when he was here. To guarantee a hospitable welcome I always lined up Cahir McGeady and Danny McNally as suitable opponents.

Sergeant Gabriel Plower was given a salutary lesson in bad manners when he played at Lisfannon recently.

It was idyllic, a cead mile failte to my guest from Bray. Little was that poor man to know that I had put him in to a bear pit, with bears which had been specially isolated because they were schizophrenic.

Love was in the air

It all happened right outside the clubhouse, the 9th green. This had been our third encounter and love was still very much in the air. With his usual delicate touch, unusual for a profession renowned for splitting heads on a busy Saturday night in Dublin, Gabriel rolled his putt up to six inches from the hole and duly gave himself the next.

"Jesus, Mary and Joseph", said I to myself, "he has fallen into the trap". The two buckos said nothing, holed out and went to the 10th tee. In the vain hope that they knew I was entertaining my daughter's father-in-law, they would make an exception. My arse they would. Gabriel teed up at the 10th, ready to unleash another bruiser when he was politely asked why he had teed off first – "because I halved the hole" came the reply. You know the rest – they made the poor man pick up his ball and teed off first themselves - pure unadulterated evil.

Lack of breeding

As I walked alongside him going down the 10th, I tried to explain the reason – a simple lack of breeding which I had had to contend with for more years than I care to remember. But he was beside himself with rage – he had never experienced anything so malevolent in all his born days. I believe to this day that if he had his baton in the bag, the two mahoods would have ended up in Letterkenny A&E.

I explained to him that I was actually the person at fault. Never make an assumption was a lesson I was so cruelly taught by my father and I had passed it on to McGeady and McNally. And sadly, on that day, it had come back to bite me.

Michael´s presentation nights were wonderful occasions where the organiser demonstrated both his unique sense of humour and his command of the English language.

It was usually at night time that Barney McDaid kept bad company. Beside him today are two tour members who have been awarded 'honorary membership of the dawn patrol', they've been in it so often, Oliver Logue and Bob Smyth.

Declan – give my head peace

I am sure that many City of Derry members will know the former principal of that prestigious school up in Bishop Street, Lumen Christi. His name is Declan O'Kelly and he will not give my head peace. Every night I go into Da Vinci's I have to listen to him whingeing and it's all down to a single shot I played, yes one single shot.

The occasion was a big Charity Open at Foyle and, as a novelty, they had a long-driving competition at the final hole. We were walking up the 17th and I couldn't help but notice that the little flag which indicated the longest drive so far was about 275 yards from the tee. I turned to McGeady and remarked that it must be "ould women" taking part in the competition.

Unleashed a "monster"

I did a few body pumps as I waited for my fourball to finish the 17th, before setting about my task.

Biceps bulging, triceps trembling, I unleashed a 'monster' which was only rising as it past the 'big girl's blouse's tee shot which had travelled a measly 275 yards. When mine finally came to its resting place, crucially in the middle of the fairway, it had travelled 302 yards. As McGeady and myself walked up to find out who I had gazumped, we looked at the list of best drives and started to laugh – out loud. Who had I 'done the dog on'? It was none other than a top academic who, apparently from what I was told, was waiting in the clubhouse to collect his prize.

Declan – get over it. It happened 25 years ago when I was 14 stones worth of rippling muscle and you were weighing in at about 8 and a half stones and no Charles Atlas. It was no contest then and it certainly isn't now. And you know why – it's me that is sitting at the computer and you're not.

Right hand man

WHEN I DECIDED that I wanted to write a fully fledged account of Michael's remarkable life and about golf in the north-west, I contacted my son Colm to ask would he be able to help me in the design and production. He is vastly experienced, having spent five years along with his brother Niall in the production of the 'Derry News'. To have had him by my side for the past few months has been a joy. Nothing has been too much for him - he has worked long, long hours seven days a week, knowing how much it meant to me. I just couldn't have done it without him. I am so grateful to him for making what seemed an impossible task so straightforward.

A joy

With none of the pressure of having to run a business, I have been given the freedom to allow my memories of a wonderful man and his incredible life flow free and that has been such a joy. And to have Colm by my side to keep me right, I can ask for no greater a gift.

Always get your facts right

In the beautiful tribute which Michael paid to my father on 14th January, 1994, he commented that when he "met the man in person it was still the era of "Upstairs Downstairs", where golf clubs were concerned. Rigid protocols existed governing the relationship of the professional with club members who were, by and large, of the awe inspiring variety – solicitors, bankers, doctors, army officers, clergy – and particularly so to a young assistant pro. Where Frank McCarroll was concerned, however, no barriers existed."

My father was a man who detested snobbery, people looking down on others they considered inferior. And he fought fearlessly for equality, no matter whose nose he put out of joint.

Dismissed the proposal

A classic example of that came in the early 1980's at North-West when long-time green keeper Plunkett Duffy was proposed for full membership at a club AGM. In opposition to the motion a long established member told the membership that such a proposal had to be rejected because it was contrary to rules and regulations laid down by the Golfing Union of Ireland.

I mentioned what had happened to my father when I met him the following Monday and he was incensed – what a load of rubbish was his observation, a comment my father would only make when he was absolutely sure of his ground.

Sealed envelope

Fast forward to the next year's AGM. On the day of the meeting he handed me a sealed envelope and told me to open it if the same proposal regarding Plunkett was made. And sure enough it was. And up jumps the large figure to admonish the proposer for bringing this up two years in succession.

As instructed by my old man, I opened the letter – from the GUI and signed by its then General Secretary, Mr. Bill Menton. It clearly stated that no such rule existed and in any case the GUI would have no authority to instruct individual clubs what they could or could not do.

I brought it up to the honorary secretary to read it – I realised very quickly that my popularity rating with the powers that be at North-West were at an all time low. But to tell you the truth, I couldn't care less. The objection to the proposal collapsed and Plunkett became a member that night. I was very proud to be able to have played my part in righting an obvious wrong.

Plunkett Duffy

For Sheila and myself it was our first-ever trip abroad to Marbella in 1979. From left are Mary McCarroll, myself, Eugene O'Doherty, Kathleen O'Doherty, Michael and Sheila.

So lucky

I have had the pleasure of meeting many great names from the world of sport other than golf – Floyd Patterson, Brian Clough, Johnny Giles, Dennis Taylor, Rio Ferdinand, David Moyes and the inimitable Alex Higgins to name but a few.

I met Alex Higgins through an invitation from the late Oliver Simpson who was running a snooker exhibition in the Tulnaree Inn in Carndonagh. As it so happened Alex was mad keen on golf and wanted to play while he was in Inishowen. What a character – when I was introduced to him, all he wanted to talk about was his golf swing and ways to get his handicap down from 18.

I remember thinking (but not saying) that there would be an immediate improvement if he slowed down on the consumption of a lethal cocktail which included Green Chartreuse and vodka. It didn't affect his snooker however, giving an exhibition which thrilled the packed Tulnaree.

Do not disturb

He was staying in the Lough Swilly Hotel in Buncrana, so I arranged to collect him at 10.30am the following day to bring him to North-West for a game. I arrived at 10.30 only to be told that Mr. Higgins had left instructions not to be disturbed. I called him a "wee shite" on my way back to Derry but I wasn't too surprised – when I left him in Carndonagh he was 'three sheets to the wind'.

About 2.30 that afternoon I got an excited call from someone at North-West to say that Alex Higgins was in the pro's shop asking could I be contacted regarding a game. Sadly I had made another arrangement I couldn't get out of and had to pass up a great opportunity to take a 'fiver' off the most exciting snooker player who ever graced the planet.

Floyd Patterson

What an experience to meet the boxing legend Floyd Patterson, heavyweight champion of the world from 1956 to 1962. He was staying in the Lough Swilly Hotel, so the 'Journal' was invited to meet him. The Journal's chief photographer, Larry Doherty, Derry's great lightweight, Charlie Nash and myself headed off to Buncrana to meet him.

Why he was in Inishowen I don't remember but what an experience to sit and talk to a most gracious man. Of course we asked him the inevitable question – who, in his opinion, was the best boxer he had ever fought against. Without hesitation, it was Muhammad Ali who he fought in Madison Square Garden in 1972. It was to be his final fight losing by a technical knock-out in the 7th round.

Nash v Watt

Charlie at the time was due to meet Scotland's Jim Watt for the World Boxing Council's lightweight title in Glasgow and Floyd gave him some very good advice – unfortunately I can't recall the conversation in detail, but I do remember that it was sound for his forthcoming tussle with Watt. But I do remember his advice if he did win the WBC title – avoid at all costs avoid a fighter called Roberto Duran.

Chilling

His description of Duran was chilling. He told us he was commentating for a TV station and was ringside at a fight involving Duran. When the Panamanian came into the ring, he started to act like a deranged animal – screaming obscenities at his opponent. This is as true as I am sitting here – he told us that he was genuinely intimidated by Duran's antics. I was in awe as he told this story.

The egos of 'golfers'

In hindsight I thought of some of the four ball matches I have been involved in - some of my opponents would make Duran look like a pussycat. And that is the nature of sport. You don't have to deliver blows to the solar plexus when you can deliver an even lower blow – to the ego of 'golfers' who think they can play golf.

A very proud moment for me, pictured with Brian McElhinney at Royal Birkdale after he had just won the 2005 British Amateur Championship.

Thanks for the memories

When I think back on the various performances of note competitors down through the years, my memory is a little bit hazy but there are quite a few which come to mind. The earliest was in 1981, the era of Liam McCaul. In that particular year he was so far ahead he could have walked in at any stage on the back nine and still won. He margin was an amazing 13 pts.

Take Eamon McCourt's performance in 2014. Fabulous is the only word to describe how he managed to score 157 pts off 11 on two formidable tests of golf. When I look back on his win, it was his discipline which made the difference – a ball on the fairway off the tee is a great way to tackle any hole and his precision driving, mostly with a 3 wood, was the foundation for a great victory. Apart from that I love him and he has told me on so many occasions that he feels the same way.

A true gem

And then there was the three-way play-off in 2013, a nerve-wracking experience. When Sean McKane dropped out at the 1st tie hole, it was down to a shoot-out between Maurice Quigg and Eamon McCourt on the brutal par five 2nd at Santa Ponsa. The third shot which Maurice played was a true gem – a beautifully struck 7 iron within fifteen feet to settle the issue. Great stuff.

Another shot that comes to mind was Stevie Wray's chip at the 18th in 2003 to get him into a play-off with Ernie Heywood. It was a thing of beauty, played to perfection to 'gimme' distance. And as Ernie described it "the dirty dog did it again at the play-off hole". Conceding a shot, Ernie could only stand and watch as young Wray tidied the job up with three points at the 73rd hole.

A 'stunner'

What about Eugene Dunbar's shot at the last hole in 2015. Needing a hot finish he was to play a 'stunner' at the final hole. When the pressure is on, anything can happen – no one is immune, and amateurs feel it so much more than professionals who have that vast experience needed under pressure.

An 8 iron was the club selected and I must say, as an old hand looking on, he swung the club so rhythmically. We waited for the result as it had vanished into the sky – 12 inches from the hole and a classy one point victory over his club mate Brendan Coyle.

Dead duck

And the worst shot ever played. I wasn't there to witness it but I will accept the veracity of it because of who told the story to me – Paul Gallagher. Playing his second shot to the 16th at Santa Ponsa, Danny Cooley unleashed an 'exocet', flying so low it didn't get higher than three inches from the ground. As it crossed the pond it hit a duck on the back of the head causing a brain haemorrhage and instant death.

Two very special putters

I have two putters in my possession which I will never part with. One was bequeathed to me by Freda Craig, who also left me some old documents from the City of Derry Ladies Branch and six of the very old balata balls, which include three still encased in their original black paper covers.

The other is my father's beautiful old Fred Daly putter, made by the famous club makers of their day, John Letters. It came into my possession in a most unusual manner – North-West club member Noel Smyth brought it into the bar at Lisfannon and asked me "Do you recognise this putter? I replied that of course I did, it was my father's old putter and if possible I would like to buy it. Noel very kindly gave it to me and it is now a prized possession. **Since writing this article I have learned that Noel passed away. Just days before Brendan Burke had been telling me that he was very unwell and when I** rang Brendan again two weeks later to enquire how he was, his funeral had already taken place at Cockhill.

From Dundalk, the former customs officer was a renowned athlete, a gift he passed on to his daughter Roisin who represented Ireland in the Olympic Games. To all at Lisfannon who knew the Smyth family, and his wife Una in particular, goes their deepest sympathy. I always think of my father when I occasionally take the putter for a test run – from now on I will also think of Noel.

Two old pals who will be there every May as long as the good Lord spares them, Brian McClure and Willie Barrett.

They are both past winners, Brian Long and Steven Wray, but there is a difference between the two of them. Can you spot it? — one is good looking and one is not.

John Hasson, Peter Villa, Michael McCullough and Peter Doherty on the 1st tee at Santa Ponsa.

Overcame a 5 point deficit

BRIAN McClure overcame a five point deficit to claim the 39th Michael Doherty Spanish Golf Tournament last week in Majorca.

A regular member of the local tour, Brian (8) was in the final fourball on Day 4 to take his chance in a battle over the challenging Santa Ponsa course and he eventually emerged victorious enjoying a three points cushion over runner-up Mark O'Doherty from Greencastle.

Brian's superb score of 39 points also gave him the day prize to mark his first victory in 21 attempts to claim this much sought after trophy.

Third place in the overall tournament was secured by North West's Brendan Coyle (12) who finished runner-up in 2015. Brendan defeated City of

Derry's tour rookie, Neil Duncan (13) on break of tie.

McClure's daily points total was matched on the day by the City of Derry Professional, Sam Smallwoods, who has played once before on this tour and he was very pleased with his three under score in difficult conditions.

The other amateur day prize winners were Greencastle's Maurice Brennan (8) with 35 points and City of Derry's Karl Doherty (15) with 34 points.

The winning team over the four days was that led by Brian McClure and included Portadown's Stephen Wray, City of Derry's Shane Kelly and Sean McKane with 355 points.

The runner-up team with 334 points was that captained by the City of Derry professional Sam Smallwoods, including Neil Duncan, Newtownstewart's

Trevor Finlay and North West's Danny McCloskey.

The results were

1, Brian McClure (8) 146 pts (37,37,33,39); 2, Mark O'Doherty (5) 143 pts (38,38,36,31); 3, Brendan Coyle (11) 141 pts (41,31,37,32); 4, Neil Duncan (13) 141 pts (39,35,36,31) 5, Stephen Wray (11) 139 pts (36,33,37,33).

Daily winners

Poniente – Brendan Coyle (11) 41 pts; Santa Ponsa – Sean McKane (18) 39 pts; Poniente – John Hasson (21) 38 pts; Santa Ponsa – Brian McClure (8) 39 pts.

Team results

1, Brian McClure, Stephen Wray, Shane Kelly and Sean McKane 355 pts; 2, Sam Smallwoods, Neil Duncan, Trevor Finlay and Danny McCloskey 334 pts.

The current holder, the champion golfer of 2016 is Ballynahinch eight handicapper, Brian McClure who won in style last year with a 146 pts total. From left are Brendan Coyle (3rd), Maurice Quigg, president, Brian McClure, Eugene Dunbar who presented the prizes, Mark O'Doherty (2nd) and Neil Duncan (4th).

Dominic McGale from Omagh, a regular on earlier tours takes the weight off his feet as does another tour regular, Joe Foley.

The last time Colm played in the Michael Doherty Tour. I feel very sad about that. He is pictured with his great friend Cahir McGeady, Sean McKane and Brendan Coyle.

The Hall

By Michael Doherty

In conversation with Veronica a few months ago, she happened by chance to say that Michael had written a little book called "The Hall" and that his daughter Mary had produced it as a 16 page A5 publication in his honour as a Christmas gift in 2006. It had been intended for the family's eyes only, but when I finally sat down to read it, I was on the phone to Jim straight away – "I just have to include this in "A Gentle Man Passed By." It is a treasure and has to be shared." And of course, the Doherty family were delighted. Now sit back, read the book and see just how multi-talented a man he was.

"Christ it's coul", Jim 'The Bug' Doherty stamped his feet in the porch of Callaghan's bar. "Aye and the bloody snow's goin' tae last a while yet accordin' tae the wireless." The Bug's companion, Joseph 'Nadger' McLaughlin shoved his hands deeper into his trouser pockets as he tongued the Woodbine to the corner of his mouth, "Sure there hasn't been a race meetin' here or across the water for over a week. If you ask me 'fifty-one could turn out to be as bad as 'forty-eight as far as the racin's concerned. Sure it's only a fortnight oul and when you think that it didn't snow 'til March in 'forty-eight and it lasted for three weeks, God knows how long its goin' tae be before the thaw comes this time."

The Bug's crepe soles squelched as he strove to bring some feeling to his freezing toes, "Wait'll I see what time it is", he turned, carefully opened the bar door and put his head in. The bar was empty and very quiet, the stillness accentuated by the ticking of the big clock hanging on the wall above the fireplace with its glowing coal fire. Though he could feel the fire's warmth on his face it didn't enter The Bug's head to step inside out of the cold. If you could not buy drink you could not partake of the comforts; an unbreakable tenet of the drinking man's code, certainly where Callaghans was concerned. "It's ten to" he said, "he'll be coming soon; is there anyone waitin' at the door?" Nadger stepped out of the porch, the biting January north wind making his eyes water as he peered around the corner of the building.

The Hall

Saint Mary's Parochial Hall, stood fifty yards away across the road and slightly downhill from Callaghan's corner. Built in 1904 as the inscription high on its facade verified, it was Buncrana's most imposing building until Saint Mary's Oratory was erected some thirty years later. Upstairs it housed the cinema, complete with Upper and Lower balconies for those who could afford the two shillings and one and sixpence respectively; while the hard-backed "popular" seats, the 'eight-pennies' filled the body of the hall. Located on the ground floor were the billiard room and card room. The hall's frontage

faced the crossroads formed by the intersection of Main Street and Castle Avenue, with Cockhill Road and Saint Mary's Road, known locally as the 'back road.'

Lengthwise, the hall ran parallel to Saint Mary's Road with the door that gave access to the billiard room and via a connecting door to the card room, located at the rear of the building facing the road. It was to this door that Nadger now directed his gaze for the briefest of glances before scurrying back to the shelter of the bar porch. As he negotiated the five yards of slippery hard-packed snow he looked up Main Street. On the footpaths on either side of the street there was not a soul to be seen. In the middle of the street a youth was transporting a half-bag of coal on a sleigh, propelling it along by pushing in unison with the six-inch nails he was using as 'guiders.'As he reached the point where the street swept downwards and around onto the Cockhill road, the deftest of touches with his right-hand guider saw him take the corner perfectly without losing the momentum that would carry him to his front gate in Saint Egney's Terrace, some quarter of a mile away.

No sign of him yet

"There's no one waitin' at the door and there's no sign of him yet" Nadger reported. At the other end of Main Street, Phillip 'Phildy' Doherty, caretaker of Saint Mary's Hall, tucked his pure-wool scarf into his ankle-length overcoat and stepped into the street. His measured pace would normally get him to the hall in exactly fifteen minutes but today as for the past week, he left home five minutes earlier than usual to allow for the conditions underfoot. With highly polished strong black shoes, navyblue suit, white shirt, perfectly knotted dark-red tie, the ensemble completed by a heavy navy-blue overcoat, grey scarf and grey tweed cap; this sartorially impressive figure bore little resemblance to that which travelled the same route at eight a.m. that morning. That figure sported a worn and frayed overcoat over a well-worn boiler-suit. Only the stride, unhurried, but never slow, identified the two as one and the same person.

From early morning until lunchtime, Phildy cleaned the hall, starting with the cinema and finishing with his beloved billiard room. His final act of the morning was to light the big coke-burning furnace in the basement, which through a vast network of pipes and radiators heated the entire building. Having prepared the comforts, which the hall's patrons would enjoy later in the day, Phildy headed for home via the "back road"; he never went home at lunchtime by the Main Street.

"Yes boys"

Now as he passed Callaghans, the figures in the bar porch said almost but not quite in unison, "yes Phil,""yes boys," Phildy replied without breaking stride as he turned sharp left around the corner. The Bug and Nadger fell in a respectful three paces behind. As they approached the Hall the railway-cart was pulling away. It's driver, Jim Kavanagh, sat front left on the long flatbodied cart, his hands holding the reins, motionless, as he allowed the horse to make its own pace over the slippery road surface. At the front door of the hall were two battered metal boxes transported there by the railway-cart from the Lough Swilly train station located three-quarters of a mile away on the outskirts of the town on the road to Derry.

"Well at least there'll be a show tonight, the films have got here anyway." Nadger was a great film fan as indeed were most of the town's inhabitants. The "pictures" were shown every night except Wednesday, at eight-thirty with five programme changes a-week . On Wednesday there were two shows at six thirty and nine o'clock and on Sunday there was a children's matinee at three o'clock.

Phildy turned the big iron key in the lock and pushed open the heavy outside door. The door opened onto a corridor : immediately to the left were the back stairs to the cinema and on the right the door to the billiard room. Further along on the left was the toilet, then the caretakers room and at the corridors end the steps that led to the basement with its all important furnace. Phildy pulled open the billiard room door and The Bug and Nadger followed him inside.

Countless trouser seats

The room was lined on all four sides with mahogany bench seating, its dark brown lustre the result of being burnished by countless trouser seats for over forty years. The seating was built on a raised step about a foot above floor level, the better to view play on the two billiards tables that dominated the room. Thanks to the ministrations of Phildy, the tables were always in pristine condition, their green baize flawless, a fact given emphasis by the bright light from the high wattage bulbs encased in the large, fringed, rectangular shades suspended above each table. The shades were at a height that allowed the light to spill just beyond the parameters of the tables; the brightness of the table lights in contrast with the room's weak ceiling lights, creating a dramatic effect akin to that engendered by a brightly lit boxing ring in a darkened arena : the comparison with boxing being an entirely valid one, as no quarter was asked or given on these tables. In this room, billiards was a serious business. Phildy proceeded to the near left corner of the room, took off his overcoat and hung it on one of the pegs that lined the wall above the seating. He then sat down exactly in the corner, from where, hardly having to turn his head, he could survey the entire room. Nadger and The Bug sat close by Phildy, one on either side. Both stooped forward as they warmed their hands on the pipes running underneath the seating. The swinging open of the door and the thump of hobnailed boots on the wooden floor announced the arrival of "Big Thomas" Mc Menamin.

Big Thomas

In the pantheon of the billiard room's cognoscenti Big Thomas truly ranked among the elite, a status attained either by exceptional skill on the table, or as in Thomas's case, a deep understanding and appreciation of the game, gained through years of attendance in the room on an almost daily basis. The Bug slid sideways on the seat away from the corner, allowing Thomas to take his customary place beside Phildy. There he would spend the rest of the day until the room closed at eleven, except for a break for his tea around six o'clock. The room was now beginning to fill up, this time it was Nadger's turn to move as Old Paddy Murphy, took his place on the other side of Phildy. As the room's regulars filtered in, the choice seats on either side of Phildy filled. Soon all the room's seating was occupied, even the least popular section close to the entrance door.

Since Christmas, the numbers of the room's daily patrons had been swollen by the lads home from the building sites "across the water", the local term for England or Scotland. Their stay at home had been extended by the weather, which had brought all building work to a halt. On the wall opposite the entrance door was the board where one affixed one's initials with the chalk supplied for the purpose. The board had two columns, each having ten spaces. Every half-hour Phildy would call "time gentlemen" and the players occupying the tables would cease play. Phildy would then go to the board and call out the initials of the next to play, then, erase their initials with his handkerchief. To the clicking of the balls and conversations never too loud in deference to those engaged on the tables, the room settled into its daily pattern and rhythm.

The boy

From his desk the boy stole a glance at the clock on the schoolroom wall; twenty-five past three, just five minutes to go. He knew that after school there would be snowball fights as the boys made their way to their respective homes. Then after a hurried dinner, most would head off with their sleighs to the slopes of either Castle Avenue, the Mill Brae or the Hillhead; the town's three main sleigh runs. But for the boy, the thoughts that occupied his mind as he waited for Master Mc Cready to ring the bell and release the class were of whether the board in the billiard room would be full. He knew that the hall would, by now, have been open for almost half-an-hour and he wondered if he had any chance of getting a game before teatime.

The boy loved the game of billiards and for a twelve-year-old he was good at it, very good indeed; so good that he often had trouble getting someone to play with him, as his opponents usually spent most of the half-hour nursing their cues while the boy ran up break after break. His skill on the table he undoubtedly inherited from his father who by some way, was the best billiards player in the town. At last the aged headmaster; sitting as was his wont, bent over, elbows splayed, his head cradled in his hands staring down at an open book the pages of which he hadn't turned in almost ten minutes; suddenly sprang to his feet, in the same movement snatching the large hand-bell from the table. While the bell clanged loudly in response to the staccato movements of his right arm the boys filed quickly out of the classroom.

The boy, running as fast as he could in the slippery conditions, made it to the billiard room in just over five minutes and headed straight to the name board. It was as he had feared – all of the spaces were filled, he had no chance of getting a table. This was the way it had been since the boys had come home from across the water.

And today of all days he really wanted a game. Later that night he was to play what would be his first ever, competitive match, in the hall's big billiards handicap. Victory in the match would go to the first player to reach two hundred points. The boy's handicap was minus thirty, so he had to score two hundred and thirty points to win. His father was minus eighty, the lowest handicap in the competition. The boy's opponent was plus thirty, which meant that he would be giving him a start of sixty points.

Too big a task

Unknown to the boy the perceived wisdom in the room was that the task would prove too much for him. It was believed by the room's aficionados that as this would be his first experience of competitive play the boy would be nervous and uptight, and this, plus giving sixty points to an older and more experienced opponent would prove too big a task.

The match was to start at eight thirty and this would be another first for the boy as primary school boys were not allowed in the room after six o'clock. Tonight however this usually strictly enforced rule would not apply as he was playing an important competitive match. With no chance of a game the boy headed for home just a short distance away on Castle Avenue.

Already some of his classmates were out on the avenue with their sleighs, their whoops and laughter filling the air as they sped down the slope, towards the lough-shore. After hurriedly disposing of a bowl of soup and potatoes from the pot which his mother had simmering on the Stanley range, the boy headed back to the billiard room.

Most of the room's regulars were now in situ. Old Paddy Murphy was sitting beside Phildy across from Big Thomas. With Paddy's full head of snow- white hair, the boy was reminded of the flashing of a lighthouse beacon Old Paddy removed his cap, scratched his head for a second, then replaced it; a gesture he would repeat continuously when engaged in serious debate, which was almost all of the time.

"The Jug" – no relation to "The Bug"

One of his main protagonists in these almost daily arguments was Johnny "The Jug" Doherty: no relation to "The Bug". In the town of Buncrana every other person seemed to be either a Doherty or a McLaughlin. Today's debate was centred on who was the best footballer the town had produced. Old Paddy was championing the cause of Paddy Hegarty, better known as "Paddy Eckie," While The Jug, was putting a forceful case for John "Teddy" Smith. The footballers in question were both known personally to the boy though their playing days were long gone before he was born.

From being present during these intensely argued and wide ranging debates, the boy had learned much. He knew that the greatest heavyweight boxer of all time was Jack Dempsey, the greatest ever footballer was Peter Doherty and the greatest singer was Count John Mc Cormack. Always a subject of much discussion was the "pictures;" as the denizens of the billiard room were the town's most discerning picture-goers. The room's favourite actor was Spencer Tracy, whom all agreed was just great in San Francisco and Boystown. In both films Tracy played a priest, a fact that did him no harm at all with the local curate Fr O'Hagan, who had much to do with what was and what was not screened in St Mary's Hall. In the context of his influence on the pictures shown, Fr O'Hagan came in for more than a little criticism, though never to his face.

Addressed to Trigger

Recently the allegiance of the room's cinema devotees had been sorely tried by what appeared to be an unending series of Roy Rogers pictures. Finally some person or persons unknown graphically made their point by leaving a bag of oats at the hall's front door addressed to Trigger, St Mary's Hall. Thus for the time being, Roy had ridden off into the sunset on his beloved Trigger, but there was little doubt but that they would return, sooner rather than later, to their old pasture in St Mary's Hall.

Tonight's feature film or "big picture" as against the preliminary "shorts," was Double Indemnity with Fred Mc Murray, Barbara Stanwyck and Edward G. Robinson. "It should be a dacent show, Edward G. is good," said Nadger, "and yer woman Stanwyck's a great actress". There was not a single dissenting voice: a rare tribute from the room's critics.

Nadger and The Bug were now almost at the end of their respective forms on either side of Phildy, as those already seated automatically moved to the side, in time honoured deference, when a more senior member of the room's hierarchy arrived. The greater one's status the closer one sat to Phildy.

The boy sat near the name-board, waiting in the vain hope that some of those whose names were in front of his might not be present when Phildy called out their names and he might yet get a game before tea. At six o'clock, with no chance of getting a table, the boy headed home for his tea. This week the boy's father was on the four-to-twelve shift in the local knitting factory and had left for work before the boy came home from school. He would really have liked to talk to his father about the match though he knew very well what his father would say as he had heard him express his philosophy on billiards on innumerable occasions, " play your own game and don't play too much safety, anyone who plays too much safety you'll find can't make a dacent break when they get the chance they're so worried about leaving something on for the other player."

After tea the boy opened his schoolbag and got out his exercise book. He had a composition to write for school tomorrow. The title of the composition was "The Circus Comes to Town." Writing this would pose no problem for the boy as reading and writing were by far his favourite subjects at school. At half past seven the boy, having finished his essay put away his exercise book. He went to the scullery and washed his hands. Though he had washed his hands before tea he now washed them again thoroughly as he felt that with clean hands the cue seemed to slide more easily over the 'bridge' of thumb and forefinger.

As he made his way back to the billiard room, the sleighing was now at full tilt on the avenue: the thump of the sleighs' iron runners on the frozen snow often drowned by the shrieks of girls as the sleighs on which they travelled – almost always as passengers- hurtled down the ever quickening run.

The match

The boy entered the billiard room and was immediately aware of an atmosphere he had never experienced before. All the ceiling lights had been switched off leaving the only source of illumination that which came from the table lights. Beyond the tables the rest of the room was in near darkness, save for the small light on the wall-mounted marking board. Although the room was almost full the boy was aware that the sound level of conversation was well below normal.

At exactly half-past-eight the boy heard his name called by Phildy, together with that of his opponent, Peter Bradley. The boy went to the cue-rack and selected a cue. To his relief his favourite was on the rack.. The day before it had not been there , having been removed by Phildy, along with others in bad need of new leather tips to replace those that had been worn, almost to the wood. Phildy, thankfully, had, with his usual expertise re-tipped and returned the cues to the rack in time for the boy's match.

Marker for the game was to be Michael Gallinagh, renowned locally for his amazing facility with mental arithmetic. The marker asked Peter Bradley to call "head or harp" as he tossed a coin over the table, catching it before it hit the green baize and slapping it onto the back of his left hand. His opponent having called 'harp' correctly, had the choice of breaking-off or asking the boy to so do. With a wave of his hand he indicated to the boy to proceed.

He leant over the table and positioned the cue ball in the centre of the 'D.' Sighting along the cue to the red ball at the other end of the table, the boy was aware that the room had gone silent. In the silence the sharp click of the cue-ball on the red reverberated around the room. It was a good break, the cue-ball coming back into baulk off two cushions, the red going safe just below the left middle pocket. The quality of the break was a sign of things to come. In just five visits to the table the boy had wiped out his opponent's sixty-point handicap advantage establishing a twenty-five-point lead of his own.

Then just as the boy was about to play a half-ball in-off the red to the top right corner pocket, there came a thunder-like sound from overhead and the table lights began to dance on the chains that secured them to the ceiling. A few tiny white flakes of plaster from the ceiling fell onto the table.

"The film's broken again" said a voice from the darkness, "Big Neil'll soon fix it" rejoined another: 'Big Neil' being Neil Doherty who worked in Swan's mill by day and at night as projectionist in the hall cinema, a labour of love he shared with his brother, John James. The thunder-like sound from overhead was the ritual stamping of feet at the break in the film. As Michael, the marker, picked the particles of plaster from the green baize, the overhead noise stopped as suddenly as it had begun.

"Wee Joe's out with the lamp" volunteered another hall regular. "Wee" Joe, being Joe Flanagan, the cinema manager who, though small in stature brooked no nonsense from anyone. When he walked slowly down the cinema's centre isle sweeping the rows of seats with his high-powered torch, no one dared make even the slightest disturbance for fear of antagonising Wee Joe, the result of which could lead to the embarrassment of being told, in no uncertain terms, to leave the cinema, or worst of all, incurring the ultimate punishment of being barred from all picture showings for the next month – a fate too awful to contemplate, particularly in wintertime. As the marker finished his clean-up of the table there came a muffled cheer from above heralding the resumption of the film. When play resumed the boy continued as before; scoring on practically every visit to the table - including a break of forty-five - he ran out an easy winner.

They had been wrong

The room's billiards connoisseurs had been wrong, he had been not been the slightest bit nervous, in fact he had loved every second of the match. He particularly enjoyed it when, on reaching the match-winning total of two-hundred points, the marker, in time honoured fashion, banged the butt of the rest three times on the floor and the spectators broke into generous applause.

The boy put his cue back on the rack and took a seat near the door. The ceiling lights were on again and he glanced over at Phildy, unsure if it was alright to stay on in the room now that his match was over. Phildy was in earnest conversation with Big Thomas and old Paddy Murphy, but the boy knew he was aware of his presence. That Phildy was pretending not to notice him was he knew a special compliment – tonight he was being treated as a grownup. At ten-o'clock the boy left the room.

On the avenue the sleighs were still out but the numbers had dwindled, the schoolboys and girls having mostly gone home,

leaving the run to the adults. After a supper of hot porridge the boy went to bed. In his little room which was just big enough to hold the bed and a small bedside table, the boy read his favourite book, "Heroes of the Sea", a collection of stories of seafaring adventures he never tired of reading. On the dot of eleven o'clock, Phildy called a halt to the day's proceedings in the billiard room.

Slowly and reluctantly its patrons filed out of the warmth of the room into the cold night air. With the help of Big Thomas, Phildy draped the billiards tables with their huge dustcovers, then as always, they left the room together. They walked the length of the hall then Phildy crossed over to the footpath that would take him around Callaghan's corner and onto the main street. Big Thomas continued on the nearside of the road, then turned left down Castle Avenue. In his bed the boy was getting drowsy; he put the book down on the bedside table and switched off the light. There was no longer the sound of sleighs or of the snow revellers coming through the small square window of his room.

As the boy pulled the blankets higher around his head, from the avenue came the crunching sound of a heavy foot on the frozen snow. On the edge of sleep the boy knew it was Big Thomas heading home. He also knew that this meant that the hall was now closed and that Phildy would also be making his way homeward. The boy closed his eyes - he would see them both again tomorrow.

EPILOGUE

In a unique happening, the boy and his father went on to meet in the final of the billiards handicap. The room was filled to capacity for the occasion; no one could remember such a crowd for a billiards match. Even Father O'Hagan - who did not as a rule frequent the room - came to watch. Though the boy's father had been displaying his expertise on the billiards table since he too was a boy, that night he gave one of his greatest performances in contriving to lose while apparently trying to win.

This he accomplished by missing particular shots by the merest of fractions, in the process leaving the boy opportunities to score. When the match was over, amid the warm applause, Phildy, Big Thomas and Old Paddy, applauded more than most, for they knew and appreciated just how skilful a performance the boy's father had given.   So too did the boy.

On the back page there are five tributes from people who loved Michael dearly.

"All things!" Veronica Doherty, Chief Cook and Bottle Washer

"Touching and evocative portrayal of the way we were. Very well crafted...leaves you wanting more". Jim Doherty, Project Manager HSE

"Beautifully weighted, but the wait was worth it". Kevin Doherty, Songwriter, SCR

"A story to warm even the coldest heart – I can actually place myself in that room, I can hear the chatter of the men and smell of dampness of their wet clothes". Mary Doherty, Managing Director, Red Dog.

"It is a simple and ordinary story, calmly, wryly crafted with subtle detail – and therein lies Doherty's genius". Patricia Doherty, lecturer. Head of Department of Business Studies in LYIT.

Photograph taken of the City of Derry team prior to the all-Ireland Finals of the Pierce Purcell Shield at Portmarnock Golf Club in 1972. Front row, from left, Hector Kirk, Bobbie Bell, Jim Hamill and Des Wright; Back Row, from left, George Simms, John Gallagher, Edgar Walker, Lexie Michell, Don O´Doherty, (Club Captain), Ted Hegarty, Colin Dixon, Cahir Fitzpatrick and John Bradley

Group taken at Longniddry on the final day of the second Michael Doherty Tour in 1977. The two other venues were the magnificent Muirfield links and Gullane. Front row: Danny McNally, Hugh Quigley (N.W.), Hugh McQuilken, George Taylor, Michael Doherty. Second row: Frank Guckian, Pius Carey, Sam Anthony, Pat Loughrey, Billy Hanna, Peter McCready, Pat Doherty, Patsy Fagan, Billy Rodden (standing behind) Jock Balmer. Third row: Colm Duffy, Frank McCarroll Jun., Jim Stewart, Sam Hestor, Christy McWilliams, Gerry Coyle, Don O'Doherty, Ronnie Dougherty, Cahir Fitzpatrick, John Louden, Frank McCarroll Sen., Hector Simpson, Laurence Deeney, Bill Wright. Fourth row: Billy Elliott, Joe Ramsey, Fred Aicken, Sean Doherty (1987 N.W. Captain) Cahir McGeady, John Monaghan. Fifth row: Stanley McDermott, Ken McConomy, Cathal McKeever, Eugene O'Doherty, Brian McCarroll, Joe McCauley, George Sweeney. Top row: Brian Duddy, Cathal Langan, Jack Logue, Brian Duffy.

Friends we remember

When **Joe Ramsey** fell ill on Michael's trip in 2004, there was hope he would recover to play his usual role in 2005. Sadly his illness proved terminal. He was 74. As far as the trip was concerned his contribution was invaluable and he will always be appreciated by all who had the pleasure of knowing him.

In every sense of the word **Charlie McCafferty** was one of nature's gentlemen and a much loved member of the tour. Golf was the pastime he truly loved. He lived every moment of every round with the best part coming when he recounted his exploits with his famous seven wood. In Charlie's words - "I could make it talk!"

When Chief Fire Officer, **Sonny Jarvis**, emptied the "circular" contents of his bag into the "agua" which surrounded the par three 11th in Las Brisas, he was hopeful that the word would not get back to the organiser. He was wrong. On the night of the presentation, he received a wonderful little memento – a bottle of water from the very same pond he had hitherto bombarded relentlessly. His son Ian tells me it has pride of place in the Jarvis household.

Eamon "Lisowen" Doherty was another very popular member of early Michael Tours. He was a lovely man with a most gentle demeanour. The great tragedy of his life was the untimely death of his daughter Marguerite who had lost a brave battle against leukaemia. In typical fashion he set about honouring her memory by running an annual competition in aid of St. Mary's Hospital for Sick Children in Dublin.

Sam Anthony was also a regular on Michael Doherty's earlier tours of both Scotland and Spain. He took up golf in 1959 when his cricketing days were over and took to it like a duck to water. Although he preferred to stay clear of office, his proudest moment in golf came when his son Rob was honoured with the captaincy of City of Derry in 1981.

Frank "Mousey" Murphy passed away when he was just 53 years old. Although he knew that he was ill for some time, Frank had the remarkable capacity to remain in the best of spirits. Those who had the pleasure of travelling with him to Spain will remember his marvellous sense of humour. He played for both Derry City and Sligo Rovers in the early 1960's and when his football career finished, he turned his skills to both cycling and marathon running including the completion of the gruelling Dublin marathon.

Paddy Morrison didn't suffer fools gladly, but behind the gruff exterior was a kindly soul with a heart of gold. His life changed dramatically when he fell victim to asbestosis, a hazard of the industry in which he worked. I can't remember the last time he played in Majorca but it was by sheer willpower and determination that he made the journey. He had not lifted a club for many months before and never played again. I remember well his simple comment as he walked off Santa Ponsa on the final day - "Well kid, I made it".

Frankie Campbell will be remembered as an outstanding sportsman, excelling at every sport he played. A sporting giant in Derry, he played in the great Derry City team of the 1960's. The highlight of his career came when he led Derry to victory in the 1964 Irish Cup. A capable golfer, the highlight of his golfing career came in 2001 on the fairways of Santa Ponsa when he won the "Travellers Trophy" in a play-off.

As far as the "Tour" was concerned, **Seamus McDevitt** was a legend. A superb tenor, he would sing till the cows came home – who could possibly forget the wonderful afternoon of music in Santa Ponsa in the Pionero Hotel. Not a single request was refused by a marvellous singer who gave so generously of his time and talent.

I just loved **Gilbert McLaughlin**. Whatever special grace God gave him he exuded kindness and calmness. Inhibitions flung out the window when he was holidays, he got up to all sorts of devilment. His masterpiece must surely be the day he turned up in multi-coloured garb, dressed in a wig, and pretending to be an Arab sheik. Now there's a man who knew how to enjoy himself.

Another lovely mannered man was **Jimmy McCloskey** who went on the early tours. He was definitely on the 1980 trip to Fuengirola as he took advantage on the day off to travel many hundreds of kilometres to order marble for his business – how's that for entrepreneurial flair!

Dickson Ward and **Walter "the Brad" Brady** were inseparable. Along with Les Carruthers and Liam McCaul, they liked nothing more than to dine in all the fancy restaurants while the rest of us lived like paupers. In actual fact we were round the corner where the even fancier restaurants were.

I could go on and on, but I felt it would be nice to acknowledge some of the Tour's 'characters'. It is also nice for all of the families to know their loved ones are still remembered, particularly by the 'old-timers' who go right back to the earliest Tours. May they all rest in peace.

The Late Terry Bell

Terry Bell was born on 16th October, 1944, son of Bobby and May Bell, both former Captains of City of Derry Golf Club, Bobby being Captain in 1961 and May, the lady Captain in 1975. The first milestone in what was to be a brilliant golfing career occurred when he won his own father's Captain prize at the tender age of 16. Remarkably, not alone did he win the prize but the first three prize winners all played in the same fourball – which must be a record for a Captain's Prize at Prehen.

By 1970 he was one of a score of scratch players in the country, winning the City of Derry Club Championship off that handicap and in 1971 he won the North of Spain amateur Championship and followed up by reaching the semi-final of the Spanish Amateur Championship in the same year.

Won the Balmoral

Scratch Cup

He was a regular on the Ulster Inter-Provincial Team and in May of 1972, he shared the South of Scotland Championship with fellow Ulster Golfer Brian Hoey, there being no opportunity to stage a play off. He also won the Balmoral Scratch Cup and the Town's Cup at Royal Portrush.

What was probably his most cherished victory was the winning of the 1972 Captain's Prize at Royal Portrush off scratch. In his sub-par round of 70 he covered the second nine holes in an incredible 31 strokes. Even as late as 26th November 1972 Terry was to continue his winning ways in the North Western Alliance at North West collecting the Gross Prize on that occasion.

Untimely Death

Terry Bell suffered a cerebral haemorrhage on a car journey

Terry Bell

home from Belfast and being admitted to Atlnagelvin Hospital, never regained consciousness and died on 20th December, 1972. The shock waves that reverberated around the North West and indeed the whole of Ulster, cast a gloom over the entire golfing fraternity.
Don O'Doherty

Back in 1972 at North-West, some of the finest amateurs in Ireland played in the North-West Senior Scratch Cup. Seated, from left, are Arnold O'Connor David Corcoran, Raymond Kane, Noel Fogarty, Roddy Carr and John O'Leary. Standing, left to right, are Billy Caldwell, Michael Doherty, Jack McGinley, John Sweeney, Tommy Doherty, the legendary Joe Carr, Norman O'Hara, Brendan Kelly, Frank Friel and Vincent Grant.

Michael pictured with the five times British Open champion Peter Thomson at the Shelbourne Park, Dublin. Mr. Thompson won at Royal Birkdale in 1954, St. Andrew's in 1955, Hoylake in 1956, Royal Lytham and St. Annes in 1958 and Royal Birkdale in 1965.

Gordon Forbes

I was so sorry to learn about the untimely death of Gordon Forbes. For those of us who were lucky enough to compete in senior golf, we had the opportunity to meet such fine people as Gordon. Not only was he a formidable competitor, he was a sportsman to the fingertips. I played with him on a number of occasions and against him once – I regret to say that I came out on the losing side but that was no shame as he was a fully fledged Ulster inter-provincial and I was past my 'sell-by' date.

Totally out of the blue, he had a brain haemorrhage in Australia and had to be flown home where he was to spend his last days in Altnagelvin Hospital. When he died on 2nd February of this year he was just 53 years old. He was a very successful businessman with ventures both here in Ireland and Australia in his role as boss of Finrone Systems, Pig farm building specialists. How dominant he was at his home club is surely demonstrated by the fact that he won Newtownstewart's Club Championship at Baronscourt on no fewer than sixteen occasions! And for good measure he tore Baronscourt apart on 23rd June, 2007 when he went round in 62 shots, eight under par.

He was down to 'scratch' by the age of sixteen and his lowest GUI handicap was plus 2. Selected to play for Ulster in the Inter-provincials in 1989 at Rosses Point, the team included the exalted company of Darren Clarke (Dungannon) and Garth McGimpsey (Bangor). A sturdy competitor in the regional championships, he reached the semi-finals of the North of Ireland in 1992. Scratch Cup wins included city of Derry and Donegal and he won bronze medal in the North of Ireland for having the lowest aggregate rounds in 2004.

The Forbes name in golf will continue through the exploits of his teenage daughter, Emma. Already a junior international, she honoured her father's memory with a great victory in the Ireland Nick Faldo series at the

Gordon Forbes, who sadly passed away in early 2017.

Lough Erne resort in the first week in April. She is a star of the future.

To his loving family, wife Sharon, sons and daughters, Calvin, Russell, Emma and Alice and his mother Mary goes the sympathy of the golfing fraternity.

Best of the famous Jacksons

Daniel George Jackson was born on 29th May, 1925, one of five brothers who were destined to form a unique quintet of single figure golfers at City of Derry Golf Club. While Liam was also a scratch golfer and Patrick in low single figures, it would not be unfair to select George as the all-round best of the five.

George learned his golf at Lisfannon, his parents having a holiday home just across the road from the course. A dedicated golfer and student of the game, George continued his practice on the playing fields of St. Patrick's College, Armagh before moving to U.C.D. where he graduated with a B.D.S. degree.

George Jackson, scratch golfer

A pioneer

While George took an active interest in the administration of the club, being captain in 1957, he will be best remembered for his achievements on the course where apart from his unique playing records he pioneered the idea of playing in provincial and international tournaments, playing in the open championship at St. Andrew's in 1955 and again at Hoylake in 1956. In those days pre-qualifying allowed all amateurs of sufficiently low handicaps to pre-qualify with the tournament stars.

George twice reached the last eight of the Irish Open Amateur Championship and once led the field in the East of Ireland Championship at Baltray. During that period he claimed the scalps of several of the current Irish internationals and was certainly worthy of at least interprovincial honours.

Four records in one year

George held four course records in one year at City of Derry, North-West, Greencastle and Ballyliffin.

Ironically in the 1956 Captain's prize at City of Derry, in which he broke the record in qualifying, he again reduced his own record, shooting a 68 to win Mr. Bertie Bresland's prize. Further records were to fall to him at North West and Ballyliffin.

George emigrated to Canada with his family in June, 1969. Sadly, it was to be a short sojourn, passing away on 24th February, 1971. His remains were brought back to Derry to complete a life cycle which will long remain in the memory of those privileged to be associated with him.

Don O'Doherty

Brilliant at everything

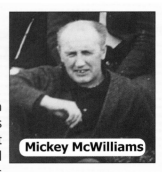

Mickey McWilliams

A man of affable temperament, City of Derry's Mickey McWilliams was just brilliant at anything he attempted. A low single figure golfer Mickey excelled on the golf course, witness to captain's prize wins in 1957 and 1960. The latter, in many ways, epitomised the man as, playing off a 1 handicap he took a disappointing 39 shots to complete the first 9 holes only to complete the second 9 in an incredible 31 shots. On the green baize he was equally at home in both billiards and snooker, and was a much sought after winger in the soccer and gaelic codes.

In entertainment he again excelled himself and was lead vocalist in the resident Carlton Swingtette in the local Corinthian Ballroom. Perhaps Mickey's finest hour was reserved for the unique City of Derry Captain's night where he entertained one and all in song 'til the early hours of the morning. Of Mickey it can be truly said, 'there never will be another'.

Don O'Doherty

One for the album. Pictured outside the clubhouse at Mijas in 1981 are front, from left, are Don O'Doherty, John Bradley, Leo Hickey, Maurice Quigg, Cahir McGeady, Eddie McCauley, Aenas McBride, Norman McMorran, Tom Cooke, Willie Dunlop, Derek McLaughlin, A.N. Other, Michael Doherty, Dixon Ward and Liam McCaul. Back, left to right, are Frank McCarroll senior, Dominic McGale, Sean O'Dwyer, Joe Foley, John Gormely, Eugene O'Doherty, Frank Guckian, A.N. Other, Pat Morrison, Denis Hegarty, Walter Brady, Norman Kane, Ted Graham, Gilbert McLaughlin and Christie McWilliams.

Charlie Begley – a great man

Another of the pioneers of senior golf at both City of Derry and North-West was the affable Charlie Begley, someone for whom I had a great deal of time. He was a man of high intelligence but so innocent at the same time. "See me hi, if I didn't have a wife and seven weans I would have won about three British Opens by now". While it was all said in great humour, it summed up the great belief he had in himself.

He was a great all rounder, excelling in golf, snooker, darts and soccer and, on a more intellectual level, he was a bridge player of considerable ability. When he passed away it was so

sudden – on the 1st fairway at North-West he collapsed and died shortly afterwards. Apart from being in the bosom of his family, perhaps Lisfannon is the only other place he may have picked.

He played in the Barton Shield for City of Derry with Frank Guckian. On the day of one particular match Charlie, who was a telecoms engineer, fell off a telegraph pole and had broken his wrist. Did he cry off? – not a chance. He produced a shoe horn, attached it firmly to the lame wrist and completed the match. I think that says it all – they don't make them like that anymore.

Charlie Begley

Frank Guckian – a truly amazing man

It had been my first trip to Majorca, in 1981, and I had been enjoying every minute of it. My father introduced me to those I hadn't met before which made it all the easier to socialise. Among the group was Frank Guckian, a successful entrepreneur, a member of many important Boards and active in a brand of politics which advocated equality for all – a very serious dude indeed, one to treat with added respect.

Frank Guckian was everything you didn't expect him to be – a wonderful raconteur, a comedian, a singer – an all-round wonderful entertainer. My abiding memory of him was standing on a stool in the Green Parrott, conducting one of the most enthusiastic choirs I have ever seen. We were on for the night until we were interrupted by three members of the Magaluf branch of the Gardai Siochana. We were making too much noise and had to quieten down as those in nearby apartments couldn't get to sleep. This was 11 pm in upmarket Magaluf. Up to now we had been told they only get up at 11 o'clock.

Fabulous in his 3-piece Versace

My main story about Frank concerns the annual presentation ceremony, a very formal occasion where you were expected to wear a jacket and tie. He was sitting out by the pool looking stunned and I naturally asked him if anything was wrong.

He said "you are not going to believe this. Just five minutes ago Ted Graham walked into the pool area on his way to the presentation ceremony. He looked fabulous – dressed in a Versace 3 piece suit, walking along without a care in

the world, with an expensive brandy in one hand and a huge cigar in the other.

The next thing he vanished from sight. Oh my God, Frank realised that Ted had not seen the swimming pool and walked straight into the deep end.

Frank Guckian

Not an experienced swimmer by any stretch of the imagination but determined to save an old friend, he jumped from his seat. But what he saw when he reached the side of the pool was, in his own words, the most extraordinary thing he had ever seen in his life. Ted must have had at least two bottles of brandy already in him and hadn't a care in the world. There he was standing fully upright on the floor of the pool with the cigar still in his right hand and the now diluted glass of brandy in his left. I often wondered in subsequent years was that an exact interpretation of what took place. I would never have doubted Mr. Guckian's word. I subsequently found out that Ted did in fact have a little altercation with the pool so Mr. Guckian's story had substance. Was it the exact truth or the work of a wonderful imagination which could make a "silk purse out of a sow's ear. The jury is still out.

Youngest ever captain

Francis Gerard Guckian joined City of Derry in the 1930s at the tender age of 9. Quickly adapting to the sport, Frank progressed until the height of his playing career, he had reduced his handicap to 4 and was a regular member of senior teams representing City of Derry. Fred Daly in fact, had ambitious plans for Frank, seeing great potential in his golf, but studies prevented him from devoting as much time as he would have liked to the game.

Diverting his attention to the administration of the club. Frank in

1954, became the youngest club captain in the history of City of Derry and highlighted his year by arranging many home and away friendlies with North West clubs. A short time later he was honoured with the presidency in 1959, again claiming the record of the club's youngest president.

To concentrate solely on Frank Guckian's golfing achievements would be to leave Hamlet out of the play. Frank added to all gatherings a great sense of presence, dignity and most of all harmless, inoffensive fun. Those of us who witnessed him in his

old auctioneer role on captain's eve, or saw him rouse a lethargic touring group to unprecedented merriment appreciate the great contribution he has made to life in general and City of Derry Golf Club in particular.

A man of singular generosity and compassion, he was at all times ready and available to listen to the troubles of his fellow travellers in life, more often than not using his astute brain to solve their particular problems.

Don O'Doherty

Paul Houston

When I think back on trips organised by Michael, I can't help but think of Greencastle past captain, Paul Houston, a truly wonderful character, so full of life. It was to Marbella in 1979. He was the life and soul of the party - when Paul was about, everybody laughed.

I remember one night in particular when we were in a restaurant where Paul was in full flow. There was just our group and another two people in the restaurant. As the jokes flowed and the pair at the next table laughed more and more, the stories went nearer and nearer the knuckle.

After an hour or so of unbridled humour, he introduced himself to the next table. They had a little surprise for him – they were two priests from Holland. Much to their added amusement, he asked one of them to hear his confession straight away. What a loss to his family, to golf and to the community.

A customary greeting from Frank Guckian who is sharing a pot of tea with Brian Duffy, older brother of Colm.

'The Legacy'

... a play by 16 years old Michael Doherty

Michael wrote a play, 'The Legacy', at the age of sixteen. That is not a misprint, he was just sixteen years old! And not only that, it was performed in St. Mary' Hall, Buncrana to a packed house and received a wonderful reception. The script is just eight pages long but it is hilarious.

To write a review which would do it justice, I asked Sinead Davis (nee O'Doherty) whom I believed had the necessary qualifications. Sinead has a B.A Hons in English, Masters in Educational Management and a PHD in Educational Neuropsychology. I only ask the crème de la crème.

Michael Doherty was evidently a very skilful and talented playwright at such a tender age; this offering is a relatively short one-act play entitled 'The Legacy' but its concise format is used as a clever dramatic device. This script leaps off the page with the dramatic conventions, characterisation and dialogue easily envisioned as a stage production.

The premise, plot and setting are simple, quickly established and immediately hook the audience. The play was written in 1954 but not time anchored in a specific era; it actually embodies a timeless, classic quality harking back to rural Ireland of yest-a-year.

The playwright presents a vivid and engaging piece; it is set in a traditional country kitchen with the two protagonists, John and Pat presented to us as somewhat stereotypical socially gauche, aging bachelors with a quintessentially rural, sheltered perspective of the world. The

genre is probably most aptly described as a Comedy of Intrigue or Situation; in fact the play has all the hallmarks of a Shakespearian comedy.

The harmony of the narrative is disrupted when John receives a letter from a firm of solicitors informing him that his uncle has died and he is the chief beneficiary of the deceased's estate; essentially, he is in line for a significant inheritance. But, beneath this seemingly straightforward premise lies a caveat and a complication. One of the conditions of the inheritance is that John must be married. Therein lies the twist of the tale and the rising action of drama and comedy ensues. John is not married. Subsequently, it

emerges that some years ago John lied to his uncle, telling him he was married and the now deceased uncle has been sending John and ' his wife' £5 a month for a number of years! And so, this situation lends itself to humour as this deception must now be perpetuated. The play's action and climax pivots on the very humorous, bizarre and farcical yet plausible context that Pat must produce a wife to the solicitor in order to claim his loot!

The characterisation is astute, creating relatable and comedic characters. John, the beneficiary coerces his friend and ally Pat into adopting a feminine persona and dressing up as Primrose his fictitious wife! The playwright captures the fun, the farcical and the clumsiness of the deceiving duo in their dialogue and stage directions. There is a tangible mood of anticipation and a collective inhalation of breath – waiting to see if the pair can pull off the deception, fool the solicitor and claim the money. It reaches a comedic crescendo when Primrose appears as the demure, quiet wife. It seems success is within their grasp. But, alas, at the very last minute, in the very last line their destiny is doomed. The final caveat is revealed in the closing line of the letter: " You will receive the legacy on the birth of your first child". This is such a tantalizing twist and ingenuous finale.

A superbly entertaining and gripping comedic play. Bravo!